Lectures on
Dynamic Macroeconomics
Methods and Applications

World Scientific Lecture Notes in Economics and Policy

ISSN: 2630-4872

The World Scientific Lecture Notes in Economics and Policy series is aimed to produce lecture note texts for a wide range of economics disciplines, both theoretical and applied at the undergraduate and graduate levels. Contributors to the series are highly ranked and experienced professors of economics who see in publication of their lectures a mission to disseminate the teaching of economics in an affordable manner to students and other readers interested in enriching their knowledge of economic topics. The series was formerly titled World Scientific Lecture Notes in Economics.

Published:

Vol. 24: *Lectures on Dynamic Macroeconomics: Methods and Applications*
by Chetan Dave and Marco M. Sorge

Vol. 23: *Lectures in Production and Supply*
by Barry K. Goodwin

Vol. 22: *Lectures on Probability and Statistics for Graduate-Level Economics*
by Antonio Jiménez-Martínez

Vol. 21: *Lecture Notes in Experimental Economics*
by John Duff

For the complete list of volumes in this series, please visit
www.worldscientific.com/series/wslnep

World Scientific Lecture Notes in Economics and Policy – Vol. 24

Lectures on Dynamic Macroeconomics

Methods and Applications

Chetan Dave
University of Alberta, Canada

Marco M Sorge
University of Salerno, Italy

World Scientific

NEW JERSEY • LONDON • SINGAPORE • BEIJING • SHANGHAI • TAIPEI • CHENNAI

Published by

World Scientific Publishing Co. Pte. Ltd.
5 Toh Tuck Link, Singapore 596224
USA office: 27 Warren Street, Suite 401-402, Hackensack, NJ 07601
UK office: 57 Shelton Street, Covent Garden, London WC2H 9HE

Library of Congress Control Number: 2024059294

British Library Cataloguing-in-Publication Data
A catalogue record for this book is available from the British Library.

World Scientific Lecture Notes in Economics and Policy — Vol. 24
LECTURES ON DYNAMIC MACROECONOMICS
Methods and Applications

ISBN 978-981-12-9620-8 (hardcover)
ISBN 978-981-12-9757-1 (paperback)
ISBN 978-981-12-9621-5 (ebook for institutions)
ISBN 978-981-12-9622-2 (ebook for individuals)

For any available supplementary material, please visit
https://www.worldscientific.com/worldscibooks/10.1142/13931#t=suppl

Desk Editors: Aanand Jayaraman/Yulin Jiang

Typeset by Stallion Press
Email: enquiries@stallionpress.com

Preface

Modern macroeconomic theory is the study of dynamic general equilibrium economic models. Models are defined broadly and allow for situations where markets do not necessarily clear and where prices do not necessarily adjust instantaneously. This text provides an introduction to the study of such models: time can either be modeled in a discrete or continuous fashion, and the environment may be either deterministic or stochastic – this generality accommodates theories of both business cycles and economic growth.

The purpose of this book is to cover *first* the tools employed in modern macroeconomic theory and *second* the topics most often encountered in macroeconomic debate. While the focus of the book is on macroeconomic modeling, the tools that are employed can also be applied to other fields in economics (e.g. natural resource/environmental economics and industrial organization). Throughout the text, the reader is exposed to both methodology and applications – the scope and reach of a reader's own application is of course entirely a function of her own ingenuity with economic questions of interest.

Modern macroeconomics employs economic models with a view to achieving various objectives. A first objective is to account for and understand, often via replication, recurrent patterns of aggregate economic activity known as stylized facts. These facts pertain to both long-run growth patterns and characteristics of short-run cyclical fluctuations. The second objective is to interpret and analyze specific socioeconomic episodes, such as the worldwide Great Depression of the 1930s, and the third is to conduct policy analyses that often cannot be conducted in reality – the so-called counterfactual exercises. For example, what are the welfare implications of a drop in income taxes in favor of consumption taxes for a nation's economy? There is limited scope for such experiments in reality, but this question can be analyzed using a model of aggregate economic behavior. Thus, this field shares the goals of the economics discipline as a whole but is somewhat specialized in the tools that it employs. The analysis of aggregate time series such as GDP, unemployment, and inflation requires models that are dynamic in nature and typically involve an element of uncertainty. As in other fields within economics, models are required to be tractable, have empirical relevance, and be internally consistent.

Textbook treatments of the tools employed in dynamic analyses abound, as do texts on various topics in macroeconomics. Existing texts sometimes presume a degree of technical expertise and familiarity with the requisite mathematical training; instructors are therefore left to fill in any gaps. While various texts do provide brief overviews of tools (often in their appendices), advanced texts are not necessarily accessible from 'day one of class' for all students. This text is designed to fill this gap – it is meant to be a unified source to a variety of tools and topics in macroeconomic theory that is also mathematically and computationally accessible.

This text, to be viewed as curated lecture notes, is styled to act as a macroeconomic-theory counterpart to the microeconomics expositions by Kreps (1990) and Varian (1992). The hope is that in following these canonical expositions in microeconomics, dissemination of the methods and topics in macroeconomic theory can be brought to both the senior undergraduate and graduate student populations as instructors see fit. The current manuscript covers many of the same topics in Romer (2018) but also acts as an introduction to Ljungqvist and Sargent (2018) – a decidedly more technical and focused treatment of core macroeconomic theory. The academic background required is minimal but standard. It is assumed that students have a background in microeconomics and macroeconomics roughly at the level of Varian (2024) and Mankiw (2018), respectively. With respect to mathematics, we assume knowledge of functions, series and sequences, multivariate differential and integral calculus, introductory matrix algebra, and basic statistics. Background or concurrent studies in mathematics at the level of de la Fuente

(2000), Dixit (1990), and/or Simon and Blume (1994) is strongly recommended.

We would like to thank our many wonderful students over the years for their patience and diligence in pointing out more effective ways for us to explain this material. In addition, we wish to thank our professional mentors, colleagues, and former professors and dissertation supervisors: we owe them an ongoing debt of gratitude as they selflessly continue to teach us economics. All remaining errors are, as expected, entirely our own.

About the Authors

Chetan Dave is a Professor in the Department of Economics at the University of Alberta. He completed his undergraduate studies at McGill, his master's at the University of British Columbia, and his PhD at the University of Pittsburgh. Professor Dave's research interests are primarily in quantitative macroeconomics and secondarily in behavioral and experimental economics. His hobbies revolve around literature, music, and travel.

Marco M. Sorge is an Associate Professor of Economic Policy at the University of Salerno, an Affiliate Professor at the University of Göttingen, and a Research Fellow at the Center for Studies in Economics and Finance (CSEF). He received his PhD in Quantitative Economics from the Bonn Graduate School of Economics (BGSE) in 2011.

His teaching and research areas are computational economics, dynamic macroeconomics, and political economy. Specific research interests focus on identification/estimation issues inherent in Dynamic Stochastic General Equilibrium (DSGE) frameworks in the presence of information heterogeneities and on theoretical mechanisms underlying wealth inequality and the evolution of wealth distributions.

Contents

Preface v

About the Authors ix

1. Introduction **1**

1.1 Aims and Objectives 1
 1.1.1 A brief history of macroeconomic thought . . . 3
1.2 A Tour of Topics and Tools 5
 1.2.1 A few real stylized facts 9
 1.2.2 A few nominal stylized facts 11
1.3 Elements of General Equilibrium 11
1.4 A Roadmap Through Notation 15
1.5 Conclusion 18

I The Tools of the Trade **19**

2. Deterministic Dynamics **21**

2.1 Continuous Time Systems 21
 2.1.1 Basic concepts and scalar dynamics 21
 2.1.2 Systems of linear equations 29
 2.1.3 Taylor series approximations and linearization 39
2.2 Dynamic Optimization: Introductory Comments 40
2.3 Constrained Optimization Theory: A Primer 41
2.4 Calculus of Variations 44
2.5 Optimal Control in Continuous Time 46

2.5.1 The continuous time present value Hamiltonian 46
2.5.2 The continuous time current value Hamiltonian 48
2.6 From Mathematics to Economics 51
2.6.1 Intertemporal choice and exponential discounting 51
2.6.2 Uncertainty and risk aversion 52
2.6.3 Aggregate data and production functions 53
2.6.4 The discount factor 55
2.6.5 Interpreting dynamic optimization problems 58
2.7 Discrete Time Systems 60
2.7.1 Basic concepts and scalar dynamics 60
2.7.2 Systems of linear equations 71
2.7.3 Steady states and stability analyses 77
2.8 Linearization Techniques: Discrete Time 77
2.8.1 Taylor series approximations and linearization 77
2.8.2 Log-linearization 79
2.9 Dynamic Optimization in Discrete Time 81
2.9.1 The discrete time lagrangian 81
2.9.2 Discrete time dynamic programming 83
2.10 From Discrete to Continuous Time 86
2.11 Conclusion 87

3. Stochastic Dynamics 89

3.1 Stochastic Processes 90
3.1.1 Univariate processes 91
3.1.2 Multivariate processes 93
3.1.3 Impulse response functions 95
3.1.4 Variance decompositions 96
3.1.5 The law of iterated expectations 98
3.2 Preparing Data 100
3.3 Optimization 100
3.4 Linear Rational Expectations Model Solutions 104
3.4.1 Univariate solutions 104
3.4.2 Multivariate solutions 107
3.5 Conclusion 115

II Topics in Aggregate Economics 117

4. Exogenous Growth 119

4.1 Origins of Growth Theory . . . 119
4.2 The Solow Model . . . 123
4.2.1 The nature of production . . . 123
4.2.2 The nature of markets and behavioral relations . . . 125
4.2.3 Solving and analyzing the model . . . 127
4.3 One Sector Optimal Growth . . . 132
4.3.1 Environment . . . 132
4.3.2 Optimal growth and risk aversion . . . 134
4.3.3 Solution method 1: Benevolent social planner . . . 136
4.3.4 Solution method 2: Decentralized equilibrium . . . 142
4.4 Labor–Leisure Choice in the Ramsey Model . . . 144
4.4.1 Environment and optimization . . . 144
4.4.2 Solution . . . 145
4.5 Conclusion . . . 146

5. Endogenous Growth 147

5.1 Introduction . . . 147
5.2 AK Growth . . . 148
5.3 An Optimizing AK Model . . . 150
5.4 Knowledge and Growth . . . 158
5.4.1 The decentralized equilibrium . . . 159
5.4.2 The benevolent social planner . . . 163
5.5 Exogenous vs. Endogenous Growth Models . . . 165
5.6 Conclusion . . . 169

6. Real Business Cycles 171

6.1 Introduction . . . 171
6.2 A Stochastic Ramsey Model . . . 173
6.2.1 Environment . . . 173
6.2.2 Optimization and the model representation . . . 174
6.3 A Real Business Cycle Model with Indivisible Labor . . . 177
6.3.1 Environment . . . 178

6.3.2 Optimization and the nonlinear representation 179
6.3.3 The stationary form of the model 180
6.3.4 The non-stochastic steady state 181
6.3.5 Linearization 183
6.3.6 Model solution under rational expectations 184
6.3.7 Calibration 186
6.3.8 Model evaluation 188
6.4 Conclusion 190

7. New Keynesian Models 193

7.1 Introduction 193
7.2 Money and Output in Competitive Equilibrium 195
7.2.1 Environment 195
7.2.2 Stochastics 197
7.2.3 Equilibrium conditions and profit maximization implications 199
7.2.4 An undetermined coefficients rational expectation solution 199
7.2.5 Model solution 203
7.2.6 Conclusions 207
7.3 Introduction to a New Keynesian Model 208
7.3.1 Economic environment 209
7.3.2 The representative household 211
7.3.3 The representative final goods-producing firm 214
7.3.4 The representative intermediate goods-producing firm 215
7.3.5 The monetary authority 217
7.3.6 Equilibrium and the linearized system 217
7.4 Conclusion 222

8. Asset Pricing 225

8.1 Introduction 225
8.2 The Lucas Model 226
8.2.1 Assumptions 226

8.2.2 Optimization 227
8.2.3 Equilibrium and analysis 227
8.3 Empirical Asset Pricing Puzzles 230
8.3.1 The equity premium puzzle 231
8.3.2 The excess volatility puzzle 232
8.4 Bubbles 233
8.5 The Price-Dividend Ratio 235
8.6 Conclusion 238

9. Overlapping Generations Models 239

9.1 Introduction 239
9.2 The Basic OLG Model 240
9.2.1 The general environment 240
9.2.2 A pure endowment economy 240
9.2.3 Dynamic efficiency 243
9.3 An Economy with Production 245
9.3.1 Household behavior 246
9.3.2 Firm behavior 246
9.3.3 Market clearing 246
9.3.4 The model solution and the savings function 247
9.3.5 The fundamental difference equation 248
9.4 Dynamic Efficiency and the Golden Rule 251
9.5 Bequests and Dynamic Efficiency 253
9.6 Social Security and Optimal Capital 257
9.7 Conclusion 259

10. Heterogeneous-Agent Models 261

10.1 Introduction 261
10.2 Household Income Heterogeneity 263
10.2.1 Income fluctuation 264
10.2.2 The endogenous grid method: Remarks 268
10.2.3 Endogenous labor income heterogeneity 269
10.3 Heterogeneous Expectations 271
10.3.1 Limited information and heterogeneous expectations 273
10.3.2 Heterogeneous forecast rules 275

10.4 Heterogeneous-Agent New Keynesian Models 278
10.4.1 A short review 278
10.4.2 Two-agent new Keynesian model insights 281
10.5 Conclusion 292

References 293

Chapter 1

Introduction

1.1 Aims and Objectives

Macroeconomic theory is concerned with the study of aggregate economies, for example, a country or a group of countries. Economic activity is typically characterized by a series of aggregate variables, such as the gross domestic product (GDP), consumption, investment, interest rates, and inflation. These variables are usually provided for a country in its national income and product accounts (NIPA); for the United States (U.S.), NIPA data are produced by the Department of Commerce. An excellent free data source for U.S. macroeconomic variables is the FRED database, available online at the website of the Federal Reserve Bank of St. Louis.[1] NIPA data for other countries can be found in the databases of international organizations such as the IMF and are sometimes available from a country's central bank and/or statistical agency websites (e.g. via Statistics Canada). The aggregate economy, as described by these aggregate variables, exhibits certain empirical regularities motivating the study of macroeconomics.

The main empirical regularity seen across nations has to do with growth and cycles in real GDP. The broad aim of macroeconomic theory is to understand and explain such economic growth and business cycles, as measured by various statistical representations of aggregate variables. For economic growth, the challenge involves

[1] See http://research.stlouisfed.org/fred2/.

identifying economic processes that allow nations to exhibit long-run growth in per capita GDP and explain why GDP growth rates vary across nations; the long run here refers to decades or more. In the seminal contributions of Solow (1956) and Swan (1956), the economic model postulates a 'capital accumulation equation', which, when combined with the assumption of technological progress in the production of goods and services, explains growth in per capita incomes of a particular nation. The same model when applied across countries predicts that nations that share similar economic characteristics will eventually reach the same long-run economic growth rate in terms of per capita income. Thus, differences in growth outcomes across countries are attributed to differences in economic characteristics (e.g. savings rates). For business cycles, the 'short run' is typically measured in quarters. There, the challenge lies in explaining and predicting a number of fluctuations (around their respective trends) exhibited by a large number of aggregate variables. An early and important example of this type of analysis is the economic model developed by Kydland and Prescott (1982), which attributes business cycles to fluctuations in productivity.

Underlying both types of analyses is a common methodological theme involving the use of dynamic general equilibrium models. An analysis can take place in either a deterministic setting, as in many standard growth models, or it can take place in a stochastic setting, as in Kydland and Prescott's (1982) business cycle model. These models can then be evaluated using statistical techniques to determine the extent to which they match data and can eventually inform policy-making and be used for forecasting (see DeJong and Dave (2011) for an introduction to this field). No model is intended to perfectly capture all of the processes and dynamics comprising the economy. The process of developing an economic model is typically informed by a specific policy question; if the data turn out to be consistent with the model, then the latter can be used to inform the direction of public policy. Finally, economic models are also developed to highlight and explain particular features of the data; these contributions have an inherent value as they allow for a better understanding of the economic forces shaping national economies.

This chapter first provides a very brief overview of the history of macroeconomic thought, with a particular focus on methodology.

Next, we discuss the tools employed throughout this text. The chapter also provides a brief introduction to general equilibrium theory – a central focus in macroeconomic theory. This is followed by a tour of the notation employed. Finally, the chapter concludes with a brief discussion of the stylized facts drawn from data that motivate much of macroeconomic practice and research.

Following the introduction, the first part of the text lays out the tools that are most commonly encountered when analyzing macroeconomic phenomena. These mathematical tools allow one to analyze economies in a dynamic setting, with or without uncertainty. The techniques will be useful throughout this book and form the basis of advanced economic analyses. In the second part of the text, we cover a series of basic topics that every economics student should know. These topics range from theories of exogenous growth to new Keynesian business cycles. This book, like others, necessarily reflects the choice and treatment of topics as we usually teach them. The interested reader should therefore actively search the vast literature for alternative viewpoints of both the history of this field and the topics covered.[2]

1.1.1 A brief history of macroeconomic thought

The traditional approach for studying empirical regularities began with the specification of a (static or dynamic) system of equations consisting of accounting identities, *ad hoc* behavioral equations (for example Keynes' consumption function), and 'forcing processes' for exogenous variables. The two main theoretical paradigms that each gave a framework for analysis were termed the classical and Keynesian paradigms. Under the classical paradigm, markets comprising an aggregate economy reach an equilibrium through smooth relative price adjustments and generate a real-nominal dichotomy. In the wake of the Great Depression, the Keynesian paradigm did away with market clearing assumptions (especially in the short run) and explained why nominal and real variables influenced one another due to a number of processes that were inconsistent with classical viewpoints. The mathematics behind both schools of thought were

[2]For particularly interesting reviews, see Blanchard (2000) and Woodford (2000).

however very similar: the specification of a system of equations reflecting views on the interaction of aggregate variables.[3]

The modern approach for studying empirical regularities requires construction of explicit, dynamic optimization problems solved by different economic actors, where prices are determined in general equilibrium. Modern economists believe that explicit constrained optimization explains human behavior is now reflected by the importance placed on 'microfoundations' in the study of economic problems. A careful specification of the assumptions underlying an economic model is considered to be of utmost importance in understanding the model's implications and predictions. Optimization problems are consistent with microeconomic principles and endogenous variables are clearly identified relative to exogenous and predetermined ones. Further, expectations of variables are often required to be consistent with the economic model at hand, reflecting the 'rational expectations' revolution. The result is a system of equations with no *ad hoc* behavioral equations, but rather equations that explicitly reflect economic behavior of agents across time.[4] This change in methods gave birth to new classical and new Keynesian schools of thought operating under new methodological principles: clear specification of preferences, constraints, policies, and external factors that yield a system of equations with a direct link to optimization problems facing agents.[5]

Modern macroeconomics typically employs economic models to achieve one or more of three major goals. The first is to account for and replicate recurrent patterns of aggregate economic activity known as stylized facts. These stylized facts not only describe salient features of long-run relationships among macroeconomic aggregates

---

[3]See Chapters 1–6 of Sargent (1987) for an exposition of the traditional approach to studying aggregate economies.

[4]An early exposition of this approach was provided in Sargent (1987).

[5]The specification of a preference maximization problem where preferences are represented by a utility function is not viewed as *ad hoc* because it is based on an axiomatic description of the economic agent's preferences. See for example the first few chapters of Mas-Collel *et al.* (1995). While one may view these axioms as *ad hoc*, the economist now has a clear understanding of the characterization of the agent's preferences and can change specific features of her behavior by changing the (clearly specified) axioms.

but also describe broad characteristics of short-run, cyclical fluctuations. The second goal is to interpret and analyze specific socio-economic or historical episodes, for example the Great Depression of the 1930s. The third goal is to conduct policy analyses that cannot be conducted in reality: for example, what would be the societal welfare implications of the U.S. government dropping income taxes in favor of sales taxes? Such a question cannot be answered through an experimental but still real-world policy change, but can be analyzed using a macroeconomic model that describes the aggregate behavior of all of the major actors in the economy. The field, not surprisingly, thus shares the goals of other fields in economics. However, the focus of the methodology is on the analysis of economies in a dynamic (deterministic or stochastic) setting designed to analyze relationships among aggregate time series. Model requirements share the same characteristics as in other fields, namely that models be simple (tractable), empirically relevant, and 'internally consistent'.[6] Macroeconomic models that share such characteristics can be surprisingly good at prediction. Finally, since macroeconomic models are dynamic in nature, dynamic tools are often imported from the fields of mathematics (and engineering) and subsequently modified for use in economics by macroeconomists, but other fields use these tools as well. In this text, the main set of tools are discussed first, followed by a series of standard topics in macroeconomic theory that illustrate them.

1.2 A Tour of Topics and Tools

The general macroeconomic environment is dynamic since we are interested in modeling the behavior of variables through time; and since these time series exhibit 'persistence',[7] we must account for the notion that economic decisions made today affect future choices and outcomes. So, the tools learned in macroeconomics are also applicable to other fields in economics. The dynamic nature of macroeconomics

[6]Internal consistency refers to a logic within models. That is, given a clear specification of assumptions, conclusions are derived from the working model at hand.

[7]Persistence means that a decline in a variable is followed by further declines and growth in a variable is followed by subsequent growth.

means that we must learn how to: describe the evolution of variables through continuous and discrete time, understand the properties of our descriptive dynamic equations, and finally be able to optimize functions that vary through time.

In both models of economic growth and business cycles, macroeconomists employ time series data. A time series represents the value of a variable (e.g. real GDP, denoted y) over time. We denote a time series as a function of time, e.g. $y(t) = y_t$, because as time changes the value of real GDP changes with it. Next, macroeconomists often use logarithmic versions of a time series represented in levels. This is because changes in the natural logarithm (denoted as log) of a variable y_t over time represent the growth rate of that variable, that is,

$$\frac{\partial \log y(t)}{\partial t} = \frac{\partial \log y_t}{\partial t} = \frac{\partial \widetilde{y}_t}{\partial t} = \frac{\frac{\partial y_t}{\partial t}}{y_t} \equiv \frac{\overset{\bullet}{y}_t}{y_t} \equiv g_{y_t}, \tag{1.1}$$

where $\overset{\bullet}{y}_t = \frac{\partial y_t}{\partial t}$.

Growth models try to explain the pattern of g_{y_t} within and across nations. As an example of growth for one nation, consider the U.S. real gross domestic product (GDPC1 in the FRED database). The time series plots presented here in Figures 1.1 and 1.2 are in billions of 2017 dollars (y_t) and in natural logarithms ($\log y_t$). The gray shaded bars represent recessions, as determined by the U.S. National Bureau of Economic Research (NBER) business cycle dating committee (USRECQM in the FRED database).

These figures clearly reflect the positive experience of the U.S. in terms of the growth of y_t since World War II. Why this trend has been the case is often the topic of models of economic growth. Equivalently and more importantly, many nations have not experienced such growth, and economic growth models may also try to address that fact as well.

In contrast to models of economic growth, business cycle models try to explain fluctuations in time series variables around their trends. As an example, nominal GDP (Y_t) for the U.S. can be thought of as real GDP (y_t) multiplied by some measure of the aggregate price level (p_t):

$$Y_t = p_t \times y_t. \tag{1.2}$$

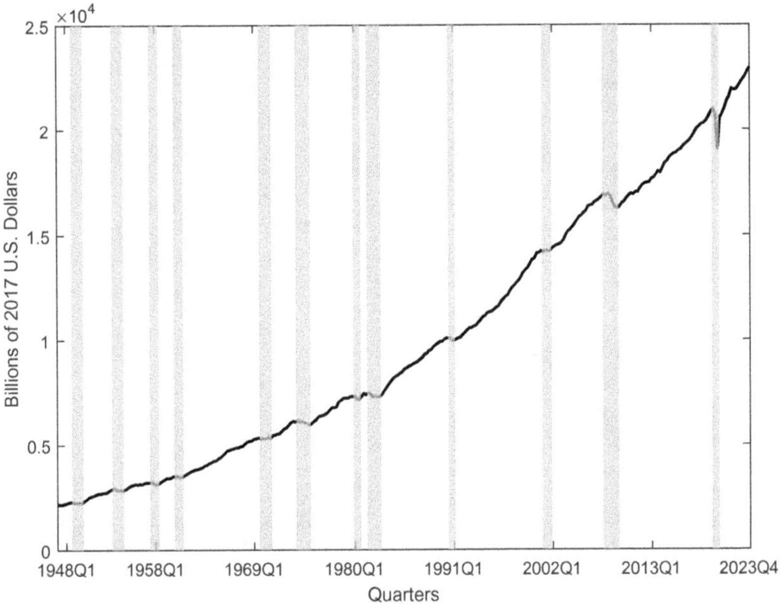

Figure 1.1. U.S. real GDP in billions of 2017 dollars (y_t).

Let us look at these two components separately (i.e. fluctuations in real GDP and a measure of inflation). Consider the GDP implicit price deflator as a measure of the aggregate price level (p_t, GDPDEF in the FRED database). For time series plots of cycles, consider fluctuations around the growth rate in terms of annualized[8] percentage changes in y_t,

$$\widehat{y}_t = \left\{\left[\left(\frac{y_t}{y_{t-1}}\right)^4\right] - 1\right\} \times 100, \tag{1.3}$$

and consider inflation (π_t) measured as the annualized percentage change in p_t,

$$\pi_t = \left\{\left[\left(\frac{p_t}{p_{t-1}}\right)^4\right] - 1\right\} \times 100. \tag{1.4}$$

[8]Since the data have a quarterly frequency, annualization incorporates an exponential of 4.

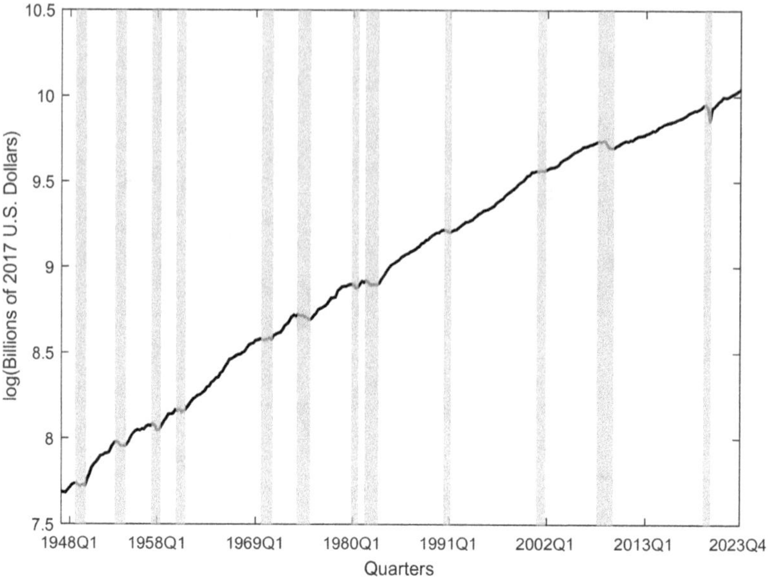

Figure 1.2. Log of U.S. real GDP in trillions of 2017 dollars ($\log y_t$).

Even without any statistical analysis, one immediately notes several features of the data in Figures 1.3 and 1.4. First, $\widehat{y}_t$ typically drops during periods highlighted by the gray bars. As mentioned, these periods are what the NBER considers to be recessionary periods. Second, $\widehat{y}_t$ seems to have fluctuated a fair bit (i.e. wide swings) early on in the post-WWII years, but since the mid-1980s or so the swings seem to be less dramatic. Third, π_t also seems to exhibit a decrease in dramatic swings in later time periods. Some have termed this feature of the data, common to several macroeconomic time series, the 'Great Moderation'.[9] Fourth, π_t seems to trend up until the 1980s and then trend down rather quickly. Such observations, often derived via statistical methods (some of which we will study in this text), are known as stylized facts. The objective of much of macroeconomic modeling is to write down models that deliver these stylized facts, be they growth facts and/or business cycle facts. If a

[9]See Clarida *et al.* (2000) and Cogley and Sargent (2001, 2005) for analyses concerning declines in macroeconomic volatility.

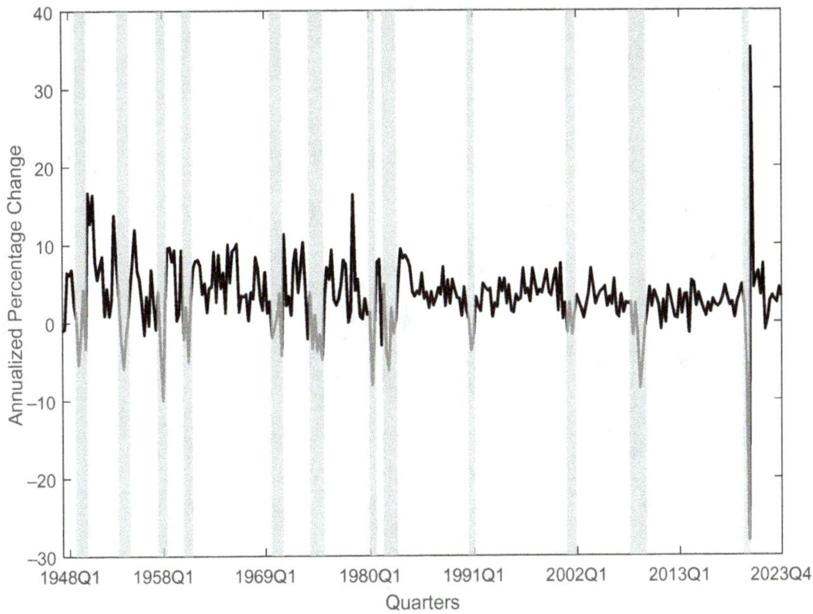

Figure 1.3. Annualized percentage change in U.S. real GDP in billions of 2017 dollars ($\widehat{y}_t$).

model does a good job of accounting for and replicating stylized facts, then it is said to be useful for prediction and policy experiments.

1.2.1 A few real stylized facts

The key feature of data that needs to be addressed by macroeconomists when they examine economic growth is the notion of balanced growth. Specifically for the U.S., in the long-run (usually measured on a five-year basis), output and physical capital per worker grow at almost constant rates that show no diminishment. The ratio of physical capital to output and the rate of return to capital are almost constant quantities. The return to labor (wages) grows at the same rate as output, and the output shares of capital and labor are almost constant. Further, the ratio of investment to output is constant, the ratio of labor income to output is constant, and the ratio of consumption to output is constant. These are the basic stylized facts for U.S. growth, and so growth models need to incorporate them.

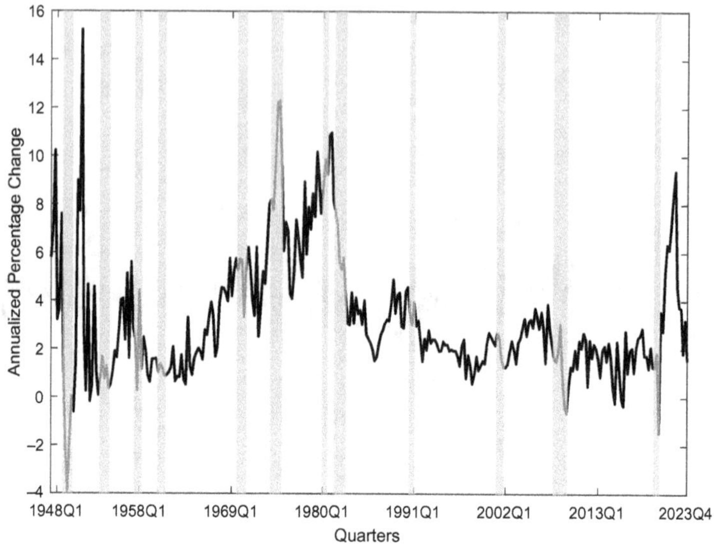

Figure 1.4. Annualized percentage change in the U.S. GDP implicit price deflator (π_t).

Additionally, there are cross-country differences in levels and growth rates of GDP. Indeed, persistent international differences exist: unconditional convergence of poor countries to rich ones is non-existent. But, groups of countries that share certain socioeconomic characteristics do show convergence to the same living standards, which is called conditional convergence. Indeed, in discussing models of growth, attempts to verify whether a model exhibits this conditional convergence property is a first step in validating a growth theory when confronted with data.

Next, what are the real business cycle stylized facts that must be explained by models? As noted above, business cycles are defined as the deviation of real GDP from its trend. Business cycle facts are reported in terms of volatility (the standard deviation of a variable relative to the standard deviation of real GDP), co-movement (correlation of a variable with other variables), and persistence (correlation of the variable with its own past values). Further, these business cycle stylized facts can be pro-cyclical, counter-cyclical, or a-cyclical in terms of co-movement with the cycle of real GDP. Finally, some variables are leading, coincident, or lagging indicators of changes in the cycle of real GDP. Specifically, in the U.S., consumption of non-durables and services is less volatile than real output, real investment is three times as volatile than real output, and hours worked are much less volatile than output. Once again, for existing or new business cycle models, replication of stylized facts is a standard against which competing models are adjudicated.

1.2.2 A few nominal stylized facts

In the long run, money growth (in terms of growth in, say, M2) typically moves one-for-one with inflation in the U.S. In the short run, money growth is leading and pro-cyclical, whereas inflation is leading and pro-cyclical and nominal interest rates are lagging and pro-cyclical. With respect to equity markets, stock prices, as measured by a host of indices, are leading and pro-cyclical and trend upward in the long run. In general, most macroeconomic variables tend to be pro-cyclical and almost all macroeconomic aggregates tend to be highly persistent at the quarterly frequency. A key item with respect to macroeconomic modeling in the short run is that the long-run growth stylized facts and the short-run stylized facts need to be jointly accounted for in any business cycle model.

Several researchers have documented these and other stylized facts for a number of nations. Such documentation continues, as facts can change over time. Indeed, much of macroeconomic research begins with the stylized facts that are to be explained by the model built by the researcher. As a result, several sources exist for such documentation; a good place to start is the collection of facts outlined by Cooley and Prescott (1995). Having established the stylized facts to be addressed, the next step is to specify a general equilibrium model that might have a chance of replicating those facts; such modeling is briefly discussed as follows.[10]

1.3 Elements of General Equilibrium

Most macroeconomic models are of the general equilibrium variety. The definition and interpretation of a general equilibrium (hereafter, GE) is explained in a typical core microeconomic and macroeconomic

---

[10]An excellent example of research that first establishes the stylized facts to be explained and then builds a model to explain them was provided by Dressler and Li (2009).

theory sequence of a doctoral program and also in advanced undergraduate economics courses. It suffices to say for now that GE models allow the researcher to simultaneously account for all of the optimization objectives of relevant agents and to analyze how these different optimization objectives impact (equilibrium) prices. A GE model allows for a clear description of the economic environment (e.g. market clearing) as well as a specification of what the researcher takes to be exogenous to the environment (e.g. shocks to an economy such as Hurricane Katrina).[11]

In typical macroeconomic environments, agents comprise: households that maximize utility from consumption and leisure subject to budget constraints that may be dynamic in nature, firms that maximize profits from selling output subject to the constraint that their production is limited by the existing level of available factors of production (i.e. production function), and governments that are assumed to maximize some welfare criterion for the well-being of all citizens. Further economic aspects of the environment typically consist of how households and firms interact within and across time and assumptions on the nature of the markets (for example, do markets clear and if so how do prices adjust?). A GE is obtained when there is a set of prices for each good and service exchanged in the economy such that households maximize utility, firms maximize profit, and any other agents attain their objectives as well. Under certain conditions, the economic outcomes of GE models have certain attractive efficiency properties, captured by the so-called 'fundamental welfare theorems'.

The first such theorem states that if markets are competitive and complete, then equilibrium prices will ensure that the allocation of goods to the households is Pareto efficient. This means that, under the current equilibrium allocation, it is not possible to make some households better off without making others worse off. A market can be described as competitive if each economic agent, while optimizing her own objective, takes prices as a given. In particular, either she is too 'small' relative to the rest of the market to influence prices or she behaves as though she cannot affect prices. In addition, we say that

---

[11]For a detailed exposition of general equilibrium theory, see Mas-Collel *et al.* (1995).

markets are complete when a market exists for all possible goods and contingencies. A complete spot market for goods and services is not a particularly unreasonable assumption; the assumption of an asset market for all possible contingencies is however more problematic, in that the assumption may be particularly unrealistic in the real world.

The second welfare theorem implies that any allocation of goods and services that is Pareto efficient can be implemented as a competitive equilibrium. For example, suppose that society considers a particular (Pareto efficient) outcome to be socially desirable, perhaps because it is deemed to be equitable. Then, the second welfare theorem says that the government can devise a lump-sum tax and transfer system between members of society that, once implemented, will allow the competitive market to allocate goods and services in exactly the way that society sees fit. Both theorems are proved in an economic setting with particular assumptions, and the reader should consult textbooks such as that by Mas Collel *et al.* (1995) to make sure that they understand the significance of all of these assumptions.

The first welfare theorem is easily the more immediately relevant of the two. First, it states that an (idealized) market economy has certain efficiency properties. More importantly, the first welfare theorem allows macroeconomists to model a theoretical social planner instead of multiple markets. It is often more tractable to model a benevolent social planner's problem, provided the conditions of the theorem are met. The first welfare theorem then assures us that the outcome obtained in the social planner's problem is in fact identical to the (typically more complicated) competitive equilibrium outcome. Therefore, as long as a macroeconomic environment contains all of the assumptions of a competitive economy, then the modeler can safely adopt the more tractable benevolent social planner's problem. If any one condition is violated, a decentralized equilibrium must be modeled; this usually implies specifying the optimization problems of all agents in the economy and solving them jointly.

As for the second welfare theorem, its implications are far less interesting from a real-world point of view: while the theorem is reassuring in that intervention by the state in the form of lump-sum taxes and transfers can yield *any* Pareto optimal outcome, its usefulness is limited by the fact that taxation systems throughout the world are almost exclusively proportional since a state's informational requirement in finding out the right kind of lump-sum taxation scheme to obtain a desired outcome could be burdensome, and government institutions may not be efficient.

Now, in order to make macroeconomic models tractable, we usually make simplifying assumptions about the specific functional forms used to describe preferences or production functions. The parameters in these functional forms can then be evaluated and used for empirical exercises. Some common functional forms for utility defined over consumption (c_t) are the constant absolute risk aversion (CARA) form,[12]

$$U(c_t) = \frac{-\exp(-\gamma c_t)}{\gamma} \quad \forall \gamma > 0, \tag{1.5}$$

and the constant relative risk aversion (CRRA) form,

$$U(c_t) = \begin{Bmatrix} \dfrac{c_t^{1-\gamma}}{1-\gamma} & \forall \gamma \neq 1 \text{ and } \gamma > 0 \\ \log(c_t) & \gamma = 1 \end{Bmatrix}. \tag{1.6}$$

We will learn why these functional forms are important later. Some common functional forms for production using as inputs capital (k_t) and labor (n_t) are the Cobb–Douglas form

$$y_t = F(k_t, n_t) = k_t^{\alpha} n_t^{1-\alpha}, \tag{1.7}$$

and the constant elasticity of substitution functional form, given by

$$y_t = F(k_t, n_t) = \left[\alpha k_t^{\zeta} + (1-\alpha) n_t^{\zeta}\right]^{\frac{1}{\zeta}}, \quad \zeta \leq -1. \tag{1.8}$$

Again, we will learn why these functional forms are important later when we discuss how the nature of real-world macroeconomic data can influence the choice of functional forms. While these functions are simple, they can be surprisingly good at replicating broad features of the data, once the parameters that characterize them are estimated. In that sense, although they may seem reductionist, these functional forms allow the researcher to reach a middle ground between matching some features of the data and tractability.

[12]The symbol $\forall$ means 'for all'.

1.4 A Roadmap Through Notation

Having specified the fundamentals of the economy (household's preferences, etc.), a first step in analyzing a model is to specify the optimization problems that reflect the economic intuition to be examined. As mentioned previously, they are dynamic in nature and may contain various stochastic elements. These specifications will allow us to introduce further notation that is used throughout the text.

A continuous time deterministic optimization problem is typically written as[13]

$$\max_{x_t} \quad \Gamma = \int_0^T e^{-\rho t} F(y_t, x_t) dt, \tag{1.9}$$

$$s.t. \quad \dot{y}_t \leq G(y_t, x_t), \quad y_{(0)} = y_0, \tag{1.10}$$

whereas a discrete time deterministic problem is written as

$$\max_{\{x_t\}} \quad \Gamma = \sum_{t=0}^{T} \beta^t F(y_t, x_t), \tag{1.11}$$

$$s.t. \quad y_{t+1} - y_t \leq G(y_t, x_t), \quad y_{(0)} = y_0. \tag{1.12}$$

For example, $F(y_t, x_t)$ could be the instantaneous utility of the household in period t, where x_t is consumption in period t and y_t represents output. In both cases, and for each period t, the objective is to maximize a discounted (integral) sum of the instantaneous objective $F(y_t, x_t)$ subject to some constraint. The dynamic nature of the problem means that choices today affect constraints later. It is useful to divide variables between control variables (here, x_t) and state variables (y_t). Control variables are those that can be chosen at a point in period t, whereas values of the state variables cannot be chosen directly: a choice of a particular value for x_t today might affect the value of the state variable next time period. State variables provide a description in period t of all of the relevant aspects of the economy that the economic agent has to take into account to choose her controls optimally.

[13]Throughout this text, *s.t.* is used as shorthand for 'such that' in specifying constraints in optimization problems.

Finally, in contrast to deterministic environments, in a discrete time *stochastic* environment, the objective to be maximized takes the form

$$\max_{\{x_t\}} \quad \Gamma = E_0 \sum_{t=0}^{T} \beta^t F(y_t, x_t, \varepsilon_t), \tag{1.13}$$

$$s.t. \quad y_{t+1} - y_t \leq G(y_t, x_t, \varepsilon_{t+1}), \quad y_{(0)} = y_0, \tag{1.14}$$

$$\varepsilon_t \sim IID(0, \sigma_\varepsilon^2 I). \tag{1.15}$$

Here, the variable ε_t is a random variable. This renders the dynamic problem probabilistic, in a sense defined precisely in subsequent chapters.

These optimization problems can be reduced to a linear system of equations that can be used to analyze certain properties of the resulting economy. An example is a standard stochastic discrete time difference equation of the form

$$z_t = \alpha + \beta z_{t-1} + \varepsilon_t, \tag{1.16}$$

$$E(\varepsilon_t) = 0, \tag{1.17}$$

$$E(\varepsilon_t \varepsilon_s) = \begin{Bmatrix} \sigma^2 & \forall\, t = s \\ 0 & \forall\, t \neq s \end{Bmatrix}. \tag{1.18}$$

Whereas, a standard system of stochastic discrete time difference equations is

$$z_t = A + B z_{t-1} + \varepsilon_t, \tag{1.19}$$

$$z_t = \left[z_{1t}\ z_{2t}\ z_{3t}\ \ldots\ z_{nt}\right]', \tag{1.20}$$

$$\varepsilon_t = \left[\varepsilon_{1t}\ \varepsilon_{2t}\ \varepsilon_{3t}\ \ldots\ \varepsilon_{nt}\right]', \tag{1.21}$$

$$E(\varepsilon_t) = 0, \tag{1.22}$$

$$E(\varepsilon_t \varepsilon_s) = \begin{Bmatrix} \Sigma & \forall\, t = s \\ 0 & \forall\, t \neq s \end{Bmatrix}. \tag{1.23}$$

These are the objects of final analysis: given a model of the economy, the solution can be used to deliver a system of stochastic discrete time difference equations. But there are some intermediate steps, which are sketched out in the following.

Let's consider for example a stochastic dynamic optimization problem in discrete time:

$$\max_{x_t} \quad \Gamma = E_0 \sum_{t=0}^{\infty} \beta^t F(y_t, x_t, \varepsilon_t), \tag{1.24}$$

$$s.t. \quad y_{t+1} - y_t \leq G(y_t, x_t, \varepsilon_{t+1}), \tag{1.25}$$

where ε_t is a random shock with zero mean and finite variance, observed at the start of time $t+1$. The solution of the model will usually be a system of nonlinear expectational difference equations,

$$\Psi(z_t, z_{t-1}|\theta) = 0, \tag{1.26}$$

such that θ denotes the parameters in the model and z_t may contain random variables as well as variables in expectations (e.g. $E_t(y_{t+1})$, where y_{t+1} is, say, real GDP in period $t+1$, so $E_t(y_{t+1})$ is period t's expectation of real output in period $t+1$). The nonlinear system will be linearized and expressed as a system of expectational linear difference equations:

$$\Gamma E_t(z_{t+1}) = \Xi z_t + \Phi \varepsilon_t. \tag{1.27}$$

Here, Γ represents a conformable matrix. This system will be solved under 'rational expectations' to yield

$$z_t = A + B z_{t-1} + \varepsilon_t, \tag{1.28}$$

which in turn can be analyzed and tested against the data.

Similarly, in continuous time non-stochastic environments, an optimization problem will be solved to yield systems of nonlinear differential equations,

$$\Psi(z_t, \dot{z}_t|\theta) = 0, \tag{1.29}$$

or, systems of nonlinear difference equations,

$$\Psi(z_t, z_{t+1}|\theta) = 0, \tag{1.30}$$

in the case of a discrete time deterministic environments. These nonlinear systems will then be linearized to yield systems of linear differential equations,

$$\dot{z}_t = A + Bz_t, \tag{1.31}$$

in the case of a continuous time deterministic environment, or systems of linear difference equations,

$$z_{t+1} = A + Bz_t, \tag{1.32}$$

in the case of a discrete time deterministic environment. Note that A and B in the notation above are matrices with the parameters of a model as elements.

1.5 Conclusion

Answers to economic questions will be given through analyses of the linear systems briefly described in this chapter, although methods do exist to analyze nonlinear systems directly. So, in this text, first we study linear systems; second, linearization, and third, we study optimization for deterministic and stochastic environments in discrete and continuous time settings. Once we have the mathematics, we can turn to the study of various macroeconomic models. That is, given our dynamic toolkit developed in the following two chapters, we will discuss models of economic growth, business cycles, asset pricing, and other topics.

Part I

The Tools of the Trade

Chapter 2

Deterministic Dynamics

2.1 Continuous Time Systems

2.1.1 Basic concepts and scalar dynamics

Most environments in macroeconomics are dynamic in nature, that is, they examine economic phenomena that evolve over time. Time can be modeled in two forms: discrete, where $t \in \{0, 1, 2, 3, \ldots\}$, and continuous, where $t \in \Re$ or some interval thereof. Discrete time is useful when modeling period-to-period changes, while continuous time is useful when modeling longer-term time-averaged environments that are nevertheless dynamic. For example, a quarterly business cycle is often analyzed in discrete time, especially since data are often reported at that frequency. In contrast, growth of output in the long-run as measured by time-averaged GDP is often examined in a continuous time setting. Growth modeling is also conducted assuming continuous time because solutions to continuous time models (something of the form $\dot{y}_t = f(y_t)$) are often easier to derive than in discrete time. In particular, it is straightforward to get an explicit solution to the optimization problem at hand. Finally, growth models are typically not 'taken to the data' directly. Instead, the empirical analysis is informed by the growth model, but the model itself is (typically) not tested. This is in contrast to business cycle models, where it is sensible to have a discrete time model because each period can be thought of as a quarter or a month, etc. The (linearized) solutions to business cycle models are often estimated directly, so having a discrete time model in this case is particularly useful. Finally, a word of caution: while for many economic problems, analyzing a model in continuous time or in discrete time doesn't make much of a difference in terms of the dynamics you obtain, this is not true for all models. So, the setting that you choose has to be informed by the question being asked and also by the methodology you intend to use when you take your model to the data.

In this chapter, we focus on the tools employed when modeling continuous and discrete times in deterministic (i.e. nothing is probabilistic) environments; in a subsequent chapter, we focus on stochastic tools. We do this by first describing the relationship of a variable measured in continuous time with its own time derivatives, analyzing single linear equations, deriving solutions, and drawing 'phase' diagrams to determine 'stability' graphically and analytically. Given an analysis of single equations, systems of linear equations are discussed next, 'phase' diagrams demonstrated for small systems, and systems solutions derived. Next, linearization tools employed when encountering nonlinear equations and/or systems are discussed. These continuous time tools conclude with optimization theory as applied to continuous time dynamic problems in finite and infinite horizons.[1]

2.1.1.1 *A taxonomy of differential equations*

In economics, one will often encounter a variable, say y (or x or z), being described over time. The simplest such relationship is a linear function. The variable is denoted y_t and is a *function* of time i.e. $y_t = y(t)$, where t is measured in continuous time $t \in \Re$. One will typically find y_t expressed in the same equation with its own time derivatives. This relationship is known as a differential equation. Depending on their functional form, differential equations fall into one or more broad categories. If the differential equation depends only on total time derivatives of one variable, then it is classified as an ordinary differential equation (ODE). If the differential equation depends on partial derivatives, it is classified as a partial

[1] An authoritative treatment of many of the topics covered in this part of the book is available in de la Fuente (2000).

differential equation (PDE). In continuous time, the standard notation for describing time derivatives of a variable y_t is

$$\dot{y}_t = y_t' = \frac{dy_t}{dt}. \tag{2.1}$$

This notation can be applied to higher-order derivatives such as

$$\ddot{y}_t = y_t'' = \frac{d^2y_t}{dt^2}, \tag{2.2}$$

although for orders larger than two, dot superscripts can become unwieldy, so primes ($'$'s) are often used instead.

Differential equations come in multiple classifications. The first classification has to do with autonomy with respect to time. If time does not appear explicitly in the expression, then the differential equation is considered autonomous: this means that the equation can be analyzed without referring to a specific time period. If time appears as an argument, then the differential equation is called non-autonomous. To illustrate, the differential equation $\dot{y}_t = ay_t$ is classified as autonomous, while $\dot{y}_t = a_1y_t + a_2t$ is non-autonomous due to the presence of time (t).

The second classification has to do with homogeneity. If there are no constant terms or other time-dependent variables in the relationship, then the differential equation is homogeneous. For example, the relationship $\dot{y}_t = ay_t$ is a homogeneous differential equation. The following are non-homogeneous differential equations:

$$\dot{y}_t = a_1y_t + a_2x_t, \tag{2.3}$$

$$\dot{y}_t = ay_t + b, \tag{2.4}$$

$$\dot{y}_t = a_1y_t + a_2x_t + b. \tag{2.5}$$

Third, differential equations are classified by order. The order of a differential equation is the highest derivative that appears in the relationship. As a result,

$$\dot{y}_t = ay_t + b, \tag{2.6}$$

is considered to be a first-order differential equation, while

$$\ddot{y}_t + a_1\dot{y}_t + a_2y_t = b, \tag{2.7}$$

is of second order. In general, a kth-order linear differential equation is written as

$$a_1 y_t + a_2 y_t'' + a_3 y_t''' + \cdots + a_k y_t^k = b, \tag{2.8}$$

where $a_1, a_2, \ldots, a_k$ and b are given constants. The simplest differential equations are of the homogeneous, autonomous, first-order differential variety. One can also take a kth-order differential equation and transform it into a first-order *system* of differential equations, simply by relabeling the variables and using matrix algebra. Lastly, differential equations can be classified based on whether the coefficients are constant or not; here, our focus is on constant coefficient differential equations of the types described above. We describe the solution and analysis of first-order equations since higher-order equations can be analyzed using matrix methods described in the section on systems of equations.

2.1.1.2 *Solutions of differential equations*

The solution to a differential equation describes the time path of the relevant variable as a function of time and other associated parameters. A differential equation can be solved by describing its general solution y_t^g as the sum of its complementary solution y_t^c and any particular solution y_t^p. That is,

$$y_t^g = y_t^c + y_t^p. \tag{2.9}$$

The complementary solution is obtained by solving the original equation in its homogeneous form. The resulting equation is sometimes called the complementary equation and is used to solve for y_t^c. The particular solution is a selected solution of the original equation and is often solved through the method of undetermined coefficients. The method is best explained via examples, as follows.

Consider the first-order, homogeneous differential equation

$$\overset{\bullet}{y}_t = \frac{dy_t}{dt} = ay_t, \tag{2.10}$$

with y_0 given as an initial condition.[2] Write (2.10) as

$$\frac{dy_t}{y_t} = adt. \tag{2.11}$$

[2]That is, the value of y at time $t = 0$ is some number y_0.

In this instance, the general solution will be the same as the homogeneous solution since the original differential equation is in fact homogeneous. Therefore, solving (2.11) by integrating both sides of (2.11) yields

$$y_t^g = ke^{at}, \tag{2.12}$$

where k is a constant of integration. This is because the left-hand side of (2.11) integrates to $\ln y_t$ and the right-hand side integrates to $at + k'$, where k' is a constant. Exponentiating both sides gives equation (2.12), where $k = \exp(k')$. It's not surprising that the solution involves an exponential function in time, after all, the original differential equation implies that the rate of change of y is proportional to the size of y whenever a is positive. As y becomes larger with time, the rate of change increases with it.

The value of k depends on the initial condition. In order to determine k, use the initial condition by setting $t = 0$, that is, $y_0 = ke^{a\times 0}$. Therefore,

$$y_0 = k, \tag{2.13}$$

and

$$y_t^g = y_0 e^{at}. \tag{2.14}$$

Next, consider the first-order, non-homogeneous equation

$$\overset{\bullet}{y}_t = ay_t + b, \tag{2.15}$$

with y_0 given and b as some constant. To solve, first obtain the complementary equation

$$\overset{\bullet}{y}{}_t^c = ay_t, \tag{2.16}$$

and as seen above, the solution to this is simply

$$y_t^c = k_1 e^{at}, \tag{2.17}$$

where k_1 is an integration constant. Second, write (2.15) as

$$\overset{\bullet}{y}{}_t^p - ay_t^p = b \tag{2.18}$$

to solve for a particular solution. Guess that y_t^p takes the form

$$y_t^p = k_2 t + k_3, \tag{2.19}$$

because the constant b can result from taking the derivative of an expression with respect to time that contains both t and a constant. Thus,

$$\overset{\bullet}{y}{}_t^p = k_2, \tag{2.20}$$

and substitute (2.19) and (2.20) into (2.15). This gives the relationship

$$k_2 - a(k_2 t + k_3) = b, \tag{2.21}$$

which can be solved by undetermined coefficients, as follows.

Since time does not appear on the right-hand side of (2.21), set k_2 equal to zero. Simplifying produces

$$k_3 = -\frac{b}{a}, \tag{2.22}$$

and so the particular solution is

$$y_t^p = k_2 t + k_3 = -\frac{b}{a}. \tag{2.23}$$

Adding the complementary solution with the particular solution results in the general solution

$$y_t^g = k_1 e^{at} - \frac{b}{a}, \tag{2.24}$$

which can be expressed as

$$y_t^g = \left(y_0 + \frac{b}{a}\right) e^{at} - \frac{b}{a} \tag{2.25}$$

after imposing the initial condition.

In summary, a differential equation such as

$$\overset{\bullet}{y}_t = a y_t - b, \tag{2.26}$$

with an initial condition $y(0) = y_0$, is called an initial value problem. The general solution for (2.26) is given by

$$y_t = \left(y_0 - \frac{b}{a}\right) e^{at} + \frac{b}{a} \tag{2.27}$$

and consists of a complementary solution and a particular solution. By specifying y_0, the equation is 'started' and the general solution then provides the entire path of y_t as a function of time and values for parameters. Finally, in order to obtain a solution, the method of undetermined coefficients is used. In this method, integration constants are pinned down by using the initial condition of the variable.

2.1.1.3 *Steady states and stability analyses*

In continuous time, a steady state is achieved when

$$\dot{y}_t = 0. \tag{2.28}$$

Therefore, a non-homogeneous differential equation

$$\dot{y}_t = ay_t - b \tag{2.29}$$

has a steady state equal to

$$\overline{y} = \frac{b}{a}. \tag{2.30}$$

It is often useful to find out if the steady state is unique (an example is provided in the following). Given uniqueness, it is important to find out the stability of the differential equation around a given steady state. In particular, we're interested in knowing how the variable y_t evolves near the steady state and whether trajectories of y_t tend to converge to, or diverge from, the steady state. Since the differential equation is borne out of economic modeling, the steady-state value of y_t will tell you something about the relationship of all of the economic parameters of your model and the equation of motion when it is at rest. Steady states often correspond to equilibrium concepts in macroeconomic models and typically serve as a 'benchmark' of the behavior of the economic system being considered.

Going back to stability analysis, we say that there is local stability for a first-order differential equation if

$$\frac{d\dot{y}_t}{dy_t} < 0, \tag{2.31}$$

while there is local instability when

$$\frac{d\dot{y}_t}{dy_t} > 0. \tag{2.32}$$

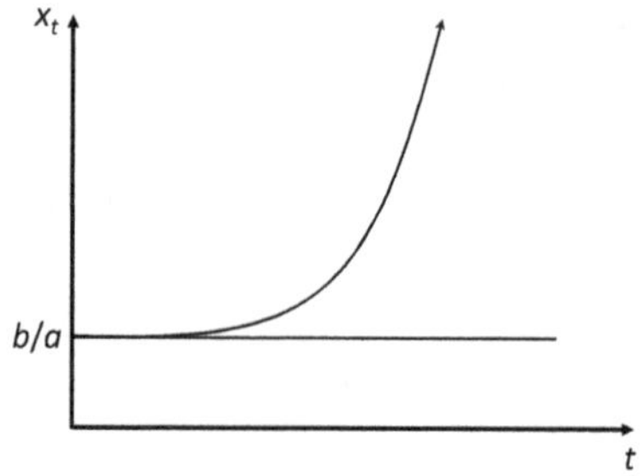

Figure 2.1. Solution of $\dot{x}_t = ax_t - b$ for $a > 0$.

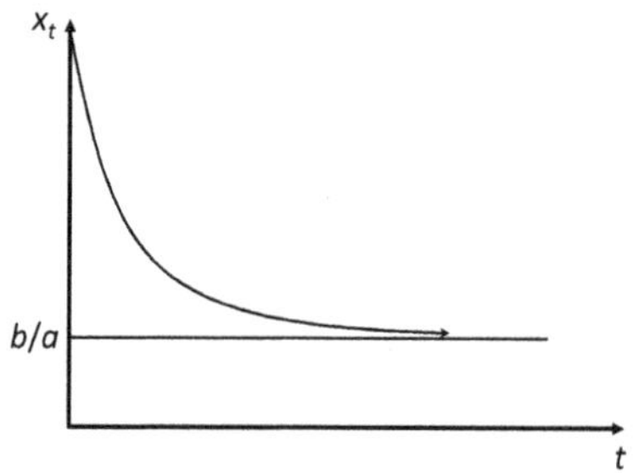

Figure 2.2. Solution of $\dot{x}_t = ax_t - b$ when $a < 0$.

One can understand these stability rules using time-path diagrams. Consider as an example the relationship

$$\dot{x}_t = ax_t - b. \tag{2.33}$$

The time-path diagram for this equation when $a > 0$ is plotted in Figure 2.1.

As one can see, all values of x_t move away from the steady state, $\overline{x} = \frac{b}{a}$. Therefore, the differential equation is locally unstable. By contrast, examine the time-path diagram when $a < 0$ plotted in Figure 2.2.

In this case, $\dot{x}_t$ approaches $\overline{x} = \frac{b}{a}$; as such, the differential equation is locally stable.

2.1.1.4 *Unidimensional phase diagrams*

The stability of differential equations can be seen through the use of unidimensional phase diagrams. This involves finding the steady

Figure 2.3. Phase of $\dot{y}_t = a_1 y_t - y_t^2$.

state(s) of a differential equation and determining the behavior of the time-dependent variable in the neighborhood of the steady states. For instance, consider the nonlinear differential equation

$$\dot{y}_t = a_1 y_t - y_t^2 = y_t(a_1 - y_t), \quad a_1 > 0. \tag{2.34}$$

When $\dot{y}_t = 0$, the equation becomes

$$y_t^2 = a_1 y_t, \tag{2.35}$$

with the following multiple steady states:

$$\bar{y} = a_1 \quad \text{and,} \tag{2.36}$$

$$\bar{y} = 0. \tag{2.37}$$

When $\dot{y}_t > 0$, it can be shown that $0 < y_t < a_1$ and when $\dot{y}_t < 0$ that $y_t < 0$ or $y_t > a_1$. These results can be illustrated on a unidimensional phase diagram as shown in Figure 2.3, in which the arrows indicate the movement of y_t through time.

2.1.2 Systems of linear equations

It is usually easier to solve a higher-order differential equation by translating it into a system of lower-order equations. Indeed, nth-order differential equations can be written as a first-order system of n equations and n variables. Additionally, non-autonomous equations can be written as autonomous systems by introducing a new variable, e.g. $y_t = t$.

2.1.2.1 *A taxonomy of systems*

The taxonomy of systems of differential equations follows that of single differential equations: they can be classified in terms of autonomy, homogeneity, and order. When classifying systems of equations, all the equations must share the same classification for the system as a whole to obtain that label. For instance, the system of differential equations

$$\dot{y}_{1t} = a_1 y_{1t} + a_2 y_{2t} + b_1, \tag{2.38}$$

$$\dot{y}_{2t} = a_3 y_{1t} + a_4 y_{2t} + b_2 \tag{2.39}$$

is autonomous, while

$$\dot{y}_{1t} = a_1 y_{1t} + a_2 y_{2t} + a_3 t + b_1, \tag{2.40}$$

$$\dot{y}_{2t} = a_4 y_{1t} + a_5 y_{2t} + b_2 \tag{2.41}$$

is non-autonomous because time appears explicitly in the form of the term $a_3 t$.

With respect to classifying systems in terms of homogeneity, the following system is found to be homogeneous:

$$\dot{y}_{1t} = a_1 y_{1t} + a_2 y_{2t} + a_3 y_{3t}, \tag{2.42}$$

$$\dot{y}_{2t} = a_4 y_{1t} + a_5 y_{2t} + a_6 y_{3t}, \tag{2.43}$$

$$\dot{y}_{3t} = a_7 y_{1t} + a_8 y_{2t} + a_9 y_{3t}, \tag{2.44}$$

since there are no constant terms or other time-dependent variables in any of the equations. In contrast, the system

$$\dot{y}_{1t} = a_1 y_{1t} + a_2 y_{2t} + a_3 y_{3t} + b_1, \tag{2.45}$$

$$\dot{y}_{2t} = a_4 y_{1t} + a_5 y_{2t} + a_6 y_{3t}, \tag{2.46}$$

$$\dot{y}_{3t} = a_7 y_{1t} + a_8 y_{2t} + a_9 y_{3t} + b_2 \tag{2.47}$$

is non-homogeneous due to the presence of constant terms.

Next, the order of a system is determined by the highest derivative that appears in any of the equations; we focus on only constant coefficient systems. Hence,

$$\ddot{y}_{2t} + a_1 \dot{y}_{2t} + a_2 y_{2t} = b, \tag{2.48}$$

$$\dot{y}_{1t} = y_{2t} \tag{2.49}$$

is considered to be a second-order system of differential equations. Of course, one can convert this second-order system into a first-order system by setting

$$\dot{y}_{2t} = y_{3t}. \tag{2.50}$$

The system then becomes

$$\ddot{y}_{2t} + a_1\dot{y}_{2t} + a_2 y_{2t} = b, \tag{2.51}$$

$$\dot{y}_{1t} = y_{2t}, \tag{2.52}$$

$$\dot{y}_{2t} = y_{3t}, \tag{2.53}$$

which can be put into the form of a first-order system:

$$\dot{y}_{1t} = y_{2t}, \tag{2.54}$$

$$\dot{y}_{2t} = y_{3t}, \tag{2.55}$$

$$\dot{y}_{3t} = b - a_1 y_{3t} - a_2 y_{2t}. \tag{2.56}$$

This transformation is useful because the analysis of a first-order system of equations is a lot like the analysis of a first-order single equation.

2.1.2.2 *Solutions of deterministic systems*

There are two methods of solving systems of differential equations. One solves each equation separately, while the other uses a matrix approach; both approaches of course are related. Consider the 2×2 first-order system

$$\dot{y}_{1t} = a_1 y_{1t} + a_2 y_{2t} + b_1, \tag{2.57}$$

$$\dot{y}_{2t} = a_3 y_{1t} + a_4 y_{2t} + b_2. \tag{2.58}$$

To solve, one must first isolate y_{2t} in terms of y_{1t} (or vice versa), differentiate, solve a second-order equation, and substitute back to obtain solutions. Clearly, this method is unwieldy as the number of variables and equations increases. The matrix method is much simpler, as follows. The above equations can be expressed as

$$\dot{Y}_t = AY_t + B, \tag{2.59}$$

where capitalized letters denote a matrix. That is,

$$\overset{\bullet}{Y}_t = \begin{bmatrix} \overset{\bullet}{y}_{1t} \\ \overset{\bullet}{y}_{2t} \end{bmatrix}, \quad Y_t = \begin{bmatrix} y_{1t} \\ y_{2t} \end{bmatrix}, \tag{2.60}$$

$$A = \begin{bmatrix} a_1 & a_2 \\ a_3 & a_4 \end{bmatrix}, \quad B = \begin{bmatrix} b_1 \\ b_2 \end{bmatrix}. \tag{2.61}$$

If A is diagonal (i.e. $a_2 = a_3 = 0$), then the system becomes

$$\overset{\bullet}{y}_{1t} = a_1 y_{1t} + b_1, \tag{2.62}$$

$$\overset{\bullet}{y}_{2t} = a_4 y_{2t} + b_2. \tag{2.63}$$

The complementary solutions are simply

$$y_{1t}^c = k_1 e^{a_1 t}, \tag{2.64}$$

$$y_{2t}^c = k_2 e^{a_4 t}, \tag{2.65}$$

where k_i are arbitrary integration constants.

Solving around the steady state, the particular solutions are

$$y_{1t}^p = -\frac{b_1}{a_1}, \tag{2.66}$$

$$y_{2t}^p = -\frac{b_2}{a_4}. \tag{2.67}$$

Together, these produce the general solutions

$$y_{1t}^g = k_1 e^{a_1 t} - \frac{b_1}{a_1}, \tag{2.68}$$

$$y_{2t}^g = k_2 e^{a_4 t} - \frac{b_2}{a_4}. \tag{2.69}$$

Thus, an advantage of having A as diagonal is that the system is 'uncoupled': the dynamic evolution of the variables y_{1t} and y_{2t} are separated from one another so that if A is not diagonal, then one must find a way to diagonalize it, as follows.

First, let r_1 and r_2 be the eigenvalues of A and v_1 and v_2 be the eigenvectors associated with the eigenvalues. Next, let D be the diagonal matrix,

$$D = \begin{bmatrix} r_1 & 0 \\ 0 & r_2 \end{bmatrix}, \tag{2.70}$$

and P be the matrix of eigenvalues,

$$P = \{v_1, v_2\} = \begin{bmatrix} v_{11} & v_{21} \\ v_{12} & v_{22} \end{bmatrix}. \tag{2.71}$$

If r_i are distinct and the v_i are linearly independent, then

$$P^{-1}AP = D. \tag{2.72}$$

Define

$$Z_t = P^{-1}Y_t, \tag{2.73}$$

which can be written as

$$PZ_t = Y_t. \tag{2.74}$$

Similarly, we get the relationships

$$\dot{Z}_t = P^{-1}\dot{Y}_t, \tag{2.75}$$

$$P\dot{Z}_t = \dot{Y}_t. \tag{2.76}$$

Substitute (2.74) and (2.76) into (2.59). Ignore B to obtain the complementary matrix equation

$$P\dot{Z}_t^c = APZ_t^c. \tag{2.77}$$

This can be rewritten as

$$\dot{Z}_t^c = P^{-1}APZ_t^c. \tag{2.78}$$

Using (2.72) yields the relationship

$$\dot{Z}_t^c = DZ_t^c, \tag{2.79}$$

which has the solutions

$$z_{1t}^{c} = k_1 e^{r_1 t}, \tag{2.80}$$

$$z_{2t}^{c} = k_2 e^{r_2 t}. \tag{2.81}$$

To have the complementary solutions in terms of Y_t, the transform must be undone as follows:

$$Y_t = PZ_t, \tag{2.82}$$

$$Y_t = P\begin{bmatrix} z_{1t}^{c} \\ z_{2t}^{c} \end{bmatrix}, \quad Y_t = P\begin{bmatrix} k_1 e^{r_1 t} \\ k_2 e^{r_2 t} \end{bmatrix}, \tag{2.83}$$

$$Y_t = \begin{bmatrix} v_{11} & v_{21} \\ v_{12} & v_{22} \end{bmatrix} \begin{bmatrix} k_1 e^{r_1 t} \\ k_2 e^{r_2 t} \end{bmatrix}, \tag{2.84}$$

which means

$$y_{1t}^{c} = v_{11} k_1 e^{r_1 t} + v_{21} k_2 e^{r_2 t}, \tag{2.85}$$

$$y_{2t}^{c} = v_{12} k_1 e^{r_1 t} + v_{22} k_2 e^{r_2 t}. \tag{2.86}$$

To obtain a particular solution, first solve for the steady-state values by setting $\dot{y}_{1t} = \dot{y}_{2t} = 0$. The system becomes

$$a_1 y_{1t}^{p} + a_2 y_{2t}^{p} = -b_1, \tag{2.87}$$

$$a_3 y_{1t}^{p} + a_4 y_{2t}^{p} = -b_2. \tag{2.88}$$

Solving for y_{2t}^{p},

$$y_{2t}^{p} = \frac{-b_2 - a_3 y_{1t}^{p}}{a_4}, \tag{2.89}$$

and inserting this expression back into (2.87) gives

$$a_1 y_{1t}^{p} + a_2 \left(\frac{-b_2 - a_3 y_{1t}^{p}}{a_4} \right) = -b_1. \tag{2.90}$$

Solving for y_{1t}^{p},

$$y_{1t}^{p} = \frac{-b_1 + \frac{a_2 b_2}{a_4}}{a_1 - \frac{a_2 a_3}{a_4}}, \tag{2.91}$$

which simplifies to

$$y_{1t}^{p} = \frac{a_2 b_2 - a_4 b_1}{a_1 a_4 - a_2 a_3}. \tag{2.92}$$

Therefore, the general solutions are

$$y_{1t}^{g} = v_{11} k_1 e^{r_1 t} + v_{21} k_2 e^{r_2 t} + \frac{a_2 b_2 - a_4 b_1}{a_1 a_4 - a_2 a_3}, \tag{2.93}$$

$$y_{2t}^{g} = v_{12} k_1 e^{r_1 t} + v_{22} k_2 e^{r_2 t} + \frac{a_3 b_1 - a_1 b_2}{a_1 a_4 - a_2 a_3}. \tag{2.94}$$

To find the specific values of k_i, set $t = 0$ and solve.

2.1.2.3 *Steady states and stability analyses*

The steady state of a system of differential equations is found by setting $\dot{Y}_t = 0$ and then solving for Y_t, which may involve solving a system of equations. As an example, consider the 2×2 system

$$\dot{y}_{2t} = f(y_{1t}, y_{2t}), \tag{2.95}$$

$$\dot{y}_{2t} = g(y_{1t}, y_{2t}). \tag{2.96}$$

Then, the steady-state values $(\overline{y}_1, \overline{y}_2)$ are those which solve

$$f(\overline{y}_1, \overline{y}_2) = g(\overline{y}_1, \overline{y}_2) = 0. \tag{2.97}$$

In general, the stability of the steady state can be found by computing the Jacobian of a system of differential equations. Thus, for a 2×2 system

$$\dot{y}_{1t} = f(y_{1t}, y_{2t}), \tag{2.98}$$

$$\dot{y}_{2t} = g(y_{1t}, y_{2t}), \tag{2.99}$$

the Jacobian is equal to

$$J = \begin{bmatrix} f'_{y_{1t}} & f'_{y_{2t}} \\ g'_{y_{1t}} & g'_{y_{2t}} \end{bmatrix} = \begin{bmatrix} \dfrac{\partial f}{\partial y_{1t}} & \dfrac{\partial f}{\partial y_{2t}} \\ \dfrac{\partial g}{\partial y_{1t}} & \dfrac{\partial g}{\partial y_{2t}} \end{bmatrix}. \tag{2.100}$$

Let r_1 and r_2 be the eigenvalues of J. We use the following terminology to describe stability around the steady state based on the eigenvalues:

$$\text{Stable } \textit{node} \text{ if } r_1, r_2 \text{ both real and distinct and } r_1, r_2 < 0, \tag{2.101}$$

$$\text{Stable } \textit{focus} \text{ if } r_1, r_2 \text{ both complex and } Re(r_1),\ Re(r_2) < 0, \tag{2.102}$$

$$\textit{Saddle path} \text{ if } r_1, r_2 \text{ both real and } r_1 > 0,\ r_2 < 0, \tag{2.103}$$

$$\textit{Center} \text{ if } r_1, r_2 \text{ both complex and } Re(r_1),\ Re(r_2) = 0, \tag{2.104}$$

$$\text{Stable } \textit{improper node} \text{ if } r_1, r_2 \text{ both real and } r_1 = r_2 < 0, \tag{2.105}$$

$$\hookrightarrow J \text{ is not diagonal}, \tag{2.106}$$

$$\text{Stable } \textit{star node} \text{ if } r_1, r_2 \text{ both real and } r_1 = r_2 < 0, \tag{2.107}$$

$$\hookrightarrow J \text{ is diagonal}, \tag{2.108}$$

where $Re(r_1)$ denotes the real part of the root. Thus, an unstable focus occurs if r_1 and r_2 are both complex and $Re(r_1)$ and $Re(r_2)$ are both positive. This text deals frequently with linear systems of the form

$$\overset{\bullet}{y}_{1t} = a_1 y_{1t} + a_2 y_{2t} + b_1, \tag{2.109}$$

$$\overset{\bullet}{y}_{2t} = a_3 y_{1t} + a_4 y_{2t} + b_2. \tag{2.110}$$

In this case, the Jacobian of the system is the matrix A in the notation

$$\overset{\bullet}{Y}_t = AY_t + B. \tag{2.111}$$

Consequently, to find the stability of the system, find the eigenvalues of A and apply the stability rules stated above. Usually, we will focus exclusively on stability (roots both negative), instability (roots both positive), and saddle path stability (roots alternating in sign). Phase diagrams make the notion of saddle-path stability come alive, as discussed in the following.

2.1.2.4 *Multi-dimensional phase diagrams*

The behavior of a system in the vicinity of its steady state can be examined using graphical techniques (multi-phase diagrams). Consider the system

$$\dot{x}_{1t} = x_{1t} + 2x_{2t} - 8, \tag{2.112}$$

$$\dot{x}_{2t} = 2x_{1t} - 2x_{2t} - 4. \tag{2.113}$$

The steady state for this system is $(\overline{x}_1, \overline{x}_2) = (4, 2)$.

To analyze this system using a phase diagram, plot in 2D space the equations

$$x_{1t} + 2x_{2t} - 8 = 0, \tag{2.114}$$

$$2x_{1t} - 2x_{2t} - 4 = 0 \tag{2.115}$$

and denote these lines, as shown in Figure 2.4, as pertaining to $\dot{x}_{1t} = 0$ and $\dot{x}_{2t} = 0$, respectively.[3]

To find the phase arrows, pick a point along one of the steady-state lines. Then, move away from this point in one axial direction, say x_{2t}, while keeping the other constant (x_{1t}). In this example, one would use (2.113) to determine whether $\dot{x}_{2t}$ is increasing or decreasing depending on how x_{2t} is being changed. This process is repeated

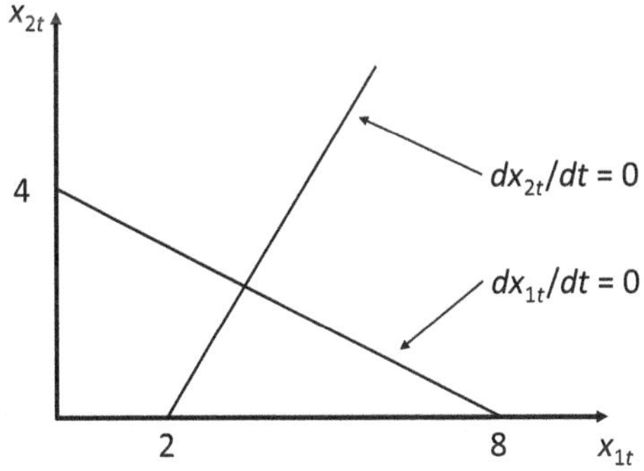

Figure 2.4. Phase lines.

[3]These equations are often referred to as nullclines.

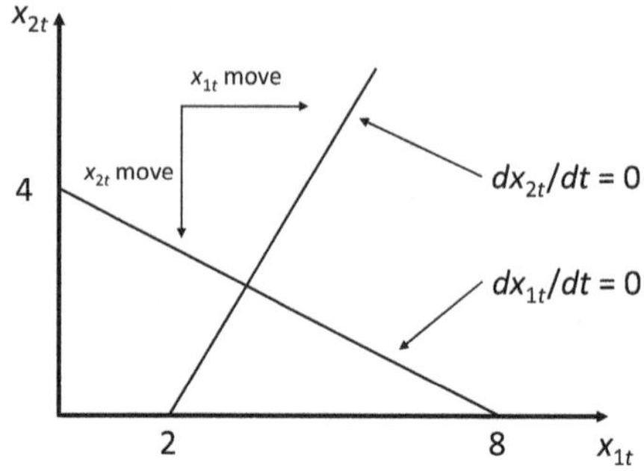

Figure 2.5. Movement directions for phase lines.

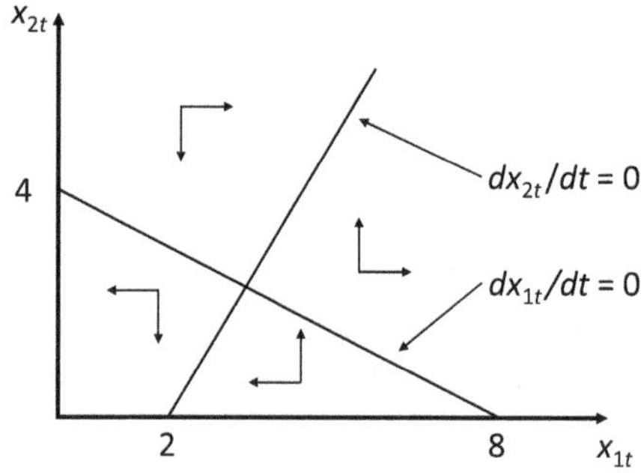

Figure 2.6. Direction arrows combined.

by changing x_{1t} while keeping x_{2t} constant. The phase arrows, which when plotted are known as the phase plane, are shown in Figure 2.5.

In a 2×2 system, there will be four regions, each having two corresponding phase arrows. Combining these arrows indicates visually whether the system, starting from any point in the two-dimensional plane, is stable, unstable or saddle-path stable, as shown in Figure 2.6.

Through linking these phase arrows, one can establish the saddle path through the steady state, as shown in Figure 2.7.

The term 'saddle-path stability' describes a situation where, for each value of x_{1t} (or conversely x_{2t}), there is a unique value of x_{2t} (or conversely x_{1t}) that ensures that the dynamics of the system tend

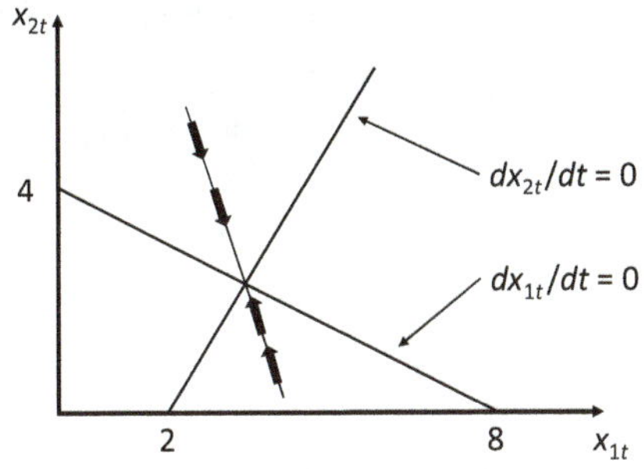

Figure 2.7. Saddle path.

toward the steady state: this is the 'saddle' pictured in the above diagram.

2.1.3 Taylor series approximations and linearization

Nonlinear systems of differential equations need to be linearized around their steady state, as nonlinear systems are notoriously difficult to analyze, especially in large dimensions. One can then analyze the behavior of each time-dependent variable in the neighborhood of this point. The linearized version of the system provides a good description of the dynamics in a small neighborhood around the steady state. However, the dynamics of the linearized system become increasingly inaccurate as one moves away from the point around which the linearization is computed. Often, the steady state is all that we are interested in. In some dynamic microeconomic applications where a system of differential equations is derived by considering jointly the best responses of individuals in a game, one may wish instead to linearize around the Nash equilibrium if it exists – the methodology for linearizing is therefore useful in many different settings. Since linear systems are easier to handle than nonlinear ones, linearization techniques are a crucial tool; the only drawback is that one is forced to analyze local solutions versus global ones. The linearization of differential equations can be accomplished using a method called Taylor series approximation (TSA).

Suppose one is given the relationship

$$\dot{x}_t - f(x_t) + b, \quad f(\cdot) \text{ nonlinear.} \tag{2.116}$$

Then, the jth-order TSA around the steady state $\overline{x}$ is given by[4]

$$\overset{\bullet}{x}_t \approx f(\overline{x}) + f'(\overline{x})(x_t - \overline{x}) + \frac{1}{2}f''(\overline{x})(x_t - \overline{x})^2 + \cdots + \frac{1}{j!}f^j(\overline{x})(x_t - \overline{x})^j. \tag{2.117}$$

Usually, only a first-order TSA (hereafter TSA1) is needed, allowing one to ignore other higher-order terms.

Therefore, the TSA1 of (2.116) is simply

$$\overset{\bullet}{x}_t \approx f(\bar{x}) + f'(\bar{x})(x_t - \bar{x}). \tag{2.118}$$

Next, consider the system

$$\overset{\bullet}{X}_t = F(X_t) + B, \quad F(\cdot) \text{ nonlinear.} \tag{2.119}$$

The jth-order TSA around the system's steady state $\overline{X}$ is given by

$$\overset{\bullet}{X}_t \approx F(\overline{X}) + JF(\overline{X})(X_t - \overline{X}) + \frac{1}{2}J^2F(\overline{X})(X_t - \overline{X})^2 + \cdots + \frac{1}{j!}J^jF(\overline{X})(X_t - \overline{X})^j, \tag{2.120}$$

and the TSA1 is equal to

$$\overset{\bullet}{X}_t \approx F(\overline{X}) + JF(\overline{X}) \times (X_t - \overline{X}). \tag{2.121}$$

Note that $JF(\overline{X})$ is the Jacobian of F evaluated at $\overline{X}$ and that $J^2F(\overline{X})$ is the Hessian of F evaluated at $\overline{X}$.

2.2 Dynamic Optimization: Introductory Comments

Many problems in economics are analyzed in a dynamic setting; the actors (households, firms, and others) are assumed to be behaving as though they are maximizing some objective subject to dynamic

[4]Note that $f(\overline{x})$ denotes the function f evaluated at $\overline{x}$. Similarly, $f'(\overline{x})$ denotes the first derivative of f evaluated at $\overline{x}$, $f''(\overline{x})$ denotes the second derivative of f evaluated at $\overline{x}$, and so on. An exclamation mark denotes factorial, e.g. $j!$ is j factorial.

constraints described by differential equations. These considerations lead us to the study of methods that allow us to formulate and solve optimization problems; these are called dynamic optimization methods and fall into two broad categories: optimal control methods (associated with Pontryagin) and dynamic programming methods (associated with Bellman). Optimal control is generally available in two forms: Lagrangians and Hamiltonians. Optimal control problems that use Lagrangians are typically not used in continuous time but rather pertain to deterministic optimization settings, as they typically involve integration techniques which are often difficult to solve. Dynamic programming methods are also not used for this setting, as they typically involve deriving and solving PDEs. Optimal control via the use of Hamiltonians, on the other hand, is usually the method of choice. For discrete time deterministic optimization problems, one can use both forms of optimal control and dynamic programming in some special cases (although rarely analytically).[5]

2.3 Constrained Optimization Theory: A Primer

We follow the discussion by Dixit (1990) and note that the Kuhn–Tucker theorem is the first central tool from optimization theory that is employed in constructing dynamic optimization concepts. Suppose x^* satisfies

$$\max_x \quad \Gamma = F(x), \quad x \in \Re, \tag{2.122}$$

$$s.t. \quad c \geq G(x), \tag{2.123}$$

where $\frac{dG(x)}{dx} = G'(x)$ is non-zero and both $F(\cdot)$ and $G(\cdot)$ are continuously differentiable. Then, the theorem states that there exists a λ^*, known as the optimal Lagrange multiplier, such that:

$$\left.\frac{dL}{dx}\right|_{(x^*,\lambda^*)} = L'_x(x^*,\lambda^*) = F'_x(x^*) - \lambda^* G'_x(x^*) = 0, \tag{2.124}$$

[5]Excellent treatments of dynamic optimization are available in Chiang (1999) and Dixit (1990).

$$\left.\frac{dL}{d\lambda}\right|_{(x^*,\lambda^*)} = L'_\lambda(x^*,\lambda^*) = c - G(x^*) \geq 0, \tag{2.125}$$

$$\lambda^* \geq 0, \tag{2.126}$$

$$\lambda^*[c - G(x^*)] = 0. \tag{2.127}$$

This theorem sets out the basic necessary but not sufficient conditions for optimizing a (multivariate) function subject to constraints; note that maximizing a function is equivalent to minimizing the negative of that function. At this point, you should note that if x^* is an optimal solution to the above maximization problem and λ^* is strictly positive, then it has to be that the constraint binds, namely that $c - G(x^*) = 0$. When this happens, the optimal value x^* does not satisfy the condition that $F'_x(x^*) = 0$. Instead, you have equation (2.124). On the other hand, if x^* is an interior solution, meaning that $c - G(x^*) > 0$, then you have the more familiar condition that $F'_x(x^*) = 0$.

The envelope theorem provides the second central tool from optimization theory that is employed typically for dynamic programming methods. Let F and G be continuously differentiable in x and y so that the optimization problem is given by

$$\max_x \quad \Gamma = F(x,y), \quad x \in \Re, \quad y \in \Re, \tag{2.128}$$

$$s.t. \quad c \geq G(x,y), \tag{2.129}$$

and let $x^*(y)$ denote the value of x that satisfies the above optimization problem. Next, let $\lambda^*(y)$ be the associated Lagrange multiplier, let $x^*(y)$ and $\lambda^*(y)$ be differentiable, and let $G'_1(x^*(y),y)$ be non-zero for all values of y. Then,

$$V(y) = \max \quad \{F(x,y) \quad s.t. \quad c \geq G(x,y)\} \tag{2.130}$$

satisfies

$$V'(y) = F'_2(x^*(y),y) - \lambda^*(y)G'_2(x^*(y),y). \tag{2.131}$$

Here, $V(y)$ is known as the value function, and the theorem states that $V(y)$ traces out the envelope of the functions $F(x^*(y_i),y)$ that are created by varying y. As mentioned above, this result is useful primarily for dynamic programming. Once again, note here that if $c > G(x^*(y), y)$ for a given value of y, meaning that $x^*(y)$ is an interior solution, then the value function satisfies $V'(y) = F_2'(x^*(y), y)$. This theorem is handy if, for example, you guess a solution $x^*(y)$ with unknown coefficients in the solution. The envelope condition, through the method of undetermined coefficients, will allow you to uncover what the coefficients are in the guess (if the guess turns out to be correct). All of the optimization methods we discuss are based, in one way or another, on these two central theorems.

Finally, as an example, let us maximize the function $f(x_1, x_2) = x_1 x_2$ subject to the constraints $x_1 + x_2 \leq 6$, and $x_i \geq 0, i = 1, 2$. Note first that, since the constraints identify a compact set and the function is continuous, global maximizers (and minimizers) will exist. The Lagrangian function is

$$L = x_1 x_2 + \lambda_1(6 - x_1 - x_2) + \lambda_2 x_1 + \lambda_2 x_2, \tag{2.132}$$

and the first-order necessary conditions are

$$L'_{x_1} = x_2 - \lambda_1 + \lambda_2 = 0, \tag{2.133}$$

$$L'_{x_2} = x_1 - \lambda_1 + \lambda_3 = 0, \tag{2.134}$$

$$\lambda_1, \lambda_2, \lambda_3 \geq 0, \tag{2.135}$$

$$\lambda_1 \times (6 - x_1 - x_2) = 0, \quad \lambda_2 \times x_1 = 0, \quad \lambda_3 \times x_2 = 0. \tag{2.136}$$

We can solve for (x_1^*, x_2^*) as follows:

- If $x_1^* = x_2^* = 0$, then $\lambda_1 = 0$ and thus $\lambda_2 = \lambda_3 = 0$, meaning all conditions are satisfied.
- If $x_1^* \neq 0$ and $x_2^* = 0$, then $\lambda_2 = 0$ and $\lambda_1 = 0$; this however implies $\lambda_3 = -x_1^* < 0$, violating the condition requiring that the Lagrange multipliers be all non-negative.
- If $x_1^* = 0$ and $x_2^* \neq 0$, then $\lambda_3 = 0$ and $\lambda_1 = 0$; this however implies $\lambda_2 = -x_2^* < 0$, violating the condition requiring that the Lagrange multipliers be all non-negative.
- If $x_1^* \neq 0$ and $x_2^* \neq 0$, then $\lambda_2 = \lambda_3 = 0$, and thus $\lambda_1 = x_1^* = x_2^* > 0$, which in turn delivers $x_1^* = x_2^* = 3$.

Since $f(0,0) = 0 < 9 = f(3,3)$, the constrained optimization problem is solved at $x_i^* = 3$, $i = 1, 2$.

2.4 Calculus of Variations

The calculus of variations is a field of mathematical analysis concerned with the maxima or minima (or extreme points) of *functionals*, i.e. of mappings whose domain consists of a well-defined set of admissible functions. Formally, let $F(t, x_t, \overset{\bullet}{x}_t)$ be a twice-continuously differentiable function on $\mathcal{I} \times \mathbb{R}^2$, with $x_t : \mathcal{I} \subset \Re \mapsto \Re$ and $t \in \mathcal{I} = [a, b]$. A classical problem addressed via variational methods is

$$\max_{\{x_t\}} / \min \qquad \Gamma = \int_a^b F(t, x_t, \overset{\bullet}{x}_t) dt, \tag{2.137}$$

$$s.t. \quad x_a = \kappa_1, \quad x_b = \kappa_2, \tag{2.138}$$

where x_t is a scalar, real-valued function (called a *trajectory*) under the condition of fixed extremes of integration (x_a and x_b are given constants κ_1 and κ_2). The so-called *Euler–Lagrange principle* states that a necessary condition for a twice-continuously differentiable function x_t^* defined on $\mathcal{I}$ to be an optimizing trajectory for the above problem, with $x_a^* = \kappa_1$ and $x_b^* = \kappa_2$, is that it solves

$$\frac{\partial F}{\partial \overset{\bullet}{x}} \left(t, x_t^*, \overset{\bullet}{x^*}_t \right) = \frac{d}{dt} \frac{\partial F}{\partial \overset{\bullet}{x}} \left(t, x_t^*, \overset{\bullet}{x^*}_t \right), \quad t \in \mathcal{I}. \tag{2.139}$$

In words, if an optimal solution x_t^* to (2.137)–(2.138) exists, then the partial derivative of the functional F with respect to the state variable x_t is equal to the time derivative of the partial derivative of F with respect to the perturbation (variation) $\overset{\bullet}{x}_t$, both evaluated at $(x_t^*, \overset{\bullet}{x^*}_t)$ at any instant time in the interval $\mathcal{I}$ under scrutiny.

Assume that the object of interest is the trajectory, if it exists, that *maximizes* the objective Γ. The following sufficient condition then allows us to find the optimal solution x_t^*: if x_t^* satisfies the Euler–Lagrange principle and is consistent with the fixed extremes of integration, then it solves (2.137)–(2.138) provided F is jointly concave with respect to x_t and $\overset{\bullet}{x}_t$ for each $t \in \mathcal{I}$. If F is strictly (and jointly) concave in its second and third arguments, then x_t^* is the unique trajectory solving the underlying problem. To search for a trajectory *minimizing* γ, the sufficient condition requires that F be jointly convex in $(x_t, \overset{\bullet}{x}_t)$ (with uniqueness ensured by strict convexity).

It is worth mentioning that, provided the second-order partial derivative $\partial^2 F/\partial \overset{\bullet}{x}^2 \neq 0$ in its domain, all possible trajectories x_t^* are necessarily twice-continuously differentiable on $\mathcal{I}$. When either of the extremes of integration is not known, an alternative condition must be invoked to solve the Cauchy problem associated with the optimization program (2.137)–(2.138); when, e.g. x_a is not assigned, then such a condition simply reads as

$$\frac{\partial F}{\partial \overset{\bullet}{x}}\left(a, x_a^*, \overset{\bullet}{x}^*{}_a\right) = 0. \tag{2.140}$$

As an example, let us solve

$$\min \Gamma = \int_0^1 \left(\overset{\bullet}{x}{}_t^2 + 2x_t t\right) dt \quad s.t. \, x_0 = 1, \; x_1 = 2. \tag{2.141}$$

Note first that $\partial^2 F/\partial \overset{\bullet}{x} \neq 0$, so that all possible trajectories x_t^* are necessarily twice-continuously differentiable on $[0,1]$. Note also that the Hessian of F with respect to $(x_t, \overset{\bullet}{x}_t)$ is a positive semidefinite square matrix (i.e. the function F is jointly convex in those variables); the Euler–Lagrange condition – provided it is satisfied by an admissible trajectory – will be necessary and sufficient for the identification of the unique minimizer for the problem at hand. The condition reads as

$$\frac{\partial F}{\partial \overset{\bullet}{x}} = \frac{d}{dt}\frac{\partial F}{\partial \overset{\bullet}{x}} \implies t = x_t^{(2)}, \tag{2.142}$$

from which by integration one has

$$\begin{aligned}
\overset{\bullet}{x}_t &= \int t dt = \frac{t^2}{2} + \kappa_1 \implies x_t = \int \left(\frac{t^2}{2} + \kappa_1\right) dt \\
&= \frac{t^3}{6} + \kappa_1 t + \kappa_2, \quad \kappa_1, \kappa_2 \in \Re,
\end{aligned} \tag{2.143}$$

with κ_1, κ_2 being arbitrary integration constants. Using the boundary conditions, obtain

$$x_0 = \kappa_2 = 1, \quad x_1 = \frac{1}{6} + \kappa_1 + \kappa_2 = 2 \implies \kappa_1 = \frac{5}{6}, \quad \kappa_2 = 1, \tag{2.144}$$

and thus the optimal trajectory solving the problem will be

$$x_t^* = \frac{t^3}{6} + \frac{5}{6}t + 1. \tag{2.145}$$

2.5 Optimal Control in Continuous Time

To set up a dynamic optimization model, variables are assigned to one of four classifications: endogenous or exogenous state, control, and co-state. Endogenous state variables cannot be changed at time t; however, current choices can impact how such variables evolve in the future. Exogenous state variables are taken as given for all time; they may also evolve; however, since they are exogenous to the system, they cannot be influenced by choices made in the optimization. State variables are also known as stock or predetermined variables, typically expressed as a differential equation or a system of differential equations when one considers a continuous time setting. Control variables can be changed at time t and are also known as flow or non-predetermined variables. Lastly, co-state variables are 'shadow prices' of state variables.

2.5.1 The continuous time present value Hamiltonian

A tool to express dynamic optimization problems is the Hamiltonian. Like the Lagrangian in the Kuhn–Tucker theorem, the mechanics of a Hamiltonian involve the maximization of some objective function subject to a set of constraints. Consider for example the following optimization problem expressed in a continuous time format:

$$\max_{\{x_t\}} \quad \Gamma = \int_{t=0}^{T} e^{-\rho t} F(y_t, x_t) dt, \tag{2.146}$$

$$s.t. \quad \dot{y}_t \leq G(y_t, x_t) \quad \forall\, t \in [0, T], \tag{2.147}$$

$$y_T \geq \widetilde{y}, \quad y_{(0)} = y_0, \tag{2.148}$$

where ρ is the (exponential) discount factor and is greater than zero ($\rho > 0$) and $F(\cdot)$ is concave while $G(\cdot)$ is linear or convex (which are sufficiency conditions for a solution to (2.146)–(2.148)).

Here, y_t is the state variable, x_t is the control variable, and π_t is the co-state or shadow price of the state variable. Note that there is no distinction made between whether y_t is an endogenous or exogenous state; such distinctions are made once we give economic content to the optimization problem. Unlike in static optimization, the objective is to obtain the optimal path of the control variable (x_t).

A present value Hamiltonian (PVH) takes the form

$$\widetilde{H}(y_t, \pi_t) = e^{-\rho t}F(y_t, x_t) + \pi_t G(y_t, x_t). \tag{2.149}$$

Note that $\widetilde{H}$ is the value function for the dynamic optimization problem. It represents the optimal value of the objective function having followed the optimal path of the control variable in present value terms.

Consider the addition of a non-dynamic or intratemporal constraint, such as

$$c \geq Q(y_t, x_t), \tag{2.150}$$

then the PVH becomes

$$\widetilde{H}(y_t, \pi_t) = e^{-\rho t}F(y_t, x_t) + \pi_t G(y_t, x_t) + \zeta_t[c - Q(y_t, x_t)], \tag{2.151}$$

where ζ_t is the shadow price of the intratemporal constraint.

The first-order conditions for (2.149) are

$$\frac{\partial \widetilde{H}}{\partial x_t} = e^{-\rho t}F'_x + \pi_t G'_x = 0, \tag{2.152}$$

$$\frac{\partial \widetilde{H}}{\partial y_t} = -\dot{\pi}_t, \tag{2.153}$$

$$\frac{\partial \widetilde{H}}{\partial \pi_t} = \dot{y}_t, \tag{2.154}$$

where (2.152) represents taking the derivative of $\widetilde{H}$ with respect to the control variable (x_t) and setting it equal to zero (represents intratemporal optimality (ITA)). Equation (2.153) represents taking the derivative of $\widetilde{H}$ with respect to the state variable (y_t) and setting it equal to $-\overset{\bullet}{\pi}_t$ (represents intertemporal optimality (ITO)), and (2.154) represents taking the derivative of $\widetilde{H}$ with respect to the co-state variable (π_t) and setting it equal to $\overset{\bullet}{y}_t$ (represents recovery of the dynamic constraint (CON)). Furthermore, the associated transversality condition (TVC) is

$$\pi_T(y_T - \widetilde{y}) = 0 \quad \forall\, T < \infty \tag{2.155}$$

in finite horizons or

$$\lim_{t \to \infty} \pi_t(y_t - \widetilde{y}) = 0 \tag{2.156}$$

in an infinite horizon.

Note that a dynamic optimization problem expressed as a PVH and solved using its associated first-order conditions will often be nonlinear in nature due to the presence of $e^{-\rho t}$ in the PVH and the first-order conditions. The term $e^{-\rho t}$ is called the discount function and reflects the assumption that economists value a dynamic problem in present value terms, discussed further later. The intuition of the FONC (often called the Pontryagin conditions) in general is as follows:

- ITA: If the solution to the dynamic optimization is found, say x_t^*, then it must be the case that infinitesimal (with respect to time) or marginal benefits equal total costs in present value terms at any given point in time.
- ITO: The depreciation of the value of the dynamic constraint ($-\overset{\bullet}{\pi}_t$) equals the total intertemporal contribution of using the state to achieve the optimal control x_t^*.
- CON: The dynamic constraint must be satisfied.
- TVC: At the end of the time horizon, the state variable has no remaining value whether in finite or continuous time. If it did, it could have been used up in selecting x_t^*.

2.5.2 The continuous time current value Hamiltonian

To illustrate the current value Hamiltonian (CVH), consider the same maximization problem as in (2.146)–(2.148). The CVH is then

$$H(y_t, \lambda_t) = F(y_t, x_t) + \lambda_t G(y_t, x_t), \tag{2.157}$$

where

$$\lambda_t = \frac{\pi_t}{e^{-\rho t}}. \tag{2.158}$$

The Pontryagin conditions and the infinite horizon TVC for the CVH are

$$\frac{\partial H}{\partial x_t} = F_x' + \lambda_t G_x' = 0 \quad \textbf{[ITA]}, \tag{2.159}$$

$$\frac{\partial H}{\partial y_t} = \rho\lambda_t - \dot{\lambda}_t \quad \textbf{[ITO]}, \tag{2.160}$$

$$\frac{\partial H}{\partial \lambda_t} = \dot{y}_t \quad \textbf{[CON]}, \tag{2.161}$$

$$\lim_{t\to\infty} \lambda_t y_t e^{-\rho t} = 0 \quad \textbf{[TVC]}. \tag{2.162}$$

Again, these optimality conditions form a system of dynamic equations to be analyzed.

Dynamic optimization problems need not be discounted and can be multivariate problems. Such problems can have bounded controls and/or bounded states. For bounded controls, the optimal control must satisfy *a priori* bounds, e.g. $a < x_t < b$. For bounded states, y_t must satisfy *a priori* bounds, e.g. $a < y_t < b$. Aside from initial conditions, the state variables may have fixed endpoints (e.g. $y_{(T)} \leq \xi$) as well. In summary, given an optimization problem, say,

$$\max_{\{x_t\}} \quad \Gamma = \int_{t=0}^{T} e^{-\rho t} F(y_t, x_t)dt, \tag{2.163}$$

$$s.t. \quad \dot{y}_t \leq G(y_t, x_t) \quad \forall\, t \in [0, T], \tag{2.164}$$

$$y_t \geq \widetilde{y}, \quad y_{(0)} = y_0, \tag{2.165}$$

the first step is to formulate a PVH or CVH. Use the PVH or CVH to obtain first-order or Pontryagin conditions; these may be a system of nonlinear differential equations. Next, linearize the system and put it into first-order form if it is not in such form. Finally, solve the system for the optimal control x_t^* and analyze it for stability and uniqueness of steady states.

Finally, as an example, let us solve

$$\max \Gamma = \int_0^1 \left(y_t - x_t^2\right) dt, \quad y_0 = 2 \quad s.t. \overset{\bullet}{y}_t = x_t. \tag{2.166}$$

Since there is no discounting (i.e. $\rho = 0$) and the control x_t is not constrained to vary in a specific subset of the real interval, we can write the CVH as

$$H(y_t, \lambda_t) = y_t - x_t^2 + \lambda_t x_t \tag{2.167}$$

and then derive the optimal control x_t^* that maximizes the CVH for given (t, y_t, λ_t) using the first- and second-order conditions

$$\frac{\partial H}{\partial x_t} = -2x_t^* + \lambda_t = 0, \quad \frac{\partial^2 H}{\partial x_t^2} = -2 < 0, \tag{2.168}$$

which delivers $x_t^* = \lambda_t/2$. We thus have

$$\frac{\partial H}{\partial \lambda_t} = \overset{\bullet}{y}(t) = \frac{\lambda_t}{2}, \tag{2.169}$$

$$\frac{\partial H}{\partial y_t} = -\overset{\bullet}{\lambda}_t = 1. \tag{2.170}$$

Hence, $\lambda_t^* = \int -dt = -t + \kappa_1$, $\kappa_1 \in \Re$, and since $\lambda_1^* = 0$, one has $\kappa_1 = 1$, where

$$\lambda_t^* = 1 - t, \quad u_t^* = \frac{1-t}{2}. \tag{2.171}$$

Finally, for the optimal trajectory, we obtain

$$y_t^* = \int \frac{1-t}{2} dt = \frac{t}{2} - \frac{t^2}{4} + \kappa_2, \quad \kappa_2 \in \Re, \tag{2.172}$$

where $y_0^* = 2$ implies $\kappa_2 = 2$. The necessary conditions are in this case also sufficient, the constraint being linear and the function F being jointly concave in (y, x).

2.6 From Mathematics to Economics

This chapter has described some of the most basic mathematical tools that will be employed throughout this text. The description has been largely devoid of the economic intuition behind why these tools are predominant in economic theory. In so far as economics can be described as the study of optimal decision-making under constraints, these tools have a direct intuitive link to the study of economics. This section describes some of the very basic intuitive links between dynamic optimization and its relation to basic economics.

2.6.1 Intertemporal choice and exponential discounting

Consider a two-period utility maximization problem (in discrete time)

$$\max_{C_t, C_{t+1}} \quad U(C_t, C_{t+1}), \tag{2.173}$$

$$s.t. \quad C_t + \frac{C_{t+1}}{1+r} = Y_t + \frac{Y_{t+1}}{1+r}. \tag{2.174}$$

Then, the price of present consumption (i.e. at time t) is $1 + r$ units of future consumption. So, what would make this problem an intertemporal one?

Suppose preferences over consumption don't change over time, that is, trade-offs between C_t and C_{t+1} are not a function of the actual date of consumption. This would imply that $U(C_t, C_{t+1})$ be separable in C_t and C_{t+1}, that is, $U(C_t, C_{t+1}) = V(C_t) + V(C_{t+1})$. Next, if wealth (out of which consumption takes place) can be stored costlessly without depreciating, then one should prefer, say, W at time t versus the same W at time $t + 1$. Thus present value matters. However, it should matter over the *utility* of consumption, not necessarily consumption itself. This is because economic agents are not said to value consumption in and of itself, but rather the *utility* they derive from it. Therefore, utility should also be discounted, not necessarily at rate r though:

$$U(C_t, C_{t+1}) = V(C_t) + \frac{V(C_{t+1})}{1+\rho}, \quad \rho \geq 0, \tag{2.175}$$

where $\frac{1}{1+\rho}$ in continuous time becomes the discount function $f(t) = e^{-\rho t}$.

This is a reflection of the more general principle of dynamic consistency: 'rationally', the ratio of marginal utilities $U'(C_t)/U'(C_{t+1})$ should be independent of time such that impatience of utility holds as a principle. However, in altering present consumption (C_t), one gives up the discounted through time utility of future consumption (C_{t+1}); it is this feature of the decision that makes the problem an intertemporal one.

2.6.2 Uncertainty and risk aversion

Suppose that there are two uncertain states of the world (1 and 2) occurring with probability $p \in [0, 1]$ and $1-p$, respectively. In state 1, wealth is W_1, and in state 2, it is W_2. Utility from wealth is $U(pW_1 + (1-p)W_2)$, and the corresponding actuarial amount of wealth is $pW_1 + (1-p)W_2$.

Suppose one is 'risk averse', i.e. one would prefer (utility from) a certain amount of wealth versus waiting to see what state of the world actually takes place. In this case, $U(pW_1 + (1-p)W_2) > pU(W_1) + (1-p)U(W_2)$, implying U is concave, and so $U' > 0$ and $U'' < 0$. If U is concave, then indifference curves are convex. The degree of convexity, measured by the slope of indifference curve, $\frac{-U''}{U'}$, quantifies risk aversion. Several assumptions can be made about this convexity or curvature of the utility function, leading to various definitions for risk aversion, as follows.

Suppose that the curvature of the utility function is such that it is independent of wealth levels, then we have the constant absolute risk aversion (CARA) parameter, being defined as

$$\sigma_{CARA} = \frac{-U''}{U'}. \tag{2.176}$$

However, why should curvature be independent of wealth levels? Should the degree of risk aversion not be proportionate to wealth in some way? In this case, the constant relative risk aversion (CRRA) parameter is defined as

$$\sigma_{CRRA} = \frac{-W \times U''}{U'}. \tag{2.177}$$

So, based on the existence of σ_{CRRA}, how do we get an actual utility function? Functional forms are after all important in modeling. Well, consider the following calculation based upon the definition of σ_{CRRA}:

$$-\sigma = \frac{W \times U''}{U'} \tag{2.178}$$

$$\rightarrow \frac{\frac{dU'}{U'}}{\frac{dW}{W}} = -\sigma \tag{2.179}$$

$$\rightarrow d\log U' = -\sigma \log W \tag{2.180}$$

$$\rightarrow \int d\log U' = \int -\sigma \log W dW \tag{2.181}$$

$$\rightarrow \log U' = -\sigma \log W + \log k_1 \tag{2.182}$$

$$\rightarrow U' = W^{-\sigma} k_1, \tag{2.183}$$

where k_1 (and later k_2) are constants of integration.

Use this result to note that

$$U' = \frac{dU}{dW} \rightarrow \frac{dU}{dW} = W^{-\sigma} k_1 \tag{2.184}$$

$$\rightarrow dU = W^{-\sigma} k_1 dW \tag{2.185}$$

$$\rightarrow \int dU = \int W^{-\sigma} k_1 dW \tag{2.186}$$

$$\rightarrow U = \left\{ \begin{array}{ll} \frac{W^{1-\sigma}}{1-\sigma} k_1 + k_2 & if\ \sigma \neq 1 \\ k_1 \log W + k_2 & if\ \sigma = 1 \end{array} \right\}. \tag{2.187}$$

Thus, it is often the case that macroeconomists employ the CRRA form of utility.

2.6.3 Aggregate data and production functions

Recall from the introductory chapter that one of the stylized facts is that the ratio of output to capital (Y/K) is constant in the long run. This fact can be used to figure out the most appropriate form for a production function.

Consider a production function of the form

$$Y_t = F(\kappa_t K_t, \lambda_t L_t), \tag{2.188}$$

such that κ_t and λ_t are exogenous technological growth processes of the form

$$\kappa_t = \kappa_0 e^{\zeta t}, \tag{2.189}$$

$$\lambda_t = \lambda_0 e^{\xi t}, \tag{2.190}$$

where ζ and ξ are positive if we believe in technological progress (i.e. growth) in both capital and labor.

Since in a steady state $\frac{Y}{K}$ is constant, we have that $\frac{d(\frac{Y}{K})}{dt} = 0$; therefore, assuming that the function F is homogeneous of degree 1, we have

$$\frac{Y_t}{K_t} = \frac{\kappa_0 e^{\zeta t} K_t F\left(1, \frac{\lambda_0 e^{\xi t} L_t}{\kappa_0 e^{\zeta t} K_t}\right)}{K_t}, \tag{2.191}$$

$$\frac{Y}{K} = \kappa_0 e^{\zeta t} F\left(1, \frac{\lambda_0 e^{(\xi-\zeta)t}\overline{L}}{\kappa_0 \overline{K}}\right) \quad \text{in steady state} \tag{2.192}$$

$$= \kappa_0 e^{\zeta t} G(e^{(\xi-\zeta)t}), \tag{2.193}$$

where $G(\cdot)$ is some function that is yet to be determined. Suppose now that $\zeta \neq 0$, then $\frac{d(\frac{Y}{K})}{dt} = 0$ if and only if

$$\zeta e^{\zeta t} G(\cdot) + e^{\zeta t}(\xi - \zeta) e^{(\xi-\zeta)t} G'(\cdot) = 0, \tag{2.194}$$

where $G' = \frac{dG}{de^{(\xi-\zeta)t}}$. This result implies

$$\zeta G + (\xi - \zeta) e^{(\xi-\zeta)t} G'(\cdot) = 0. \tag{2.195}$$

This can be written as

$$\int \frac{dG}{G} = \int \frac{-\zeta}{\xi - \zeta} d\log e^{(\xi-\zeta)t} \tag{2.196}$$

$$= \int \frac{-\zeta}{\xi - \zeta} d\log x \tag{2.197}$$

$$\rightarrow \log G(x) = \log x^{\frac{-\zeta}{\xi-\zeta}} + \log h \tag{2.198}$$

$$\rightarrow G(x) = hx^{\frac{\zeta}{\xi-\zeta}} \rightarrow \frac{Y}{K} = e^{\zeta t}\overline{h}x^{\frac{\zeta}{\xi-\zeta}} \tag{2.199}$$

$$\rightarrow Y_t = \widetilde{h}\kappa_0 e^{\zeta t} K_t \left[\frac{\lambda_t L_t}{\kappa_t K_t}\right]^{\frac{\zeta}{\xi-\zeta}} \tag{2.200}$$

$$= \widetilde{h}(\kappa_t K_t)^{1-\alpha}(\lambda_t L_t)^{\alpha}, \quad \alpha = \frac{\zeta}{\xi - \zeta}. \tag{2.201}$$

Therefore, production should take a Cobb–Douglas form if $\zeta \neq 0$ and $\xi - \zeta > 0$, assuming that you believe there is technical progress that is both capital and labor augmenting and that the original production function you are considering is homogeneous of degree one. This last assumption looks fairly reasonable since it says that doubling both the amount of capital and labor should double production.[6]

This calculation is an important reason behind the adoption of production functional forms in macroeconomic models that allow for a degree of substitutability between factors of production; the Cobb–Douglas specification is particularly pervasive in the study of macroeconomics.

2.6.4 The discount factor

Dynamic optimization problems are 'discounted' to reflect the assumption that the present is more valuable than the future. Under exponential discounting, the assumption is that two periods in time are discounted at the same rate regardless of where they manifest themselves. This is illustrated in Figure 2.8.

However, there is experimental evidence that real-world individuals tend to be highly impatient between, say, time periods t and $t + 1$ but much more patient when evaluating intertemporal decisions between $t + \tau$ and $t + (\tau + 1)$, where $\tau > 0$. This is referred to

[6]Recall that a function, for instance $f(x_1, x_2)$, is said to be homogeneous of degree one if $f(tx_1, tx_2) = tf(x_1, x_2)$.

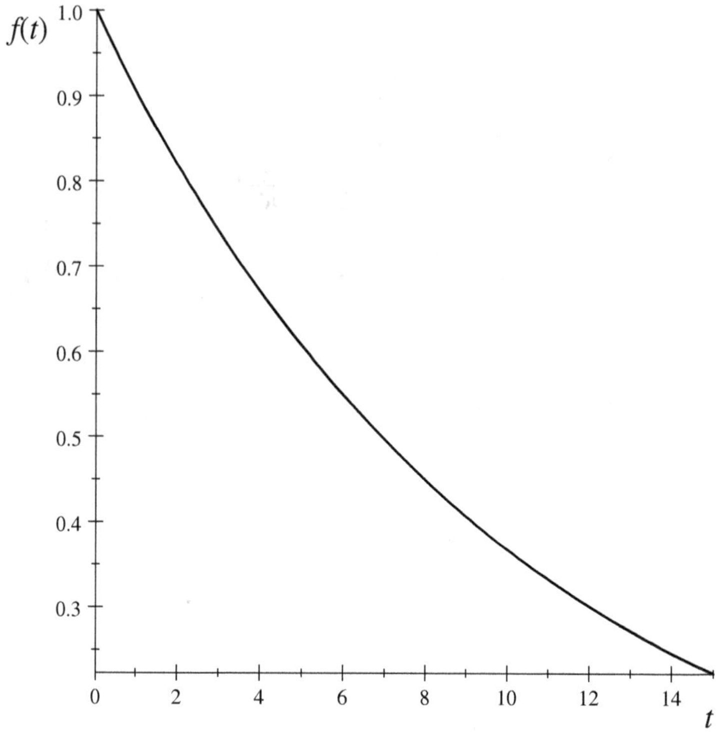

Figure 2.8. $f(t) = e^{-\rho t}$ for $\rho = 0.1$.

as hyperbolic discounting and is expressed as

$$f(t) = e^{-[\rho(t-\tau)+\phi(t-\tau)]} \tag{2.202}$$

$$\phi' \geq 0, \quad \phi'' < 0 \tag{2.203}$$

$$\lim_{(t-\tau)\to\infty} \phi'(t-\tau) = 0, \tag{2.204}$$

and illustrated in Figure 2.9.

When compared to exponential discounting, we can see the effects of short-term and long-term patience versus the same rate of impatience regardless of horizon, as illustrated in Figure 2.10.

The assumption of discounting is pervasive in economics: individuals tend to display some degree of impatience in their decisions, so including this preference characteristic in an optimization problem is crucial. Another prominent reason for assuming a

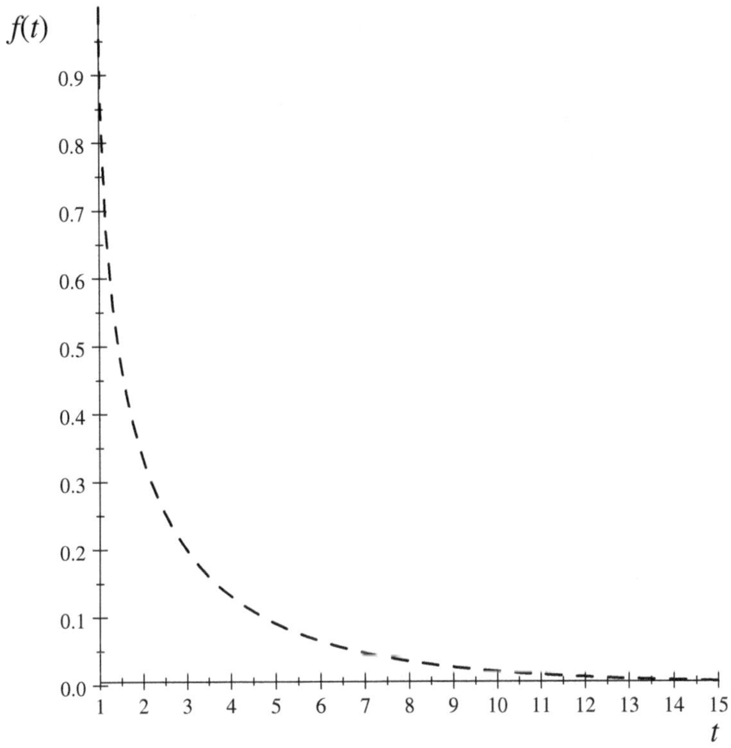

Figure 2.9. $f(t) = e^{-[\rho(t-\tau)+\phi(t-\tau)]}$ for $\phi = \sqrt{t-\tau}$, $\rho = 0.1$ and $\tau = 1$.

discounting term in optimization problems is that, otherwise, these problems will typically not have an optimal solution; indeed, the optimization problem itself will be ill-defined.

The widespread use of exponential discounting versus hyperbolic discounting in macroeconomics is more problematic from an empirical point of view. Since there is pervasive evidence that people tend to be far more patient relative to distant prospects, we should be using a hyperbolic-type discounting function; it turns out however that using them presents some computational difficulties in dynamic settings. For example, computing the steady state explicitly is sometimes impossible, unless you specify very specific functional forms for the utility function and other elements of the optimization problem. When the steady state is defined implicitly in an equation, then numerical methods may be necessary to compute it. As a result, many macroeconomists continue to use exponential over hyperbolic

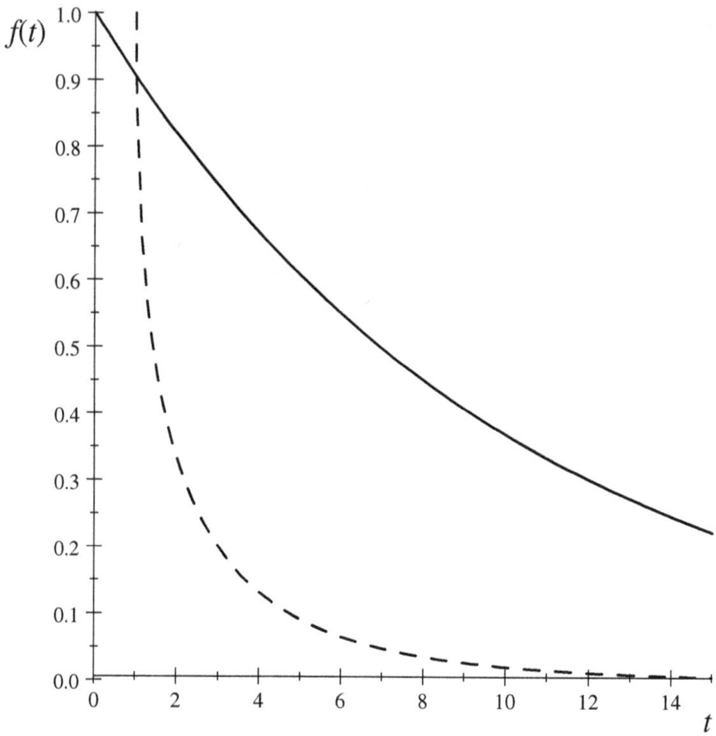

Figure 2.10. Comparing discount functions.

discounting, even though the latter tends to be more reasonable from an empirical point of view.

2.6.5 Interpreting dynamic optimization problems

Consider again the dynamic optimization problem

$$\max_{\{x_t\}} \quad \Gamma = \int_{t=0}^{T} e^{-\rho t} F(y_t, x_t) dt, \tag{2.205}$$

$$s.t. \quad \overset{\bullet}{y}_t \leq G(y_t, x_t) \quad \forall\, t \in [0, T], \tag{2.206}$$

$$y_T \geq \widetilde{y}, \quad y_{(0)} = y_0, \tag{2.207}$$

and let x_t denote consumption today, while y_t denotes the stock of some asset the agent can accumulate (e.g. wealth). How can we interpret, in economic terms, the optimization problem? If the agent is maximizing utility from consumption $F(\bullet)$, then he should make sure not to consume 'too much' today; otherwise, the asset will not accumulate sufficiently quickly for future time periods. This is the basic intuition behind the first-order conditions.

To see this, first note that equation (2.154) is simply $\overset{\bullet}{y}_t = G(y_t, x_t)$, so an optimal path of consumption should ensure that no resources are wasted in the asset accumulation function $G(\cdot)$. This is fairly intuitive. Now, suppose that the agent decides to consume more today than he usually would (say, because he is more impatient). Since $\overset{\bullet}{y}_t = G(y_t, x_t)$, we have that the change in $\overset{\bullet}{y}_t$ must be negative since there are less assets to accumulate. Also, an usually high consumption today (relative to, say, the steady state) would result in a relatively smaller value of $-\pi_t G'_x$ (because of diminishing returns and condition (2.152)). Remember that $G(\cdot)$ represents the asset accumulation equation, so one should expect G'_x to be negative. In this case, the change in π_t must be negative to be consistent with equation (2.152). Finally, equation (2.153) can be used to claim that $\overset{\bullet}{\pi}_t$ must increase. (Can you see why?)

We can now put the various pieces of the puzzle together: if the agent suddenly becomes more impatient, he will decide to consume more of the consumption good x; however, he will accumulate less capital y. Eventually though, the (shadow) price of capital π will rise, causing him to revise his optimal consumption plans accordingly. If, for example, he were in the steady state, a permanent and negative shock to his level of patience (as captured by the parameter ρ) would result in temporarily higher consumption. Eventually, the asset would become too expensive relative to the old steady state, and this would force him to revise his consumption plans downward. Thus, the optimization problem and the associated first-order conditions are entirely interpretable given an economic context.

In summary, models built in continuous time are usually specified as univariate or multivariate dynamic optimization problems, where the objective is often discounted exponentially and with initial (and/or terminal) conditions specified. These problems are solved using optimal control techniques (the PVH or the CVH just covered), and the resultant optimality conditions typically take the form of systems of differential equations. These systems, when nonlinear, need to be linearized so that they can be analyzed within the vicinity of the steady state; this can be done using TSAs. Given a linearized system around a steady state, the stability of the system can be determined (algebraically or visually via phase diagrams). The specification of the dynamics around the steady state is typically thought of as providing a characterization of the solution of the model at hand.

2.7 Discrete Time Systems

2.7.1 Basic concepts and scalar dynamics

As discussed above, time can be modeled in two forms: discrete, where $t \in \{0, 1, 2, \ldots\}$, and continuous, where $t \in \Re$ or some interval thereof. In the following, we consider the dynamics of a variable measured in discrete time and describe the features of optimization theory in dynamic problems where time is modeled in discrete form.

2.7.1.1 *A taxonomy of difference equations*

The dynamics of many economic models can be described by systems of equations featuring (a set of) variables and their lagged values. The simplest such equation is the linear relationship of a variable x_t that is measured in discrete time $t \in \{0, 1, 2, \ldots\}$, with its own past values $\{x_{t-1}, x_{t-2}, \ldots\}$; this relationship is known as a difference equation.

Depending on their functional form, difference equations fall into different categories. The first is whether time explicitly features in the equation; a difference equation that does not feature time is said to be autonomous. For example,

$$x_t = ax_{t-1} \tag{2.208}$$

is an autonomous difference equation, whereas

$$x_t = a_1 x_{t-1} + a_2 t \tag{2.209}$$

is non-autonomous due to the presence of the term $a_2 t$. We will only encounter autonomous systems of equations in our economic modeling. Macroeconomics makes heavy use of recursive techniques to both model and solve dynamic problems; these techniques are particularly useful when time does not explicitly appear as a 'state variable'. Non-autonomous difference equations are more likely to appear in problems where the time horizon explicitly matters; this is true for example of some utility maximization problems where the economic agent uses different discount factors depending on the time horizon of the prospects she is considering.

In addition, difference equations can be classified as homogeneous or non-homogeneous. Homogeneous relationships feature only one time variable and its past values, with no other variable or constant terms present. Thus,

$$x_t = ax_{t-1} \tag{2.210}$$

is a homogeneous difference equation, while

$$x_t = ax_{t-1} + y_{t-1}, \tag{2.211}$$

$$x_t = ax_{t-1} + b \tag{2.212}$$

is a non-homogeneous system of equations.

Finally, difference equations can be classified by their order. The order is determined by the extent to which a variable is dependent on its own past values. Specifically, the order is the difference between the highest and lowest time subscripts in the equation. To illustrate, consider the expression

$$x_t = ax_{t-1}. \tag{2.213}$$

This is a first-order difference equation because x_t is only affected by its value held one period ago, x_{t-1}. By contrast,

$$x_t = a_1 x_{t-1} + a_2 x_{t-2} \tag{2.214}$$

is a second-order relationship because x_t is now influenced by what happened two periods ago. In general, we can write a kth-order difference equation as

$$x_t = a_1 x_{t-1} + a_2 x_{t-2} + \cdots + a_{k-1} x_{t-k+1} + a_k x_{t-k} + b_t, \tag{2.215}$$

where $t \geq 0$ and $a_1, a_2, \ldots, a_k$ and b_t are given constants. Therefore, combining this taxonomy, we find that

$$x_t = a_1 x_{t-1} + a_2 x_{t-2} + b_{t-1} \tag{2.216}$$

is an example of an autonomous, non-homogeneous second-order difference equation.

2.7.1.2 *Solutions of difference equations*

Difference equations are often solved analytically through two different methods: recursive substitution or lag operators. A 'solution' to a difference equation describes the entire time path of the relevant variable purely as a function of parameters and time, just as in the continuous time case.

For some problems, it will be convenient to describe the general solution to difference equations x_t^g as the sum of its complementary solution x_t^c and any particular solution x_t^p. In other words,

$$x_t^g = x_t^c + x_t^p. \tag{2.217}$$

The complementary solution is achieved by taking the original expression, putting it into homogeneous form (sometimes called the complementary equation), and solving for x_t. The particular solution is a selected solution of the original equation. It is important to note that the use of lag operators may eliminate the complementary solution ($x_t^c = 0$). This term must be added back in a general functional form because it will accommodate the system's initial conditions. We now turn to descriptions of the two methods of solving difference equations.

Recursive substitution: This technique involves iterating multiple relationships from a single difference equation and then inserting these back into the original expression to find a solution. Let's illustrate this with the following first-order difference equation:

$$x_t = ax_{t-1} + c, \tag{2.218}$$

Here, x_0 is a given constant, $|a| < 1$, and c is some other constant. Begin the process of iteration by inferring that

$$x_{t-1} = ax_{t-2} + c, \tag{2.219}$$

and thus,

$$x_{t-2} = ax_{t-3} + c. \tag{2.220}$$

Plugging (2.220) into (2.219) yields

$$x_{t-1} = a(ax_{t-3}) + ac + c = a^2 x_{t-3} + ac + c. \tag{2.221}$$

In turn, substituting (2.221) into (2.218) gives

$$x_t = a^3 x_{t-3} + c(1 + a + a^2). \tag{2.222}$$

For this equation, a pattern for the solution can be seen with only three iterations. However, in general, this process can be repeated indefinitely until the form of the solution presents itself. For instance, the jth iteration of the above equation produces

$$x_t = a^j x_{t-j} + c(1 + a + a^2 + \cdots + a^{j-1}). \tag{2.223}$$

At this point, recall that for the infinite sum $1 + \lambda + \lambda^2 + \cdots$, we have the following relationship:

$$1 + \lambda + \lambda^2 + \cdots = \sum_{j=0}^{\infty} \lambda^j = \frac{1}{1-\lambda}, \; \forall \; |\lambda| < 1, \tag{2.224}$$

while for the corresponding finite sum, we have

$$\sum_{j=0}^{T} \lambda^j = \frac{1 - \lambda^{T+1}}{1 - \lambda}. \tag{2.225}$$

Using this last formula and equation (2.223) with $j = t$, we have the following solution for (2.218):

$$x_t = x_0 a^t + c\frac{1 - a^t}{1 - a}, \tag{2.226}$$

or, using $k = x_0 - c/(1 - a)$, we have

$$x_t = ka^t + \frac{c}{1 - a}. \tag{2.227}$$

Since x_0 and c are arbitrary, so is k. To check that this is the solution, replace the above formula in equation (2.218). Also, check that (2.227) holds when $t = 0$.

Alternatively, one can solve (2.218) by deriving its complementary equation

$$x_t = ax_{t-1} \tag{2.228}$$

and inferring that

$$x_{t-1} = ax_{t-2} \tag{2.229}$$

and

$$x_{t-2} = ax_{t-3}. \tag{2.230}$$

Recursive substitution produces

$$x_{t-1} = a(ax_{t-3}) = a^2 x_{t-3} \tag{2.231}$$

and, in turn,

$$x_t = a^3 x_{t-3}, \tag{2.232}$$

which gives the complementary solution

$$x_t^c = x_0 a^t, \tag{2.233}$$

or, more generally,

$$x_t^c = ka^t. \tag{2.234}$$

To find the particular solution for (2.218), one can set $x_t = x_{t-1} = x_t^p$ and solve at the steady state[7]:

$$(1 - a)x_t^p = c. \tag{2.235}$$

Thus, the particular solution is

$$x_t^p = \frac{c}{1 - a}, \tag{2.236}$$

and the general solution is

$$x_t^g = ka^t + \frac{c}{1 - a}. \tag{2.237}$$

Consider next the second-order difference equation

$$x_t = a_1 x_{t-1} + a_2 x_{t-2} + c, \tag{2.238}$$

[7]The steady state in continuous time was defined by setting $\dot{x}_t = 0$. In discrete time, the analog is $x_t = x_{t-1}(= x_{t+1}) = \overline{x}$.

whose complementary equation is

$$x_t^c = a_1 x_{t-1}^c + a_2 x_{t-2}^c. \tag{2.239}$$

Taking a page from the first-order case, guess that the solution will be of the form

$$x_t^c = kb^t, \tag{2.240}$$

(b to better distinguish from a_1 and a_2). Therefore,

$$x_{t-1}^c = kb^{t-1}, \tag{2.241}$$

$$x_{t-2}^c = kb^{t-2}. \tag{2.242}$$

Substituting into (2.239) yields

$$kb^t = a_1 kb^{t-1} + a_2 kb^{t-2}, \tag{2.243}$$

and canceling out redundant terms results in

$$b^2 = a_1 b + a_2, \tag{2.244}$$

or

$$b^2 - a_1 b - a_2 = 0. \tag{2.245}$$

This quadratic has two roots:

$$b_1, b_2 = \frac{a_1 \pm \sqrt{a_1^2 + 4a_2}}{2}. \tag{2.246}$$

If $b_1 \neq b_2$, then the complementary solution is

$$x_t^c = k_1 b_1^t + k_2 b_2^t. \tag{2.247}$$

To find a particular solution, set $x_t = x_{t-1} = x_{t-2} = x_t^p$ and solve (2.238) at the steady state to get

$$x_t^p = \frac{c}{1 - a_1 - a_2}. \tag{2.248}$$

The general solution is then

$$x_t^g = k_1 b_1^t + k_2 b_2^t + \frac{c}{1 - a_1 - a_2}. \tag{2.249}$$

Lag operators: The lag operator L acts on any time-dependent variable and reduces its period by one for each power of L. Therefore,

$$Lx_t = x_{t-1}, \tag{2.250}$$

$$L^2 x_t = x_{t-2}, \tag{2.251}$$

and in general,

$$L^j x_t = x_{t-j}. \tag{2.252}$$

If a lag operator acts on a constant or a variable that is independent of time, then it simply disappears. Further, lag operators are linear so that $L(x_t + y_t) = Lx_t + Ly_t = x_{t-1} + y_{t-1}$.

Consider again the first-order difference equation

$$x_t = ax_{t-1} + c, \tag{2.253}$$

where x_0 is given, $|a| < 1$, and c is some constant. Using the notation of lag operators, this expression can be rewritten as

$$x_t = aLx_t + c, \tag{2.254}$$

and then

$$(1 - aL)x_t = c. \tag{2.255}$$

Note that lag operators eliminate the complementary solution

$$x_t^c = \frac{1}{1 - aL} 0 = 0. \tag{2.256}$$

Therefore, define

$$x_t^c = ka^t \tag{2.257}$$

because, for any constant k,

$$(1 - aL)ka^t = ka^t - kaa^{t-1} = 0. \tag{2.258}$$

Note this is the expression derived using recursive substitution. To find the particular solution, write (2.255) as

$$x_t^p = \frac{c}{1 - aL}. \tag{2.259}$$

Next, realize that

$$x_t = (1 + aL + a^2L^2 + \cdots + a^jL^j)c = \sum_{j=0}^{\infty} a^jL^jc, \tag{2.260}$$

which can be rewritten as

$$x_t^p = c\sum_{j=0}^{\infty} a^jL^j = \frac{c}{1-a}. \tag{2.261}$$

Adding (2.257) to (2.261) produces the general solution

$$x_t^g = ka^t + \frac{c}{1-a}, \tag{2.262}$$

as shown earlier using the recursive substitution method.

Consider next the first-order difference equation

$$x_t = ax_{t-1} + y_t + c, \tag{2.263}$$

where x_0 is given, $|a| < 1$, y_t is some other variable, and c is a constant. This expression can be rewritten as

$$x_t = aLx_t + y_t + c \tag{2.264}$$

and then rearranged into the form

$$x_t(1 - aL) = y_t + c. \tag{2.265}$$

As before, the complementary solution is defined as

$$x_t^c = ka^t. \tag{2.266}$$

To find the particular solution, write (2.255) as

$$x_t^p = \frac{y_t}{1-aL} + \frac{c}{1-aL}. \tag{2.267}$$

Using the same technique as before produces

$$x_t^p = (1 + aL + a^2L^2 + \cdots + a^jL^j)y_t + (1 + aL + a^2L^2 + \cdots + a^jL^j)c \tag{2.268}$$

$$= \sum_{j=0}^{\infty} a^jL^jy_t + \sum_{j=0}^{\infty} a^jL^jc, \tag{2.269}$$

which can be expressed as

$$x_t^p = \sum_{j=0}^{\infty} a^j y_{t-j} + c\sum_{j=0}^{\infty} a^j = \frac{1}{1-a}\sum_{j=0}^{\infty} y_{t-j} + \frac{c}{1-a}. \tag{2.270}$$

Thus, the general solution is

$$x_t^g = ka^t + \frac{1}{1-a}\sum_{j=0}^{\infty} y_{t-j} + \frac{c}{1-a}. \tag{2.271}$$

Consider now the second-order difference equation

$$x_t = a_1 x_{t-1} + a_2 x_{t-2} + y_t + c. \tag{2.272}$$

This can be rewritten as

$$(1 - a_1 L - a_2 L^2)x_t = y_t + c. \tag{2.273}$$

The complementary solution is defined as

$$x_t^c = k_1 a_1^t + k_2 a_2^t, \tag{2.274}$$

because, for any arbitrary constants k_1 and k_2,

$$(1 - \lambda_1 L)(1 - \lambda_2 L)k_1 a_1^t = (1 - \lambda_1 L)(1 - \lambda_2 L)k_2 a_2^t = 0. \tag{2.275}$$

To find the particular solution, factorize the left-hand side of the equation

$$(1 - \lambda_1 L)(1 - \lambda_2 L)x_t = y_t + c, \tag{2.276}$$

where $\lambda_1 + \lambda_2 = a_1$ and $-\lambda_1\lambda_2 = a_2$. Note that λ_i are related to the roots of the quadratic equation $1 - a_1 L - a_2 L^2$:

$$\lambda_1^{-1}, \lambda_2^{-1} = \frac{a_1 \pm \sqrt{a_1^2 + 4a_2}}{2a_2}. \tag{2.277}$$

Assume that $\lambda_1 \neq \lambda_2$ and $\lambda_1 \neq 1$. Dividing through yields

$$x_t^p = \frac{y_t}{(1 - \lambda_1 L)(1 - \lambda_2 L)} + \frac{c}{(1 - \lambda_1 L)(1 - \lambda_2 L)}. \tag{2.278}$$

Note that

$$\frac{1}{(1-\lambda_1 L)(1-\lambda_2 L)} = \frac{1}{\lambda_1-\lambda_2}\left(\frac{\lambda_1}{1-\lambda_1 L} - \frac{\lambda_2}{1-\lambda_2 L}\right), \tag{2.279}$$

and apply this to (2.278) to get

$$x_t = \frac{1}{\lambda_1-\lambda_2}\frac{\lambda_1 y_t}{(1-\lambda_1 L)} - \frac{1}{\lambda_1-\lambda_2}\frac{\lambda_2 y_t}{(1-\lambda_2 L)} + \frac{c}{(1-\lambda_1)(1-\lambda_2)}, \tag{2.280}$$

which is equal to

$$x_t = \frac{\lambda_1}{\lambda_1-\lambda_2}\frac{1}{(1-\lambda_1)}\sum_{j=0}^{\infty} y_{t-j} - \frac{\lambda_2}{\lambda_1-\lambda_2}\frac{1}{(1-\lambda_2)}\sum_{j=0}^{\infty} y_{t-j} + \frac{c}{(1-\lambda_1)(1-\lambda_2)}. \tag{2.281}$$

Therefore, the general solution is equal to

$$x_t = k_1 a_1^t + k_2 a_2^t + \frac{\lambda_1}{\lambda_1-\lambda_2}\frac{1}{(1-\lambda_1)}\sum_{j=0}^{\infty} y_{t-j} - \frac{\lambda_2}{\lambda_1-\lambda_2}\frac{1}{(1-\lambda_2)}\sum_{j=0}^{\infty} y_{t-j} + \frac{c}{(1-\lambda_1)(1-\lambda_2)}. \tag{2.282}$$

The inverse of a lag operator, L^{-1}, is called a forward operator, F, and has the same properties as the lag operator. Forward operators are useful when $|\lambda| > 1$, a condition that is related to the stability of a difference equation (discussed in the following). Applying this notation to the above solution method is straightforward and illustrated as follows.

Consider the difference equation

$$x_t = a x_{t-1} + y_t + c, \tag{2.283}$$

where x_0 is given, $|a| > 1$, and y_t is some other variable (exogenous process) and c is some constant. Since we cannot use $\sum_{j=0}^{\infty} a^j = \frac{1}{1-a}$, as $|a| > 1$, we get around this problem by using forward operators. We can infer that

$$x_{t+1} = ax_t + y_{t+1} + c, \tag{2.284}$$

which can be rewritten as

$$(-a + F)x_t = y_{t+1} + c. \tag{2.285}$$

By dividing through by $-a$, this expression can be rearranged into

$$(1 - a^{-1}F)x_t = -\frac{y_{t+1} + c}{a}. \tag{2.286}$$

The complementary solution is defined as

$$x_t^c = k(a^{-1})^t = da^{-t} \tag{2.287}$$

because

$$(1 - a^{-1}F)ka^{-t} = ka^{-t} - ka^{-1}a^{-t+1} = 0. \tag{2.288}$$

Solving for the particular solution yields

$$x_t^p = -\frac{\frac{y_{t+1}}{a}}{(1 - a^{-1}F)} - \frac{\frac{c}{a}}{(1 - a^{-1}F)}. \tag{2.289}$$

Since $|a| > 1$, then logically $|a^{-1}| < 1$; therefore, by setting $a^{-1}F$ equal to λ for the convergent case, we get

$$\begin{aligned} x_t^p &= -\frac{1}{a}\sum_{j=0}^{\infty} a^{-j}F^j y_{t+1} - \frac{c}{a}\sum_{j=0}^{\infty} a^{-j}F^j \\ &= -\frac{1}{a(1 - a^{-1})}\sum_{j=0}^{\infty} y_{t+j+1} - \frac{c}{a(1 - a^{-1})}. \end{aligned} \tag{2.290}$$

and the general solution is

$$x_t^g = ka^{-t} - \frac{1}{a(1 - a^{-1})}\sum_{j=0}^{\infty} y_{t+j+1} - \frac{c}{a(1 - a^{-1})}. \tag{2.291}$$

2.7.1.3 *Steady states and stability analyses*

In discrete time, a steady state is achieved when

$$\Delta x_t = x_t - x_{t-1} = 0. \tag{2.292}$$

There are two key characteristics of a steady state. First, it is usually of interest to determine whether the steady state is unique. That is, does there exist only one point at which the system is in long-run equilibrium? Second, it is important to determine whether a difference equation is stable or not around the steady state. That is, if the value of a variable is moved away from steady state, does it return to the steady state and, if so, what path does it take?

As an example, for a homogeneous difference equation,

$$x_t = ax_{t-1}, \tag{2.293}$$

we observe stability if $|a| < 1$ and instability if $|a| > 1$.

2.7.2 Systems of linear equations

Due to the complexity of solving a higher-order difference equation, it is often convenient to translate it into a lower-order system of equations. In fact, nth order difference equations can always be written as a first-order system of n equations and n variables. Since many economic models consist of systems of higher-order equations, analysis of this class of systems is particularly useful.

2.7.2.1 *A taxonomy of systems of difference equations*

Like difference equations, systems of difference equations can be classified as autonomous or non-autonomous and homogeneous or non-homogeneous. When classifying systems of equations in this way, all equations must share the same classification for the system as a whole to obtain that label.

For instance, the system of difference equations

$$x_{1t} = a_{11}x_{1t-1} + a_{12}x_{2t-1}, \tag{2.294}$$

$$x_{2t} = a_{21}x_{1t-1} + a_{22}x_{2t-1}, \tag{2.295}$$

is autonomous, while

$$x_{1t} = a_{11}x_{1t-1} + a_{12}x_{2t-1} + a_{13}t, \tag{2.296}$$

$$x_{2t} = a_{21}x_{1t-1} + a_{22}x_{2t-1}, \tag{2.297}$$

is non-autonomous due to the explicit presence of time in at least one equation. Similarly,

$$x_{1t} = a_{11}x_{1t-1}, \tag{2.298}$$

$$x_{2t} = a_{21}x_{2t-1}, \tag{2.299}$$

$$x_{3t} = a_{31}x_{3t-1} \tag{2.300}$$

is a homogeneous system, whereas

$$x_{1t} = a_{11}x_{1t-1}, \tag{2.301}$$

$$x_{2t} = a_{21}x_{2t-1} + c_2, \tag{2.302}$$

$$x_{3t} = a_{31}x_{3t-1} + c_3 \tag{2.303}$$

is non-homogeneous due to the presence of constant terms, c_2 and c_3. In addition, systems of difference equations are assigned an order based on the difference between the highest and lowest time subscripts appearing in any one equation. For example,

$$x_{1t} = a_{11}x_{1t-1} + a_{12}x_{1t-2}, \tag{2.304}$$

$$x_{2t} = a_{21}x_{1t-1}, \tag{2.305}$$

$$x_{3t} = a_{31}x_{2t-1} \tag{2.306}$$

is a second-order system of difference equations.

Consider the nth-order difference equation

$$x_{t+1} = a_1x_t + a_2x_{t-1} + \cdots + a_nx_{t-n+1}. \tag{2.307}$$

To express this higher-order difference equation as a system, let

$$z_{t+1} = \left[x_{t+1}\ x_t\ x_{t-1} \cdots x_{t-n+2}\right], \tag{2.308}$$

and thus

$$z_t = \left[x_t\ x_{t-1} \cdots x_{t-n+1}\right]. \tag{2.309}$$

This can be written in first-order form as

$$z_{t+1} - Az_t = 0, \tag{2.310}$$

or

$$\begin{bmatrix} x_{t+1} \\ x_t \\ \vdots \\ x_{t-n+2} \end{bmatrix} - \begin{bmatrix} a_1 & a_2 & \cdots & a_n \\ 1 & 0 & \cdots & 0 \\ \vdots & \vdots & \ddots & \vdots \\ 0 & 0 & 1 & 0 \end{bmatrix} \begin{bmatrix} x_t \\ x_{t-1} \\ \vdots \\ x_{t-n+1} \end{bmatrix} = 0. \tag{2.311}$$

2.7.2.2 *Solutions of deterministic systems*

Systems of difference equations can be solved by expressing the general solution X_t^g as the sum of the complementary solution X_t^c and any particular solution X_t^p:

$$X_t^g = X_t^c + X_t^p. \tag{2.312}$$

As an example, consider the following 2×2 first-order system of difference equations:

$$x_{1t} = a_{11}x_{1t-1} + a_{12}x_{2t-1} + c_1, \tag{2.313}$$

$$x_{2t} = a_{21}x_{1t-1} + a_{22}x_{2t-1} + c_2. \tag{2.314}$$

This can be expressed as

$$X_t = AX_{t-1} + C, \tag{2.315}$$

where

$$X_t = [x_{1t}\ x_{2t}], \tag{2.316}$$

$$X_{t-1} = [x_{1t-1}\ x_{2t-1}], \tag{2.317}$$

$$A = \begin{bmatrix} a_{11} & a_{12} \\ a_{21} & a_{22} \end{bmatrix}, \tag{2.318}$$

$$C = \begin{bmatrix} c_1 \\ c_2 \end{bmatrix}. \tag{2.319}$$

If A is diagonal,

$$A = \begin{bmatrix} a_{11} & 0 \\ 0 & a_{22} \end{bmatrix}, \tag{2.320}$$

then the system becomes

$$x_{1t} = a_{11}x_{1t-1} + c_1, \tag{2.321}$$

$$x_{2t} = a_{22}x_{2t-1} + c_2. \tag{2.322}$$

By looking at each equation separately, it is straightforward to find the complementary solution

$$x_{it}^c = x_{i0}a_{ii}^t = k_i a_{ii}^t, \tag{2.323}$$

where k_i are arbitrary constants, the particular solution

$$x_{it}^p = \frac{c_i}{1 - a_{ii}}, \tag{2.324}$$

and finally, the general solution

$$x_{it}^g = k_i a_{ii}^t + \frac{c_i}{1 - a_{ii}}. \tag{2.325}$$

An attractive feature of the system of equations (2.321 and 2.322) is that each equation features only one variable and a lagged value; this makes them simple to solve. Unfortunately, few relationships in economics are independent of other variables, and so diagonal relationships are rare. However, if A is not diagonal, then it can often be diagonalized. The process of diagonalization is as follows.

For the case of $n = 2$, let r_1 and r_2 be the eigenvalues of A and v_1 and v_2 be the eigenvectors of A. Moreover, let D be the diagonal matrix,

$$D = \begin{bmatrix} r_1 & 0 \\ 0 & r_2 \end{bmatrix}, \tag{2.326}$$

and P be the matrix of eigenvectors,

$$P = [v_1 \ v_2] = \begin{bmatrix} v_{11} & v_{21} \\ v_{12} & v_{22} \end{bmatrix}. \tag{2.327}$$

First, find the complementary solution. If r_1 and r_2 are distinct and v_1 and v_2 are linearly independent, then

$$P^{-1}AP = D. \tag{2.328}$$

Define

$$Z_t = P^{-1}X_t, \tag{2.329}$$

and iterate to get

$$Z_{t-1} = P^{-1}X_{t-1}. \tag{2.330}$$

Substituting these into $X_t = AX_{t-1} + C$ and ignoring the matrix C produces the complementary matrix equation

$$PZ_t^c = APZ_{t-1}^c, \tag{2.331}$$

which can be rearranged into

$$Z_t^c = P^{-1}APZ_{t-1}^c. \tag{2.332}$$

Note that this is simply

$$Z_t^c = DZ_{t\ \ 1}^c, \tag{2.333}$$

which means that

$$z_{1t}^c = r_1 z_{1t-1}^c, \tag{2.334}$$

$$z_{2t}^c = r_2 z_{2t\ \ 1}^c. \tag{2.335}$$

Therefore, the solutions for the transformed variable are

$$z_{1t}^c = k_1 r_1^t, \tag{2.336}$$

$$z_{2t}^c = k_2 r_2^t, \tag{2.337}$$

where k_i are arbitrary constants. However, to get the complementary solution, the transform must be undone, as follows.

Applying $Z_t = P^{-1}X_t$ yields

$$X_t = PZ_t, \tag{2.338}$$

$$X_t = P[z_{1t}^c\ z_{2t}^c]', \tag{2.339}$$

$$X_t = P[k_1 r_1^t \; k_2 r_2^t]', \tag{2.340}$$

$$X_t = [v_1 \; v_2][k_1 r_1^t \; k_2 r_2^t]', \tag{2.341}$$

which means

$$x_{1t}^c = v_{11} k_1 r_1^t + v_{21} k_2 r_2^t, \tag{2.342}$$

$$x_{2t}^c = v_{12} k_1 r_1^t + v_{22} k_2 r_2^t. \tag{2.343}$$

To obtain a particular solution, set $x_{it} = x_{it-1} = x_{it}^p$ and solve for the steady-state values.

The diagonalized system becomes

$$x_{1t}^p = a_{11} x_{1t}^p + a_{12} x_{2t}^p + c_1, \tag{2.344}$$

$$x_{2t}^p = a_{21} x_{1t}^p + a_{22} x_{2t}^p + c_2. \tag{2.345}$$

This is simply a system of two equations and two unknowns. Solving for x_{2t}^p,

$$x_{2t}^p = \frac{a_{21} x_{1t}^p + c_2}{1 - a_{22}}, \tag{2.346}$$

and replacing in equation (2.344) gives

$$(1 - a_{11}) x_{1t}^p = a_{12} \left(\frac{a_{21} x_{1t}^p + c_2}{1 - a_{22}} \right) + c_1. \tag{2.347}$$

Solving for x_{1t}^p,

$$x_{1t}^p = \frac{c_1 + \frac{a_{12} c_2}{1 - a_{22}}}{1 - a_{11} - \frac{a_{12} a_{21}}{1 - a_{22}}}, \tag{2.348}$$

which simplifies to

$$x_{1t}^p = \frac{(1 - a_{22}) c_1 + a_{12} c_2}{(1 - a_{22})(1 - a_{11}) - a_{12} a_{21}}. \tag{2.349}$$

Therefore, the general solutions are

$$x_{1t}^g = v_{11} k_1 r_1^t + v_{21} k_2 r_2^t + \frac{(1 - a_{22}) c_1 + a_{12} c_2}{(1 - a_{22})(1 - a_{11}) - a_{12} a_{21}}, \tag{2.350}$$

$$x_{2t}^g = v_{12} k_1 r_1^t + v_{22} k_2 r_2^t + \frac{(1 - a_{11}) c_2 + a_{21} c_1}{(1 - a_{11})(1 - a_{22}) - a_{21} a_{12}}. \tag{2.351}$$

To find the specific values of k_i, set $t = 0$ and solve.

2.7.3 Steady states and stability analyses

To determine the stability of the system, consider again the 2×2 matrix A:

$$A = \begin{bmatrix} a_{11} & a_{12} \\ a_{21} & a_{22} \end{bmatrix}. \tag{2.352}$$

Calculate the eigenvalues r_1 and r_2. If $|r_i| < 1$, then the steady state is stable; if $|r_i| > 1$, then the steady state is unstable, and if $|r_1| < 1$ and $|r_2| > 1$, then there is a saddle path through the steady state. Note the near symmetry with the continuous time case discussed above.

2.8 Linearization Techniques: Discrete Time

Nonlinear systems are notoriously difficult to deal with because one cannot use the methods for linear equations or systems provided above. Consequently, we usually linearize systems around steady states and study their local behavior.

2.8.1 Taylor series approximations and linearization

One of the more common linearization techniques is the Taylor series approximation (TSA). Consider the equation

$$x_t = f(x_{t-1}) + c. \tag{2.353}$$

The jth-order TSA around the steady state $\overline{x}$ is given by

$$x_t \approx f(\overline{x}) + f'(\overline{x})(x_t - \overline{x}) + \frac{1}{2} f''(\overline{x})(x_t - \overline{x})^2 + \cdots + \frac{1}{j!} f^j(\overline{x})(x_t - \overline{x})^j. \tag{2.354}$$

As before, we look at a first-order TSA (TSA1) and ignore other higher-order terms; the linearized system (around the steady-state) is sufficient to understand the dynamics near the steady state as long as the function f is differentiable. The TSA1 is simply

$$x_t \approx f(\overline{x}) + f'(\overline{x})(x_t - \overline{x}). \tag{2.355}$$

Similarly, given the system of difference equations

$$X_t = F(X_{t-1}) + C, \tag{2.356}$$

the jth-order TSA around the steady state $\overline{X}$ is given by

$$\begin{aligned} X_t &\approx F(\overline{X}) + JF(\overline{X})(X_t - \overline{X}) + \frac{1}{2}J^2F(\overline{X})(X_t - \overline{X})^2 + \cdots \\ &\quad + \frac{1}{j!}J^jF(\overline{X})(X_t - \overline{X})^j, \end{aligned} \tag{2.357}$$

and the TSA1 is equal to

$$X_t \approx F(\overline{X}) + JF(\overline{X})(X_t - \overline{X}). \tag{2.358}$$

As an example, consider now the first-order difference equation

$$x_t = ax_{t+1}^2 + c. \tag{2.359}$$

Prior to taking the TSA, rearrange into the form

$$0 = \underbrace{-x_t + ax_{t+1}^2 + c}_{g} \tag{2.360}$$

so that the steady-state value, $g(\overline{x})$, is equal to zero. The difference equation can now be expressed as

$$g(x_t, x_{t+1}) = -x_t + ax_{t+1}^2 + c = 0. \tag{2.361}$$

Therefore, the TSA1 is equal to

$$g(x_t, x_{t+1}) = 0 + \frac{\partial f}{\partial x_t}(x_t - \overline{x}) + \frac{\partial f}{\partial x_{t+1}}(x_{t+1} - \overline{x}), \tag{2.362}$$

$$g(x_t, x_{t+1}) = -1(x_t - \overline{x}) + 2a\overline{x}(x_{t+1} - \overline{x}) = 0, \tag{2.363}$$

or re-expressed as

$$(x_t - \overline{x}) = 2a\overline{x}(x_{t+1} - \overline{x}). \tag{2.364}$$

2.8.2 Log-linearization

Another common method of linearization is taking logarithms. Consider the homogeneous difference equation

$$x_t = f(x_{t-1}). \tag{2.365}$$

With homogeneous and non-additive relationships, linearization requires only that logs are taken on both sides:

$$\log x_t = \log f(x_{t-1}). \tag{2.366}$$

As an example, consider the first-order equation

$$x_t = 2x_{t-1}^3 x_{t-2}. \tag{2.367}$$

The linearized relationship is simply

$$\log x_t = \log(2) + 3\log x_{t-1} + \log x_{t-2}. \tag{2.368}$$

However, if the difference equation is non-homogeneous or the relationship is additive, then taking a simple logarithm will be not be useful. To get around this problem, first express each term as the exponential of a logarithm. For instance, consider the following nth-order difference equation

$$x_t = f(x_{t-1}) + f(x_{t-2}) + \cdots + f(x_{t-n}) + c. \tag{2.369}$$

Rewrite as

$$e^{\log x_t} = f(e^{\log x_{t-1}}) + f(e^{\log x_{t-2}}) + \cdots + f(e^{\log x_{t-n}}) + c. \tag{2.370}$$

Relabel the variables as

$$\widetilde{x}_t = \log x_t, \tag{2.371}$$

$$\widetilde{x}_{t-1} = \log x_{t-1}, \tag{2.372}$$

$$\vdots \tag{2.373}$$

$$\widetilde{x}_{t-n} = \log x_{t-n}. \tag{2.374}$$

Second, take a TSA1 of the resulting expression.

As an example, consider the second-order, non-homogeneous equation

$$x_t = 5x_{t-1} + x_{t-2}^2 + 4. \tag{2.375}$$

To linearize, rewrite as

$$\begin{aligned} e^{\log x_t} &= e^{\log 5x_{t-1}} + e^{2\log x_{t-2}} + 4 && (2.376)\\ &= e^{\log 5} e^{\log x_{t-1}} + e^{2\log x_{t-2}} + 4, && (2.377)\end{aligned}$$

which is simply

$$e^{\widetilde{x}_t} = a_1 e^{\widetilde{x}_{t-1}} + e^{2\widetilde{x}_{t-2}} + 4, \tag{2.378}$$

where

$$a_1 = e^{\log 5}. \tag{2.379}$$

Rearranging produces

$$f(\widetilde{x}_t, \widetilde{x}_{t-1}, \widetilde{x}_{t-2}) = -e^{\widetilde{x}_t} + a_1 e^{\widetilde{x}_{t-1}} + e^{2\widetilde{x}_{t-2}} + 4 = 0. \tag{2.380}$$

Taking the TSA1 yields

$$\begin{aligned} f(\widetilde{x}_t, \widetilde{x}_{t-1}, \widetilde{x}_{t-2}) &= 0 + \frac{\partial f}{\partial \widetilde{x}_t}(\widetilde{x}_t - \overline{x}) + \frac{\partial f}{\partial \widetilde{x}_{t-1}}(\widetilde{x}_{t-1} - \overline{x})\\ &\quad + \frac{\partial f}{\partial \widetilde{x}_{t-2}}(\widetilde{x}_{t-2} - \overline{x}) && (2.381)\\ &= -e^{x}(\widetilde{x}_t - \overline{x}) + a_1 e^{x}(\widetilde{x}_{t-1} - \overline{x}) + 2e^{2x}(\widetilde{x}_{t-2} - \overline{x}). && (2.382)\end{aligned}$$

The steady state is given by $x_t = x_{t-1} = x_{t-2} = \overline{x}$, or

$$\begin{aligned} \overline{x}^2 + 4\overline{x} + 4 = 0, && (2.383)\\ \overline{x} = -2. && (2.384)\end{aligned}$$

Evaluating the partials at the steady state gives

$$\begin{aligned} f(\widetilde{x}_t, \widetilde{x}_{t-1}, \widetilde{x}_{t-2}) &= -e^{-2}(\widetilde{x}_t - \overline{x}) + a_1 e^{-2}(\widetilde{x}_{t-1} - \overline{x})\\ &\quad + 2e^{-4}(\widetilde{x}_{t-2} - \overline{x}). && (2.385)\end{aligned}$$

Let

$$\widetilde{x}_t - \overline{x} = \widehat{x}_t, \tag{2.386}$$

$$\widetilde{x}_{t-1} - \overline{x} = \widehat{x}_{t-1}, \tag{2.387}$$

$$\widetilde{x}_{t-2} - \overline{x} = \widehat{x}_{t-2}, \tag{2.388}$$

to finally express the linearized equation in terms of log deviation from steady state:

$$\widehat{x}_t = e^{\log 5}\widehat{x}_{t-1} + 2e^{-2}\widehat{x}_{t-2}. \tag{2.389}$$

2.9 Dynamic Optimization in Discrete Time

Dynamic models are employed in order to understand how current actions influence current and future values of variables. In economics, however, it is often necessary not only to understand how variables (systems) evolve over time but also how they can be optimized. As for continuous time models, there are four basic variable types: endogenous state, exogenous state, control, and co-state. State variables are those whose evolution over time is typically governed by a 'law of motion', expressed as a difference equation or a system of difference equations. More specifically, the value of the endogenous state variables cannot be changed immediately by decisions today. Rather, one can only make decisions today to alter endogenous state variables onward into the future. Finally, state variables are sometimes referred to as stock variables or predetermined variables. Conversely, control variables are those whose values are chosen directly at the current time period. These are sometimes referred to as flow, jump, or non-predetermined variables. Co-state variables are the shadow price of the state variable. Finally, whereas the distinction between state and control variables is often apparent, the distinction between endogenous and exogenous state variables is highly dependent on the economic model at hand.

2.9.1 The discrete time lagrangian

To begin setting up the Lagrangian, let

$$t \in \{0, 1, \ldots, T\}, \tag{2.390}$$

$$Y_t = \text{endogenous state variable}, \tag{2.391}$$

$$Z_t = \text{control variable}. \tag{2.392}$$

Then, given that we wish to

$$\max_{\{Z_t\},\{Y_t\}} \quad \Gamma = \sum_{t=0}^{T} \beta^t F(Y_t, Z_t), \tag{2.393}$$

where $\beta \in (0, 1]$ and subject to

$$Q(Y_t, Z_t) \geq Y_{t+1} - Y_t \quad \forall\, t \tag{2.394}$$

$$c \geq G(Y_t, Z_t) \quad \forall\, t, \tag{2.395}$$

with Y_0 given and $Y_{T+1} \geq Y^*$, the latter being the terminal condition. That is, at the end of the optimization horizon, Y_t must be no less than some threshold value. Also, note that the optimization problem has to be additively time separable: the functions F, Q, and G at time t must only depend on the values of Y_t and Z_t at time t. Finally, it is important to remember that there are actually $T + 1$ sets of constraints in this problem, one set for each time period.

The Lagrangian is

$$L = \sum_{t=0}^{T} \beta^t F(Y_t, Z_t) + \sum_{t=0}^{T} \pi_{t+1}[(Y_t - Q(Y_t, Z_t) - Y_{t+1})]$$

$$+ \sum_{t=0}^{T} \lambda_t [c - G(Y_t, Z_t)] + \varphi[Y_{T+1} - Y^*]. \tag{2.396}$$

In order to maximize the Lagrangian, take the derivative of L with respect to both the endogenous state and control variables and set them equal to zero. The first-order conditions are

$$\frac{\partial L}{\partial Y_t} = \beta^t F'_Y + \pi_{t+1} + \pi_{t+1} Q'_Y - \lambda_t G'_Y - \pi_t = 0, \tag{2.397}$$

$$\frac{\partial L}{\partial Y_{t+1}} = -\pi_{t+1} + \varphi = 0, \tag{2.398}$$

$$\frac{\partial L}{\partial Z_t} = \beta^t F'_z + \pi_{t+1} Q'_Z - \lambda_t G'_Z = 0. \tag{2.399}$$

Note that, in the first-order conditions, derivatives for Y_t come from two time periods: t and $t-1$. Along with the initial condition $Y_{(0)} = Y_0$, there are thus four equations and four unknowns: Y_t, Z_t, π_t, and λ_t. Finally, the associated transversality condition is

$$\lim_{T\to\infty} \pi_{T+1}(Y_{T+1} - Y^*) = 0, \tag{2.400}$$

and it simply states that either the constraint or the terminal condition should bind in the infinite instance.

2.9.2 Discrete time dynamic programming

The discrete time Lagrangian in the previous section exploited the Kuhn–Tucker conditions (albeit over time) discussed above. The dynamic programming solution instead exploits the envelope theorem conditions; however, the two methods yield the same solution in theory. In this section, we examine the dynamic programming method for an infinite horizon problem.

The method begins by first defining for a given value of Y_0, the 'value function'

$$V(Y_0) = \max_{\{Z_t\}_{t=0}^{\infty}} \sum_{t=0}^{\infty} \beta^t F(Y_t, Z_t) \tag{2.401}$$

$$s.t. \quad Y_{t+1} \leq Y_t + Q(Y_t, Z_t) \tag{2.402}$$

$$c \geq G(Y_t, Z_t). \tag{2.403}$$

That is, the value function $V(Y_0)$ defines the value of achieving the constrained optimum if the optimal path for Z_t is chosen from the start of the problem, which in this case is at time $t = 0$. This means that for any period t, given a value for the state variable Y_t, the value function can be written as

$$V(Y_t) = \max_{\{Z_{t+j}\}_{j=0}^{\infty}} \sum_{j=0}^{\infty} \beta^j F(Y_{t+j}, Z_{t+j}) \tag{2.404}$$

$$s.t. \quad Y_{t+j+1} \leq Y_{t+j} + Q(Y_{t+j}, Z_{t+j}), \quad Y_t \text{ known} \tag{2.405}$$

$$c \geq G(Y_{t+j}, Z_{t+j}). \tag{2.406}$$

Since t and j are effectively arbitrary indices, the time-t component can be separated from the infinite sum

$$V(Y_t) = \max_{Z_t} \left[F(Y_t, Z_t) + \max_{\{Z_{t+j}\}_{j=1}^{\infty}} \sum_{j=1}^{\infty} \beta^j F(Y_{t+j}, Z_{t+j}) \right] \tag{2.407}$$

$$s.t. \quad Y_{t+1} \leq Y_t + Q(Y_t, Z_t), \quad Y_t \text{ known} \tag{2.408}$$

$$Y_{t+j+1} \leq Y_{t+j} + Q(Y_{t+j}, Z_{t+j}), \tag{2.409}$$

$$c \geq G(Y_t, Z_t), \tag{2.410}$$

$$c \geq G(Y_{t+j}, Z_{t+j}). \tag{2.411}$$

Next, relabel the time indices:

$$V(Y_t) = \max_{Z_t} \left[F(Y_t, Z_t) + \max_{\{Z_{t+j+1}\}_{j=0}^{\infty}} \sum_{j=0}^{\infty} \beta^j F(Y_{t+j+1}, Z_{t+j+1}) \right] \tag{2.412}$$

$$s.t. \quad Y_{t+1} \leq Y_t + Q(Y_t, Z_t), \quad Y_t \text{ known} \tag{2.413}$$

$$Y_{t+j+1+1} \leq Y_{t+j+1} + Q(Y_{t+j+1}, Z_{t+j+1}), \tag{2.414}$$

$$c \geq G(Y_t, Z_t), \tag{2.415}$$

$$c \geq G(Y_{t+j+1}, Z_{t+j+1}), \tag{2.416}$$

and note that the indices $t + j + 1$ now define $V(Y_{t+1})$, which allows the following simplification:

$$V(Y_t) = \max_{Z_t} [F(Y_t, Z_t) + \beta V(Y_{t+1})] \tag{2.417}$$

$$s.t. \quad Y_{t+1} \leq Y_t + Q(Y_t, Z_t), \quad Y_t \text{ known} \tag{2.418}$$

$$c \geq G(Y_t, Z_t), \tag{2.419}$$

which when substituting in the constraint allows for a further simplification to a static-constrained optimization problem

$$V(Y_t) = \max_{Z_t}[F(Y_t, Z_t) + \beta V(Y_t + Q(Y_t, Z_t))] \quad (2.420)$$

$$s.t. \quad c \geq G(Y_t, Z_t), \quad (2.421)$$

where the equation $V(Y_t) = \max_{Z_t} F(Y_t, Z_t) + \beta V(Y_t + Q(Y_t, Z_t))$ is known as the Bellman equation, which is at the heart of this approach to dynamic optimization.

Since the dynamic optimization has been reduced to static optimization, we can now write

$$V(Y_t) = \max_{Z_t}\left[F(Y_t, Z_t) + \beta V(Y_t + Q(Y_t, Z_t)) + \lambda_t[c - G(Y_t, Z_t)]\right], \quad (2.422)$$

which yields the first-order condition

$$F'_Z(Y_t, Z_t) + \beta V(Y_t + Q(Y_t, Z_t))Q'_Z(Y_t, Z_t) - \lambda_t G'_Z(Y_t, Z_t) = 0. \quad (2.423)$$

Applying the envelope theorem yields

$$\begin{aligned} V'(Y_t) = {} & F'_Y(Y_t, Z_t) + \beta V'(Y_t + Q(Y_t, Z_t))(1 + Q'_Y(Y_t, Z_t)) \\ & - \lambda_t G'_Y(Y_t, Z_t). \end{aligned} \quad (2.424)$$

So, the system of dynamic equations that must be solved to yield a solution to the dynamic optimization problem is

$$\begin{aligned} & F'_Z(Y_t, Z_t) + \beta V(Y_t + Q(Y_t, Z_t))Q'_Z(Y_t, Z_t) \\ & \quad = \lambda_t G'_Z(Y_t, Z_t), && (2.425) \\ & F'_Y(Y_t, Z_t) + \beta V'(Y_t + Q(Y_t, Z_t))(1 + Q'_Y(Y_t, Z_t)) \\ & \quad = V'(Y_t) + \lambda_t G'_Y(Y_t, Z_t), && (2.426) \\ & Y_t + Q(Y_t, Z_t) = Y_{t+1}, && (2.427) \\ & \lambda_t[c - G(Y_t, Z_t)] = 0, && (2.428) \end{aligned}$$

which is now a system of four equations in three unknown variables (Y_t,Z_t, and λ_t) and one unknown function ($V(Y_t)$). Relative to the Kuhn–Tucker approach, which led to a system of potentially nonlinear equations, we now have a nonlinear system that also involves solving for an unknown function. An important theorem in the theory of dynamic programming says that as long the functions F and G satisfy certain properties (which we have already assumed), there exists such a function. In practice, the question remains of how can we solve for the unknown value function $V(Y_t)$? This is usually done using numerical methods in practice, although an algebraic method is available (known as 'Guess and Verify') for extremely simple problems.[8]

Typically, it is usually easier to consider a system of nonlinear equations (such as those associated with a discrete time Lagrangian) and analyze the stability and other properties of a linearized system. However doing so only allows for analysis of local behavior (since linearization is usually conducted around a steady state). On the other hand, using the dynamic programming approach requires solving (usually numerically) for a function, which can be difficult but allows the researcher to go beyond purely local analyses. Considering global dynamics is often necessary when behavior far away from the steady-state is different from what is implied by the analysis of the linearized system; this is for example the case in systems with multiple steady states. The decision of which approach to use to solve a dynamic optimization problem is therefore a function of the tastes of the researcher and the economic problem at hand.

2.10 From Discrete to Continuous Time

Recall that a time series is a function of discrete or continuous time:

$$x_t = x(t). \tag{2.429}$$

Consider a simple difference equation

$$x_{t+1} - x_t = g(x_t). \tag{2.430}$$

---

[8]Judd (1998) and Ljungqvist and Sargent (2004) provide details with respect to the methods available for obtaining the function $V(Y_t)$ in practice.

This equation states that between time t and $t+1$, the absolute growth in x is given by $g(x_t)$. Consider next the following approximation:

$$x_{t+\Delta t} - x_t \simeq \Delta t \times g(x_t), \tag{2.431}$$

for any $\Delta t \in [0,1]$. When $\Delta t = 0$, this equation is simply an identity. When $\Delta t = 1$, it gives $x_{t+1} - x_t = g(x_t)$. In between, it is a linear approximation, which should not be too bad if the distance between t and $t+1$ is not very large, so that $g(x) \simeq g(x_t)$ for all $x \in [x_t, x_{t+1}]$.

Now, divide both sides of this equation by Δt, and take limits to obtain

$$\lim_{\Delta t \to 0} \frac{x_{t+\Delta t} - x_t}{\Delta t} = \dot{x}_t \simeq g(x_t). \tag{2.432}$$

This limit is a differential equation representing the same dynamics as the difference equation above for the case in which the distance between t and $t+1$ is 'small'.

2.11 Conclusion

In summary, as in the continuous time case, models built in discrete time will begin with univariate or multivariate dynamic optimization problems, often discounted exponentially and with initial (and/or terminal) conditions specified. These problems will be solved using optimal control techniques (usually the discrete time Lagrangian), and the resultant optimality conditions will typically take the form of systems of differential equations. These systems, when nonlinear, will need to be linearized for analysis, for which TSAs are available. Given a linear system, steady states can be derived and stability determined. In a nutshell, that will typically be the solution of the model using which economic questions can be answered.

Chapter 3

Stochastic Dynamics

Analogous to deterministic analyses, linear stochastic macroeconomic time series exercises typically begin with the specification of a set of dynamic stochastic optimization problems that clearly indicate variables which the researcher takes to be strictly endogenous, strictly exogenous, and pre-determined. The problems lead to a system of a nonlinear *expectational* difference equations, as functions of the 'deep parameters' (say θ) that characterize the structure of the underlying model economy (and thereby show up in the associated optimization problems). The nonlinear system is subsequently linearized and then taken to the data for validation. The economic issue underlying the exercise may of course have multiple such optimization problems and the theory may be of a general or a partial equilibrium variety. In this chapter, we lay out the technical steps involved in a linear modeling exercise.

We first discuss the theory of stochastic processes in discrete time. In particular, given numerical values for a set of deep parameters θ, the model will reduce typically to a vector autoregression of first order ($VAR(1)$). This statistical object will usually be employed in answering questions one poses to the model; therefore, understanding this final object of analysis is of first-order importance. Second, we prepare the time series data to be employed in the evaluation of a model by modifying raw data so that they satisfy the requirements of the theory of stochastic processes. That is, given that the model will be built to deliver a $VAR(1)$ representation, if data are to be employed in specifying or estimating the deep parameters θ, then the data themselves will need to be of a $VAR(1)$ form. There are several options available to implement this step; we will discuss one common technique, namely, the Hodrick–Prescott filter. Third, we set up and solve dynamic, stochastic optimization problems in discrete time, also known as the theory of stochastic optimal control. We assume in this chapter that the researcher is restricted to optimizing exponentially discounted and otherwise well-behaved functions. Within this step, the next task is to linearize the nonlinear systems of difference equations that are the outputs of the optimization step. The fourth step is to solve the linear expectational difference equations under 'rational expectations' to obtain a (saddle-path) stable solution that takes the form of the sought after $VAR(1)$. Nonlinear analyses and attendant methods are covered by DeJong and Dave (2011).

In the subsequent fifth step, the literature diverges as one can pursue method of moments, maximum likelihood, or Bayesian techniques to estimate θ by coupling data and theory. The main technical needs in this step are the derivation and implementation of the likelihood function via a Kalman filter. This fifth step is typically termed structural macroeconometrics. Interested readers who feel equipped with the above-mentioned technical tools are also referred to DeJong and Dave (2011) for a definitive exposition to structural macroeconometrics. We now turn to a description of steps 1–4 in turn; similar in spirit to the previous chapter, the exposition is in reverse order, starting with analyses of linear stochastic systems.

3.1 Stochastic Processes

We need to know how to mathematically describe the time series behavior of macroeconomic aggregates when they fluctuate (probabilistically) around a linear trend, either by themselves or as sets of variables. In what follows, we assume that readers are familiar with the definition of a random variable, associated functions such as means, variances, and covariances, and the tools of matrix algebra. A detailed and canonical exposition of the topics covered in this section is provided by Hamilton (1994); here, we focus on the practical knowledge necessary for understanding stochastic macroeconomic theory and leave a more formal treatment of the material to other books.

3.1.1 Univariate processes

A stochastic process is a collection of random variables indexed by time. For example, a person walking on a line randomly taking one step to the right or one step to the left in each period is called a random walk, a kind of stochastic process. The motion of this person can be summarized with a random variable W_t – the position of the individual at a certain point in time:

$$W_t = \sum_{i=1}^{t} X_i. \tag{3.1}$$

This position is dependent on the sequence of steps taken, $X_i \in \{-1, 1\}$, where X_i are independent and identically distributed (*iid*) random variables such that $P(X_i = 1) = p \in (0, 1)$ and $P(X_i = -1) = 1 - p$. One can use this notation to show that $\lim_{i \to +\infty} P(W_t = W_{t+i}) = 1$. This last formula means that the person will eventually retrace her steps.

For the purposes of macroeconomic analysis, however, the most important stochastic process is a zero-mean white noise (WN) random disturbance,

$$\{\varepsilon_t\}_{-\infty}^{\infty}, \tag{3.2}$$

such that $E(\varepsilon_t) = 0 \; \forall \, t$, $E(\varepsilon_t^2) = \sigma^2 \; \forall \, t$ and $E(\varepsilon_t \varepsilon_s) = 0$ for all $s \neq t$; if $\varepsilon_t \sim N(0, \sigma^2)$, then we call it a Gaussian or normally distributed WN process. Because the expectation of ε_t is zero, one can use a law of large numbers to show that the sample mean converges to zero, so shocks eventually 'wash out'. Since the variance is bounded, one can use the central limit theorem to show that the distribution of the sample mean converges to a normal distribution.

Next, a covariance stationary stochastic process (CSSP) is a stochastic process that has a mean (possibly non-zero) that does not vary across time, a finite variance, and a covariance that is not a function of time. That is, the covariance is only dependent on $|t - s|$, i.e. the absolute distance between two time periods. That is, if for a univariate stochastic process y_t,

$$E(y_t) = E(y_s) = \mu, \tag{3.3}$$

$$V(y_t) = \sigma^2 < \infty, \tag{3.4}$$

$$E[(y_t - \mu)(y_s - \mu)] = \sigma_{t,s} = c(\tau),\ \tau = t - s, \tag{3.5}$$

hold, then y_t is called a univariate CSSP.

In both building models and analyzing data, our objective will be to model macroeconomic time series as functions of their own past values. This is because macroeconomic time series exhibit persistence: they are often functions of their own past (and sometimes expected future) values. For instance, consider the following autoregressive of order p ($AR(p)$) specification:

$$y_t = \rho_1 y_{t-1} + \rho_2 y_{t-2} + \cdots + \rho_p y_{t-p} + \varepsilon_t, \tag{3.6}$$

where ε_t is a WN process. The variable y_t could be real GDP, and the above equation is suggesting that it is a function of its own past values (up until p periods ago) plus some WN disturbance. The above expression can be written as[1]

$$\rho(L) y_t = \varepsilon_t, \tag{3.7}$$

where

$$\rho(L) = 1 - \rho_1 L - \rho_2 L^2 - \cdots - \rho_p L^p. \tag{3.8}$$

Since y_t is a function of the previous values of y_s, $s < t$, and the error term, the mean, variance, and covariance matrix of y_t should be related to the mean and variance of ε_t, but computing these values directly is challenging and depends on the order of the process (namely, p). Fortunately, the Wold decomposition theorem (WDT) can be used to compute the mean and other statistics associated with y_t. It states that any CSSP can be written instead as

$$y_t = A(L)\varepsilon_t \tag{3.9}$$

in the case of an $AR(p)$, albeit under certain (reasonable) conditions. Equation (3.9) known as the fundamental moving average (MA) representation of the $AR(p)$ process, and the main condition under

[1]Recall that L denotes a lag (also known as backshift) operator, when applied to a time series y_t, $Ly_t = y_{t-1}$, $L^2 y_t = y_{t-2}$, and so on.

which it holds is that the squared coefficients of $A(L)$, namely, a_0, a_1, a_2, etc. all sum to some number less than infinity, that is,

$$\sum_{j=0}^{\infty} a_j^2 < +\infty, \tag{3.10}$$

which is known as the square summability condition. If this condition were not to hold, then the MA process $y_t = A(L)\varepsilon_t$ could 'explode', which is not helpful and certainly at odds with how macroeconomic time series data present themselves. So, assuming that the WDT holds, the moving average representation of an $AR(p)$ process is given generically by

$$y_t = A(L)\varepsilon_t, \tag{3.11}$$

where $A(L)$ could be an infinite-order process.

3.1.2 Multivariate processes

The multivariate analog of an $AR(p)$ process is called a $VAR(p)$ and is expressed as follows:

$$y_t = \Phi_1 y_{t-1} + \cdots + \Phi_p y_{t-p} + \varepsilon_t, \tag{3.12}$$

$$E(\varepsilon_t) = 0_{n \times n}, \tag{3.13}$$

$$E(\varepsilon_t \varepsilon_s) = \begin{Bmatrix} \Omega & \forall\, t = s \\ 0 & \forall\, t \neq s \end{Bmatrix}, \tag{3.14}$$

where y_t consists of a number of variables (e.g. $y_t = [y_{1t}\ y_{2t}]'$) with an associated vector of WN processes ε_t. If we construct $Y_t = [y_t\ y_{t-1} \cdots y_{t-p+1}]'_{np \times 1}$ and if we let

$$\Theta = \begin{bmatrix} \Phi_1 & \Phi_2 & \Phi_3 & \cdots & \Phi_{p-1} & \Phi_p \\ I_n & 0 & \cdots & \cdots & \cdots & 0 \\ 0 & I_n & \cdots & \cdots & \vdots & \vdots \\ \vdots & \vdots & \cdots & \cdots & \vdots & \vdots \\ 0 & 0 & \cdots & \cdots & I_n & 0 \end{bmatrix}, \tag{3.15}$$

$$\nu_t = [\varepsilon_t\ 0 \cdots 0]', \tag{3.16}$$

then the $VAR(p)$ can be written as a $VAR(1)$

$$Y_t = \Theta Y_{t-1} + \nu_t, \tag{3.17}$$

$$E(\nu_t \nu_s) = \begin{Bmatrix} \Sigma & \forall\, t = s \\ 0 & \forall\, t \neq s \end{Bmatrix} \tag{3.18}$$

$$\Sigma = \begin{bmatrix} \Omega\, 0 \cdots\cdots\cdots 0 \\ 0\; 0 \cdots\cdots\cdots 0 \\ \vdots\;\vdots \cdots\; \vdots\;\; \vdots \\ 0\; 0 \cdots\cdots\; 0\;\; 0 \end{bmatrix}. \tag{3.19}$$

This specification implies that

$$Y_{t+s} = \nu_{t+s} + \Theta\nu_{t+s-1} + \Theta^2\nu_{t+s-2} + \cdots + \Theta^{s-1}\nu_{t+1} + \Theta^s Y_t, \tag{3.20}$$

which is a CSSP if all of the eigenvalues of Θ are less than one in absolute value. Finally, using the multivariate analog of the WDT implies that this $VAR(1)$ can be written as a $VMA(\infty)$:

$$Y_t = A(L)\nu_t. \tag{3.21}$$

In order to calculate the elements of $A(L)$, the relevant formulae using the method of undetermined coefficients are

$$A_0 = I_n \tag{3.22}$$

$$A_1 = \Phi_1 \tag{3.23}$$

$$A_s = \Phi_1 A_{s-1} + \Phi_2 A_{s-2} + \cdots + \Phi_p A_{s-p} \quad \forall s = 1, 2, \ldots. \tag{3.24}$$

Next, it is important to note that similar to how a higher-order system of dynamic equations (e.g. a $VAR(p)$) can be written as a $VAR(1)$, a higher-order equation such as an $AR(p)$ can also be written as a $VAR(1)$; thus, in all cases, we need only focus on the statistical properties of the $VAR(1)$ process:

$$Y_t = \Theta Y_{t-1} + \nu_t, \quad E(\nu_t \nu_s) = \begin{Bmatrix} \Sigma & \forall\, t = s \\ 0 & \forall\, t \neq s \end{Bmatrix}. \tag{3.25}$$

Let

$$\Gamma(0) = E(Y_t Y_t') \tag{3.26}$$

denote the contemporaneous variance-covariance matrix of Y_t, and let

$$\Gamma(s) = E(Y_t Y_{t-s}') \tag{3.27}$$

be the sth-order covariance matrix. Then, it holds that

$$\Gamma(0) = E\left[(\Theta Y_{t-1} + \nu_t)(\Theta Y_{t-1} + \nu_t)'\right] = \Theta\Gamma(0)\Theta' + \Sigma, \tag{3.28}$$

the solution to which is given by

$$vec\,[\Gamma(0)] = [I - \Theta \otimes \Theta]^{-1}\, vec[\Sigma], \tag{3.29}$$

where $\otimes$ denotes the Kronecker product. Further,

$$\begin{aligned} \Gamma(1) &= E(Y_t Y_{t-1}') && (3.30)\\ &= E((\Theta Y_{t-1} + \nu_t) Y_{t-1}') && (3.31)\\ &= \Theta\Gamma(0), && (3.32) \end{aligned}$$

and in general,

$$\Gamma(s) = \Theta\Gamma(s-1) = \Theta^s\Gamma(0), \tag{3.33}$$

so we now have all of the variance and covariance properties of a $VAR(1)$.

3.1.3 Impulse response functions

We now consider what happens to the time series path of a $VAR\,(1)$ process when it is temporarily disturbed. This is called an impulse response function (IRF). If the $VAR\,(1)$ process represents macroeconomic variables of interest (such as the linearized representation of equilibrium output or consumption), the IRF of the variable allows one to see how this variable 'reacts' to an economic shock over time. If for example this variable is equilibrium output, the IRF of output to a shock tells us something about the shape of business cycles in the economy being analyzed. More formally, given a $VAR(1)$ representation of a univariate or multivariate set of time series, we wish to see what happens to the future values of Y_t (say, $Y_{t+1}, \ldots, Y_{t+s}$) if at time t the WN process ν_t takes on some value and then is zero forever (e.g. $\nu_t = \sigma$, and then $\nu_{t+s} = 0 \;\forall\; s = 1, 2, \ldots$). This question can be answered by appealing to the $VMA(\infty)$ representation of the $VAR(1)$, namely,

$$Y_t = A(L)\nu_t = \nu_t + A_1\nu_{t-1} + A_2\nu_{t-2} + \cdots, \tag{3.34}$$

where it is important to recall that Y_t and ν_t are vectors (say, $m \times 1$) and that $A_1, A_2, \ldots$ are the corresponding $m \times m$ matrices. The question that the IRF answers can now be restated as follows: suppose that the first element of ν_t (say, ν_{1t}) changed by some amount (say, σ_1), the second element (say, ν_{2t}) changed by some amount (say, σ_2), and so on until the nth element of ν_t (say, ν_{nt}) changed by some amount (say, σ_n); what would be the impact of these changes on the value of Y_{t+s}? Given the $VMA(\infty)$ form, the answer is

$$\Delta Y_{t+s} = \frac{\partial Y_{t+s}}{\partial \nu_{1t}}\sigma_1 + \frac{\partial Y_{t+s}}{\partial \nu_{2t}}\sigma_2 + \cdots + \frac{\partial Y_{t+s}}{\partial \nu_{nt}}\sigma_n. \tag{3.35}$$

In order to implement the answer however, note that for the $VMA(\infty)$ representation above,

$$\frac{\partial Y_{t+s}}{\partial \nu_t'} = A_s, \tag{3.36}$$

and so

$$\Delta Y_{t+s} = \frac{\partial Y_{t+s}}{\partial \nu_{1t}}\sigma_1 + \frac{\partial Y_{t+s}}{\partial \nu_{2t}}\sigma_2 + \cdots + \frac{\partial Y_{t+s}}{\partial \nu_{nt}}\sigma_n = A_s\sigma, \tag{3.37}$$

where $\sigma = (\sigma_1\ \sigma_2 \cdots \sigma_n)'$. Now, in general, A_s could take on a complicated, non-analytical form. Thus, we can compute the answer instead by simulating the $VAR(1)$ and then recursively computing the implied A_s. As an example, Figures 3.1 and 3.2 plot the IRF for a univariate $AR(1)$ process under the assumption that ρ is 0.95 and 0.5, respectively.

3.1.4 Variance decompositions

Given a $VAR(1)$.

$$Y_t = \Theta Y_{t-1} + \nu_t. \tag{3.38}$$

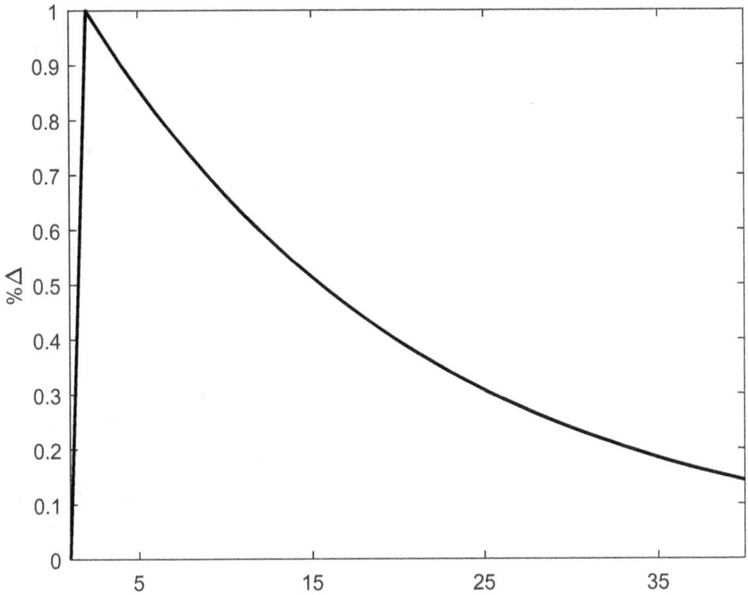

Figure 3.1. IRF for $y_t = \rho y_{t-1} + \varepsilon_t, \rho = 0.95$.

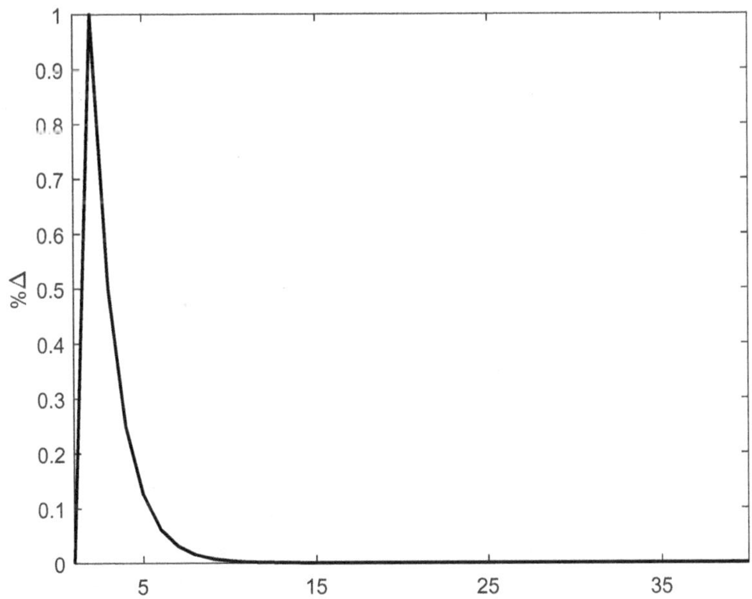

Figure 3.2. IRF for $y_t = \rho y_{t-1} + \varepsilon_t, \rho = 0.5$.

we can also ask another important question: how much of the variation in the jth variable of Y_t can be attributed to a shock to variable k at some horizon of time? For macroeconomic models, this is a particularly useful question to answer, as we can ask, for instance, how much of the variation in output is due to a demand versus a supply shock at say the 4th quarter, 8th quarter, after five years, etc.? The answer to this question is provided by the forecast error variance decomposition; the econometric theory is covered in detail by Hamilton (1994).

3.1.5 The law of iterated expectations

We conclude this section by taking a moment to understand a fundamental statistical law that will be extremely useful in the study of expectational difference equations as well as systems thereof. It is the *law of iterated expectations* (LIE), one version of which states that

$$\begin{aligned} E[E(X_{t+2} \mid \Xi_{t+1}) \mid \Xi_t] = E(X_{t+2} \mid \Xi_t) &\longleftrightarrow E_t(E_{t+1}(X_{t+2})) \\ &= E_t(X_{t+2}), \end{aligned} \tag{3.39}$$

where Ξ_t and Ξ_{t+1} are the information sets (in periods t and $t+1$, respectively) that are employed in forming the expectations as of time t and/or time $t+1$. (The information sets could include items such as the past values of the variables and in general consist of the whole sigma-algebra associated with the properly filtered probability space on which the stochastic process for X_t is defined).

The LIE states that today's expectation of tomorrow's expectation of X_{t+2} is the same as today's expectation of X_{t+2}. The intuition for this result is simple: since you do not have information about what will happen tomorrow, your best guess as to the average value today of the random variable X_{t+2} is not affected by information you do not possess. An example comes from the theory of rational expectations popularized in economics by Muth (1961) and Lucas (1972). If today someone was told that they would be given additional information tomorrow upon which to make an expectation, then she would be equally likely to revise one's current expectation of X_t upward or downward. As such, the net result of the revision would be zero, which would be equivalent to making an expectation today about X_t. Alternatively, the LIE can be understood by recognizing that the information set Ξ_t is simply a subset of Ξ_{t+1}, and so tomorrow's expectation of X_t is constrained by the knowledge held today and thus would not be any different from an expectation of X_t formulated today.

We can check the LIE using a simple example. Assume X_t follows

$$X_{t+1} = \rho X_t + \varepsilon_{t+1}, \quad E_t(\varepsilon_{t+1}) = 0. \tag{3.40}$$

Then, if we perform a forward iteration, we have that

$$X_{t+2} = \rho X_{t+1} + \varepsilon_{t+2}, \quad E_{t+1}(\varepsilon_{t+2}) = 0. \tag{3.41}$$

Substitute in the equation for X_{t+1} above and rewrite the X_{t+2} equation as

$$X_{t+2} = \rho^2 X_t + \rho\varepsilon_{t+1} + \varepsilon_{t+2}. \tag{3.42}$$

Then, taking expectations with respect to time $t+1$ would give us

$$E_{t+1}(X_{t+2}) = E_{t+1}\left[\rho^2 X_t + \rho\varepsilon_{t+1} + \varepsilon_{t+2}\right] \tag{3.43}$$

$$= \rho^2 X_t + \rho\varepsilon_{t+1}. \tag{3.44}$$

Taking expectations again with respect to time t would give us

$$E_t E_{t+1}(X_{t+2}) = E_t\left[\rho^2 X_t + \rho\varepsilon_{t+1}\right] = \rho^2 X_t, \tag{3.45}$$

but we also know that

$$E_t(X_{t+2}) = E_t\left[\rho^2 X_t + \rho\varepsilon_{t+1} + \varepsilon_{t+2}\right] = \rho^2 X_t. \tag{3.46}$$

Thus, we have shown that

$$E_t(E_{t+1}(X_{t+2})) = E_t(X_{t+2}) = \rho^2 X_t, \tag{3.47}$$

which verifies the LIE in this example.

3.2 Preparing Data

There are several ways to remove trends from macroeconomic time series. The goal under all is to transform the data into mean-zero CSSPs. One particular approach to detrending and isolating cycles is Hodrick–Prescott (hereafter, H-P) filtering, which allows for a slowly evolving trend. The H-P filter, a popular tool among macroeconomists, works as follows. First, assume that $\log y_t$ can be written as

$$\log y_t = g_t + c_t, \tag{3.48}$$

where g_t denotes the growth component of $\log y_t$ and c_t denotes the cyclical component. The H-P filter estimates g_t and c_t in order to minimize

$$\sum_{t=1}^{T} c_t^2 + \lambda \sum_{t=3}^{T} \left[(1-L)^2 g_t\right]^2, \tag{3.49}$$

taking λ as given. Trend removal is accomplished by computing

$$\widetilde{y}_t = \log y_t - \widehat{g}_t = \widehat{c}_t. \tag{3.50}$$

The parameter λ determines the importance of having a smoothly evolving growth component. For $\lambda = 0$, smoothness receives no value, and all variation in $\log y_t$ will be assigned to the cyclical component. As λ tends to ∞, the trend is maximally smooth, i.e. linear. In general, λ lies between these two extremes, e.g. for business cycle data at quarterly frequencies, the standard choice is $\lambda = 1,600$. It is important to remember that this is only one way to isolate cycles in data. There is a very large and meaningful literature on the advantages and disadvantages of a number of different methods. The choice of method is invariably up to the researcher and the empirical question at hand.

3.3 Optimization

Recall that there are two central theorems in the theory of optimization that are of relevance. The first, known as the Kuhn–Tucker theorem provides us with a Lagrangian method to solve (under some regularity conditions) an optimization problem featuring inequality constraints and delivers a system of nonlinear equations for analysis. The second, known as the envelope theorem, provides us with Bellman's method to solve a dynamic optimization problem (possibly exhibiting random components) and delivers a function along with nonlinear equations for analysis. The envelope theorem is better suited to an exposition of dynamic programming methods which are best suited for nonlinear exercises. Here, we restrict ourselves to the Kuhn–Tucker theorem, a detailed exposition of stochastic dynamic programming (which is largely a numerical methodology given a lack of closed-form analytical solutions) is provided by Ljungqvist and Sargent (2018) and DeJong and Dave (2011).

In order to apply the Kuhn–Tucker theorem to our context, consider the following standard dynamic, stochastic optimization problem in discrete time. The expected value (as at time $t = 0$) of the exponentially discounted sum of a periodic function

$$F(c_t, s_t, \varepsilon_t), \tag{3.51}$$

where c_t is the control variable, s_t is the state variable, and ε_t is a (possibly serially correlated) random shock (observed at the start of period $t+1$), is to be maximized. The notation is assumed to subsume cases in which leads and lags of the control or state variables are present in F. Further, assume that this function (and the eventual set of constraints) has the necessary continuity and differentiability characteristics as required per the Kuhn–Tucker theorem for an interior optimum. This optimization is not unconstrained; however, assume that the constraints take the form

$$G(c_t, s_t, \varepsilon_{t+1}) = s_{t+1} - s_t \quad \forall\, t, \tag{3.52}$$

with given initial conditions for s_0. The notation for the constraint described above is also assumed to subsume leads and lags of state variables subject to the fact that s_{t+1} is not known until ε_{t+1} is observed at the start of $t+1$. Also subsumed in the notation are a number of exogenous stochastic processes that might form part of the constraint set.

The optimization problem can now be written as

$$\max_{\{c_t\}} \quad E_0 \sum_{t=0}^{\infty} \beta^t F(c_t, s_t, \varepsilon_t), \quad \beta \in (0,1) \tag{3.53}$$

$$s.t. \quad G(c_t, s_t, \varepsilon_{t+1}) = s_{t+1} - s_t \quad \forall\, t, \tag{3.54}$$

where β is the exponential discount factor, and we are explicitly ignoring the fact that expected value optimization would technically require us to take the time-t expectation of the constraint as well.

We can now maximize by taking the first-order conditions of the following Lagrangian:

$$L = E_0 \left\{ \sum_{t=0}^{\infty} \beta^t F(c_t, s_t, \varepsilon_t) + \sum_{t=0}^{\infty} \lambda_{t+1} \left[s_t + G(c_t, s_t, \varepsilon_{t+1}) - s_{t+1} \right] \right\}, \tag{3.55}$$

which entails taking the derivative of L with respect to the state, control, and co-state variables and setting them equal to zero. The first-order conditions are

$$\frac{\partial L}{\partial s_t} = E_t \left\{ \beta^t F_s' + \lambda_{t+1} + \lambda_{t+1} G_s' - \lambda_t = 0 \right\}, \tag{3.56}$$

$$\frac{\partial L}{\partial c_t} = E_t \left\{ \beta^t F_c' + \lambda_{t+1} G_c' = 0 \right\}, \tag{3.57}$$

$$\frac{\partial L}{\partial \lambda_{t+1}} = E_t \left\{ s_t - G(c_t, s_t, \varepsilon_{t+1}) - s_{t+1} = 0 \right\}. \tag{3.58}$$

Note that, in the first-order conditions, derivatives for s_t can come from potentially two time periods: t and $t-1$. In fact, the way the Lagrangian has been written is not precise; indeed in the presence of uncertainty given all the possible realizations of ε_{t+1} the constraints are actually very large. What is represented above however is the *process* whereby, having carefully constructed the current period objective function (F) and substantive constraint (G) and implicitly employing the law of iterated expectations, one obtains a system of nonlinear *expectational* difference equations (note the presence of E_t). The system consists of as many first-order conditions with respect to control variables as there are controls, as many first-order conditions with respect to state variables as there are states, and all of the constraints and all of the exogenous stochastic processes implicit in the notation. Therefore, the system is by definition square (i.e. as many variables as there are equations), as in all previous deterministic analyses.

The nonlinear system is not amenable for linear analysis, obviously. In order to linearize, first keep the expectations operator outside of the equation, i.e. retain

$$E_t \left\{ \beta^t F_s' + \lambda_{t+1} + \lambda_{t+1} G_s' - \lambda_t = 0 \right\}, \tag{3.59}$$

and do *not* pull in the expectations as in

$$\beta^t E_t F_s' + E_t \lambda_{t+1} + E_t \lambda_{t+1} G_s' - E_t \lambda_t = 0. \tag{3.60}$$

Next, for each equation in the system, use a Taylor series approximation of first order to linearize around the non-stochastic steady state. You may at this step use a logarithmic approximation as well; the objective in general is to write down a set of linear equations with variables in deviations from steady states. The advantage of writing linear models so that all variables are in logarithmic deviations from steady states is that then coefficients can be generally interpreted as elasticities, which are unitless and therefore less cumbersome. Recall from the previous chapters that to do a first order approximation, one employs

$$x_t = f(\overline{x}) + f'(\overline{x})(x_t - \overline{x}) \tag{3.61}$$

in the univariate case or

$$X_t = F(\overline{X}) + JF(\overline{X})(X_t - \overline{X}) \tag{3.62}$$

in the multivariate case, where values with bars on them represent non-stochastic steady-state values and J is the Jacobian matrix of first derivatives. Since given first-order conditions, this step is a *procedure* versus a formula, the examples in the chapters that follow provide applications of this procedure.

Finally, note that the multiplier is not removed from the nonlinear system prior to linearization. Indeed, the multiplier itself is treated as a variable and linearized. The main reason for not substituting out the multiplier in order to reduce the dimensionality of the system (a process usually undertaken in deterministic analyses for growth for instance) is because, for example, $E_t(\lambda_{t+1}G_c')$ is a covariance that cannot be presumed to equal zero. Therefore, we usually keep the multiplier and not reduce the system. However, researchers who employ dynamic programming to obtain nonlinear systems do not have a multiplier because that is not usually part of the output from the dynamic programming approach in stochastic optimization.

3.4 Linear Rational Expectations Model Solutions

As with difference equations, expectational difference equations (or systems thereof) can be categorized by their order. Further, as with difference equations, higher-order expectational difference equations (or systems thereof) can always be written in first-order form; therefore, we focus on solving such linear first-order expectational difference equations and systems thereof.

An example of an expectational difference equation is

$$y_t = aE_t(y_{t+1}) + \varepsilon_t, \tag{3.63}$$

where ε_t is a WN process. In such equations, the expectations operator is defined relative to the distribution of ε_t, which via the expectations operator induces a distribution for y_t. The objective of 'solving' such an equation is to solve for the (stochastic) path of y_t, having computed the expectation $E_t(y_{t+1})$. The same applies to systems of equations.

3.4.1 Univariate solutions

There are several methods available for solving an expectational difference equation: repeated substitution, factorization, the method of undetermined coefficients, and Whiteman's (1983) method. Generally, the factorization approach involves taking the expectation (or projection) of the relationship at hand – at the lowest information set – and then factoring to isolate the expectation that needs to be evaluated. By contrast, the method of undetermined coefficients involves guessing the form of the answer and then finding coefficients that will make the solution work. These approaches (or combinations thereof) generalize to the multivariate case, discussed as follows, and even though one will rarely work with univariate expectational difference equations, it is useful to review the intuition of how to solve them, as that intuition translates to the multivariate case.

Consider

$$y_t = aE_t y_{t+1} + cx_t, \tag{3.64}$$

where x_t is an *exogenous* CSSP with an $MA(\infty)$ representation

$$x_t = \xi(L)\varepsilon_t \tag{3.65}$$

and $|a| < 1$. We seek a solution to this equation, and by solution, we mean the value or, more precisely, time path of y_t purely as a function of the parameters (a and c) and exogenous variables (x_t).[2]

3.4.1.1 *Repeated substitution*

Iterate the equation to be solved forward to obtain

$$y_{t+1} = aE_{t+1}y_{t+2} + cx_{t+1}. \tag{3.66}$$

Take expectations conditional on information known at time t to obtain, using the LIE,

$$E_t y_{t+1} = aE_t y_{t+2} + cE_t x_{t+1}. \tag{3.67}$$

Substitute this last expression into $y_t = aE_t y_{t+1} + cx_t$ to obtain

$$y_t = a^2 E_t y_{t+2} + acE_t x_{t+1} + cx_t. \tag{3.68}$$

Repeat this iterative substitution until time $t + T$:

$$y_t = c\sum_{i=0}^{T} a^i E_t x_{t+i} + a^{T+1} E_t y_{t+T+1}, \tag{3.69}$$

and if y_t is bounded, then since $|a| < 1$, we have that

$$\lim_{T\to\infty} a^{T+1} E_t y_{t+T+1} = 0; \tag{3.70}$$

[2]At this point, it is useful to review the material in Chapter 2, as many of the relevant concepts carry through to stochastic analyses.

thus, the solution is

$$y_t = c\sum_{i=0}^{\infty} a^i E_t x_{t+i}. \tag{3.71}$$

3.4.1.2 *Undetermined coefficients*

Guess a solution of the form

$$y_t = \sum_{i=0}^{\infty} \lambda_i E_t x_{t+i}, \tag{3.72}$$

where the λ's are the coefficients to be determined. If the guess is correct, then

$$E_t y_{t+1} = \sum_{i=0}^{\infty} \lambda_i E_t x_{t+i+1}, \tag{3.73}$$

and we can substitute these two equations into $y_t = aE_t y_{t+1} + cx_t$ to obtain

$$\sum_{i=0}^{\infty} \lambda_i E_t x_{t+i} = a\sum_{i=0}^{\infty} \lambda_i E_t x_{t+i+1} + cx_t. \tag{3.74}$$

This last equation can only hold if for every i the coefficient on x_{t+i} on the left-hand side is the same as the corresponding coefficient on the right-hand side. By matching the coefficients, we get

$$c = \lambda_0 \tag{3.75}$$

$$\lambda_{i+1} = a\lambda_i = a^i c, \tag{3.76}$$

which then yields

$$y_t = c\sum_{i=0}^{\infty} a^i E_t x_{t+i}. \tag{3.77}$$

3.4.1.3 *Factorization*

For

$$y_t = aE_t y_{t+1} + cx_t, \tag{3.78}$$

take expectations on both sides with respect to the oldest information set, which in this case is at time t:

$$E_t y_t = aE_t y_{t+1} + cE_t x_t. \tag{3.79}$$

Rewrite in terms of lag operators:

$$E_t y_t = aFE_t y_t + cE_t x_t \tag{3.80}$$

$$F = L^{-1}. \tag{3.81}$$

This yields

$$(1 - aF)E_t y_t = cE_t x_t, \tag{3.82}$$

$$E_t y_t = c(1 - aF)^{-1} E_t x_t, \tag{3.83}$$

$$\rightarrow y_t = c\sum_{i=0}^{\infty} a^i F^i E_t x_t \tag{3.84}$$

and hence the solution

$$y_t = c\sum_{i=0}^{\infty} a^i E_t x_{t+i}. \tag{3.85}$$

3.4.2 Multivariate solutions

Consider a model that leads to a set of linear first-order expectational difference equations. This model needs to be solved for a stable solution that takes the form of a $VAR(1)$. There are several methods for obtaining the solution; see DeJong and Dave (2011). Here, we outline one such method, that of Blanchard and Kahn (1980). The first step prior to implementing the Blanchard and Kahn (1980) procedure to obtain such a stable solution requires collecting all l static equations of the model and writing them as

$$\underset{l\times l}{A} y_t = \underset{l\times m}{B} x_t + \underset{l\times p}{C} u_t \tag{3.86}$$

and, next, writing the m dynamic equations as

$$\underset{m\times m}{D} E_t x_{t+1} + \underset{m\times l}{F} E_t y_{t+1} = \underset{m\times m}{G} x_t + \underset{m\times l}{H} y_t + \underset{m\times p}{J} u_t \tag{3.87}$$

and the p exogenous stochastic processes as

$$u_t = \underset{p\times p}{P} u_{t-1} + \varepsilon_t, \tag{3.88}$$

where the vector x_t is $m \times 1$, the vector u_t is $p \times 1$, and the vector y_t is $l \times 1$. Clearly, the model is assumed to have a total of $l + m$ equations that involve a total of $l + m$ variables aside from the p stochastic processes.

The next step is to solve for y_t and $E_t y_{t+1}$ given (3.86) and (3.88). This yields

$$y_t = A^{-1}Bx_t + A^{-1}Cu_t \tag{3.89}$$

from (3.86) and

$$E_t y_{t+1} = A^{-1}BE_t x_{t+1} + A^{-1}CE_t u_{t+1} \tag{3.90}$$

$$\rightarrow E_t y_{t+1} = A^{-1}BE_t x_{t+1} + A^{-1}CPu_t, \tag{3.91}$$

where (3.88) has been employed in the last equality above in order to substitute $E_t u_{t+1}$ with Pu_t given that from (3.88),

$$E_t u_{t+1} = PE_t u_t + E_t \varepsilon_{t+1} \tag{3.92}$$

$$= Pu_t + 0 = Pu_t. \tag{3.93}$$

Next, substitute (3.89) and (3.91) into (3.87) to obtain

$$DE_t x_{t+1} + F[A^{-1}BE_t x_{t+1} + A^{-1}CPu_t]$$
$$= Gx_t + H\left[A^{-1}Bx_t + A^{-1}Cu_t\right] + Ju_t \tag{3.94}$$

and collect terms,

$$[D + FA^{-1}B]E_t x_{t+1} = [G + HA^{-1}B]x_t$$
$$+ [J + HA^{-1}C - FA^{-1}CP]u_t, \tag{3.95}$$

and finally, obtain the form of the system that Blanchard and Kahn (1980) require as the input to their solution procedure:

$$E_t x_{t+1} = \underset{m\times m}{K} x_t + \underset{m\times p}{L} u_t \tag{3.96}$$

$$K = \left[D + FA^{-1}B\right]^{-1}\left[G + HA^{-1}B\right] \tag{3.97}$$

$$L = \left[D + FA^{-1}B\right]^{-1}\left[J + HA^{-1}C - FA^{-1}CP\right]. \tag{3.98}$$

So, consider now the $m \times m$ system of linear first-order expectational difference equations given by

$$E_t x_{t+1} = \underset{m\times m}{K} x_t + \underset{m\times p}{L} u_t, \tag{3.99}$$

where now the $m \times 1$ vector of variables x_t is ordered so that the $n_1 \times 1$ predetermined variables (i.e. those for which $E_t x_{t+1} = x_{t+1}$) are stacked on top of $n_2 \times 1$ non-predetermined variables (i.e. $m = n_1 + n_2$). Blanchard and Kahn (1980) provide a method for solving (3.99) provided that the number of explosive eigenvalues of K (i.e. the number of eigenvalues greater than one) equals n_2. There is no solution if the number of explosive eigenvalues of K is greater that n_2 and multiple solutions if the number of explosive eigenvalues of K is less than n_2. Assuming a stable solution exists, rewrite K using the Jordan decomposition as

$$K = M^{-1} N M, \tag{3.100}$$

where

$$N = \begin{bmatrix} \underset{n_1\times n_1}{N_1} & 0 \\ 0 & \underset{n_2\times n_2}{N_2} \end{bmatrix}, \quad M = \begin{bmatrix} \underset{n_1\times n_1}{M_{11}} & \underset{n_1\times n_2}{M_{12}} \\ \underset{n_2\times n_1}{M_{21}} & \underset{n_2\times n_2}{M_{22}} \end{bmatrix} \tag{3.101}$$

$$L = \begin{bmatrix} \underset{n_1\times p}{L_1} \\ \underset{n_2\times p}{L_2} \end{bmatrix} \tag{3.102}$$

and uncouple the system as

$$\begin{aligned} \begin{bmatrix} M_{11} & M_{12} \\ M_{21} & M_{22} \end{bmatrix} E_t x_{t+1} &= \begin{bmatrix} N_1 & 0 \\ 0 & N_1 \end{bmatrix} \begin{bmatrix} M_{11} & M_{12} \\ M_{21} & M_{22} \end{bmatrix} x_t \\ &\quad + \begin{bmatrix} M_{11} & M_{12} \\ M_{21} & M_{22} \end{bmatrix} \begin{bmatrix} L_1 \\ L_2 \end{bmatrix} u_t. \end{aligned} \tag{3.103}$$

The uncoupled system can now be written as

$$E_t x_{1t+1} = N_1 x_{1t} + Q_1 u_t, \tag{3.104}$$

$$E_t x_{2t+1} = N_2 x_{2t} + Q_2 u_t, \tag{3.105}$$

where

$$x_{1t} = M_{11}x_t^p + M_{12}x_t^{np}, \tag{3.106}$$

$$x_{2t} = M_{21}x_t^p + M_{22}x_t^{np}, \tag{3.107}$$

$$Q_1 = M_{11}L_1 + M_{12}L_2, \tag{3.108}$$

$$Q_2 = M_{21}L_1 + M_{22}L_2. \tag{3.109}$$

Note that the vector x_t has now been partitioned as $x_t = [x_t^p \quad x_t^{np}]'$, where x_t^p denotes all of the predetermined variables that are stacked on top of the non-predetermined variables (x_t^{np}).

Since the eigenvalues of N_2 are explosive (i.e. lie outside the unit circle), (3.105) can be solved forward to obtain

$$x_{2t} = -N_2^{-1}Ru_t, \tag{3.110}$$

where the $n_2 \times p$ matrix R is given by

$$vec\,(R) = vec\left(\sum_{j=0}^{\infty} N_2^{-j}Q_2P^j\right) = \sum_{j=0}^{\infty} vec(N_2^{-j}Q_2P^j) \tag{3.111}$$

$$= \sum_{j=0}^{\infty}[P^j \otimes (N_2^{-1})^j]vec(Q_2) = \sum_{j=0}^{\infty}[P \otimes N_2^{-1}]^j vec(Q_2) \tag{3.112}$$

$$= [I_{(n_2\times p)\times(n_2\times p)} - P \otimes N_2^{-1}]^{-1}vec(Q_2). \tag{3.113}$$

This result can be employed along with (3.107) to obtain

$$x_t^{np} = S_1x_t^p + S_2u_t, \tag{3.114}$$

where

$$S_1 = -M_{22}^{-1}M_{21}, \tag{3.115}$$

$$S_2 = -M_{22}^{-1}N_2^{-1}R. \tag{3.116}$$

Equation (3.106) now provides a solution for x_{1t}:

$$x_{1t} = (M_{11} + M_{12}S_1)x_t^p + M_{12}S_2u_t. \tag{3.117}$$

This solution can be employed in equation (3.104) to obtain

$$x_{t+1}^p = S_3 x_t^p + S_4 u_t, \tag{3.118}$$

$$S_3 = (M_{11} + M_{12}S_1)^{-1} N_1 (M_{11} + M_{12}S_1), \tag{3.119}$$

$$S_4 = (M_{11} + M_{12}S_1)^{-1} (Q_1 + N_1 M_{12} S_2 - M_{12} S_2 P). \tag{3.120}$$

Finally, in order to recover the relationship between y_t and x_t, return to (3.89):

$$y_t = A^{-1} B x_t + A^{-1} C u_t \tag{3.121}$$

$$= A^{-1} B \begin{bmatrix} I_{n_1 \times n_1} \\ S_1 \end{bmatrix} x_t^p + A^{-1} B \begin{bmatrix} 0_{n_1 \times p} \\ S_2 \end{bmatrix} u_t + A^{-1} C u_t, \tag{3.122}$$

which can be written more compactly as

$$y_t = S_5 x_t^p + S_6 u_t, \tag{3.123}$$

$$S_5 = A^{-1} B \begin{bmatrix} I_{n_1 \times n_1} \\ S_1 \end{bmatrix} \tag{3.124}$$

$$S_6 = A^{-1} B \begin{bmatrix} 0_{n_1 \times p} \\ S_2 \end{bmatrix} + A^{-1} C. \tag{3.125}$$

Equations (3.88) along with (3.114), (3.118), and (3.123) therefore provide the following stable rational expectations solution to the model:

$$z_{t+1} = \Pi z_t + W \varepsilon_{t+1}, \tag{3.126}$$

$$x_t^{np} = U z_t, \tag{3.127}$$

$$z_t = [x_t^p \quad u_t]', \tag{3.128}$$

where

$$\Pi = \begin{bmatrix} S_3 & S_4 \\ 0_{p \times n_1} & P \end{bmatrix}, \quad W = \begin{bmatrix} 0_{n_1 \times p} \\ I_{p \times p} \end{bmatrix} \tag{3.129}$$

$$U = \begin{bmatrix} S_5 & S_6 \\ S_1 & S_2 \end{bmatrix}. \tag{3.130}$$

With respect to coding the solution in Matlab, the required input matrices into the program are A, B, C, D, F, G, H, J, and P

along with the numbers n_1, n_2, and p. The program then delivers the matrices Π, W, and U along with an indicator that takes on a value of 0 if the solution found is stable and 1 if either there is no solution or multiple solutions. Finally, in order to write the solution of the model as a $VAR(1)$, let $Y_t = [x_t^p \quad u_t \quad x_t^{np}]'$. Then,

$$Y_t = \underbrace{\begin{bmatrix} \Pi \\ U^{-1} \end{bmatrix}}_{\Theta} Y_{t-1} + \underbrace{\begin{bmatrix} W \\ 0 \end{bmatrix}}_{\Upsilon} \varepsilon_t \tag{3.131}$$

$$\rightarrow Y_t = \Theta Y_{t-1} + \nu_t \tag{3.132}$$

In summary, the Blanchard and Kahn (1980) procedure requires three items. First, reduce a model into a system of static and dynamic equations (a trivial item). Second, clearly specify which variables are predetermined and which are not (which is not always abundantly clear), and finally, the key matrices which determine the extent to which this solution method can be easily implemented are the matrices A and $\left[D + FA^{-1}B\right]$. If the latter matrix cannot be easily inverted, then it is numerically difficult to implement this solution procedure on a computer.

As mentioned, there are several other methods available for solving linear systems. Given potential numerical difficulties in inverting $\left[D + FA^{-1}B\right]$, the method of Klein (2000) can be employed. Klein (2000) uses an alternate decomposition method to provide a solution but still requires that a researcher be able to specify which variables are predetermined and which are not. The method of Sims (2001) overcomes both the invertability and knowledge issue and provides a method that can be thought of as the best 'eigenvalue-decomposition' method for solving linear expectations difference equations. Further, a matrix analog to the method of undetermined coefficients is provided by Uhlig (1999). All of these methods are covered in detail by the work of DeJong and Dave (2011), and we reference the reader to that text for not only solution methods but also methodologies governing the estimation of structural parameters underlying a dynamic stochastic time series model.

Finally, we note that any linear model can be reduced to a system of equations that can be solved using the method of Sims (2001) as follows. For *any* linear model, one can collect all l static equations and write them as

$$\underset{l\times l}{A}\, y_t = \underset{l\times m}{B}\, x_t + \underset{l\times p}{C}\, u_t \tag{3.133}$$

and next write the m dynamic equations as

$$\underset{m\times m}{D}\, E_t(x_{t+1}) + \underset{m\times l}{F}\, E_t(y_{t+1}) = \underset{m\times m}{G}\, x_t + \underset{m\times l}{H}\, y_t + \underset{m\times p}{J}\, u_t \tag{3.134}$$

and the p exogenous stochastic processes as

$$u_t = \underset{p\times p}{P}\, u_{t-1} + \varepsilon_t, \tag{3.135}$$

where the vector x_t is $m \times 1$, the vector u_t is $p \times 1$, and the vector y_t is $l \times 1$. Clearly, the model is assumed to have a total of $k = l + m + p$ equations that involve a total of $k = l + m + p$ variables. The Blanchard and Kahn (1980) and Klein (2000) solution methods deal with models written as (3.86)–(3.88) directly, and so if one can construct the matrices required in (3.86)–(3.88), one can move straight to those solution procedures.

The method of Sims (2001) deals with models written as

$$\Gamma_0 \xi_{t+1} = \Gamma_1 + \Gamma_2 \xi_t + \Gamma_3 \varepsilon_{t+1} + \Gamma_4 \eta_{t+1}, \tag{3.136}$$

where η_{t+1} is an 'expectations error'. In order to see this introduction of an expectations error, consider how one might collapse the notation in (3.86)–(3.88) into that of (3.136). First, replace $E_t(x_{t+1})$ and $E_t(y_{t+1})$ with $\phi_t = E_t(x_{t+1})$ and $\lambda_t = E_t(y_{t+1})$ in (3.87). This yields the system

$$\underset{l\times l}{A}\, y_t = \underset{l\times m}{B}\, x_t + \underset{l\times p}{C}\, u_t \tag{3.137}$$

$$\underset{m\times m}{D}\, \phi_t + \underset{m\times l}{F}\, \lambda_t = \underset{m\times m}{G}\, x_t + \underset{m\times l}{H}\, y_t + \underset{m\times p}{J}\, u_t \tag{3.138}$$

$$u_t = \underset{p\times p}{P}\, u_{t-1} + \varepsilon_t. \tag{3.139}$$

However, simply relabeling variables is not sufficient; we need to recognize that variables in expectations come with idiosyncratic expectations errors, and so we also need to add to the system the matrix equations,

$$x_{t+1} = \phi_t + \eta_{xt+1}, \tag{3.140}$$

$$y_{t+1} = \lambda_t + \eta_{yt+1}, \tag{3.141}$$

where η_{xt+1} and η_{yt+1} are $m \times 1$ and $l \times 1$, respectively. Now, rewrite the entire system as

$$y_{t+1} = \lambda_t + \eta_{yt+1}, \tag{3.142}$$

$$x_{t+1} = \phi_t + \eta_{xt+1}, \tag{3.143}$$

$$u_{t+1} = \underset{p\times p}{P}\, u_t + \varepsilon_{t+1}, \tag{3.144}$$

$$\underset{l\times 1}{0} = -\underset{l\times l}{A}\, y_t + \underset{l\times m}{B}\, x_t + \underset{l\times p}{C}\, u_t, \tag{3.145}$$

$$\underset{m\times 1}{0} = \underset{m\times l}{H}\, y_t + \underset{m\times m}{G}\, x_t + \underset{m\times p}{J}\, u_t - \underset{m\times m}{D}\, \phi_t - \underset{m\times l}{F}\, \lambda_t. \tag{3.146}$$

Then, stacking the equations yields

$$\begin{bmatrix} I & 0 & 0 & 0 & 0 \\ 0 & I & 0 & 0 & 0 \\ 0 & 0 & I & 0 & 0 \\ 0 & 0 & 0 & 0 & 0 \\ 0 & 0 & 0 & 0 & 0 \end{bmatrix} \begin{bmatrix} y_{t+1} \\ x_{t+1} \\ u_{t+1} \\ \phi_{t+1} \\ \lambda_{t+1} \end{bmatrix} = \begin{bmatrix} 0 & 0 & 0 & 0 & I \\ 0 & 0 & 0 & I & 0 \\ 0 & 0 & P & 0 & 0 \\ -A & B & C & 0 & 0 \\ H & G & J & -D & -F \end{bmatrix} \begin{bmatrix} y_t \\ x_t \\ u_t \\ \phi_t \\ \lambda_t \end{bmatrix} + \begin{bmatrix} 0 \\ 0 \\ I \\ 0 \\ 0 \end{bmatrix} \varepsilon_{t+1} + \begin{bmatrix} I & 0 \\ 0 & I \\ 0 & 0 \\ 0 & 0 \\ 0 & 0 \end{bmatrix} \begin{bmatrix} \eta_{yt+1} \\ \eta_{xt+1} \end{bmatrix}, \tag{3.147}$$

and if we let $\xi_t = [y_t\ x_t\ u_t\ \phi_t\ \lambda_t]'$, $\eta_{t+1} = \left[\eta_{xt+1}\ \eta_{yt+1}\right]'$, and $k = 2(l+m)+p$, then to see the notational mapping from (3.86)–(3.88) to (3.136), in which clearly $\Gamma_1 = 0$, we have

$$\underset{k\times k}{\Gamma_0}\, \xi_{t+1} = \underset{k\times k}{\Gamma_1} + \underset{k\times k}{\Gamma_2}\, \xi_t + \underset{k\times p}{\Gamma_3}\, \varepsilon_{t+1} + \underset{k\times(l+m)}{\Gamma_4}\, \eta_{t+1}. \tag{3.148}$$

3.5 Conclusion

To conclude, we begin stochastic macroeconomics by understanding the theory of stochastic processes and what it says about the central object of interest, namely, a $VAR(1)$. In order to reduce models to such a representation, we first solve stochastic dynamic optimization problems that lead to a system of nonlinear expectational difference equations. Linearizing leads to a system of linear expectational difference equations. At this point, the system needs to be 'solved' under rational expectations, that is, the expectations need to be solved under the distribution for the exogenous stochastic processes in the model. Doing so delivers the $VAR(1)$ representation of the model upon which, given values for deep parameters, we can conduct statistical exercises in order to determine how closely the model matches data.

Part II

Topics in Aggregate Economics

Chapter 4

Exogenous Growth

4.1 Origins of Growth Theory

In two famous papers, Harrod (1939) and Domar (1946) sought to understand what determined long-run growth in GDP. Here, we discuss their economic model which ushered in the beginning of modern economic growth theory.[1] Similar to almost all models of macroeconomic growth, the Harrod–Domar model assumes the existence of an aggregate production function that combines factor inputs into an output (GDP). The model is restricted by a national income accounting constraint, an equation that describes the evolution of capital over time and a behavioral relation that specifies how much of aggregate income is consumed.

The production function for output (Y_t) is assumed to be of a Leontief form without technological progress:

$$Y_t = \min\{\kappa K_t, \lambda L_t\}, \quad \kappa > 0, \quad \lambda > 0, \tag{4.1}$$

with κ and λ as coefficients on the two factors of production: capital (K_t) and labor (L_t). Next, the economy is assumed to have a constant savings rate that is proportional to income; the model therefore assumes a consumption function that is a fixed proportion of output. Capital is accumulated in the economy and depreciates at the rate of

[1] As mentioned in the preface, the reader is assumed to have an undergraduate background in macroeconomic theory and therefore some familiarity with growth theory.

δ per (continuous time) period. With respect to the production side of the economy, note that the Leontief specification does not allow for any substitutability between capital and labor. Suppose for example that all labor is fully employed, then even if there is abundant capital, it cannot be substituted for labor in the production process. As a result, this kind of production function allows for potential non-utilization of resources. In particular, the only case where both capital and labor are fully utilized is when $\kappa K_t = \lambda L_t$. Suppose instead that the economy has 'too much capital', meaning that $\kappa K_t > \lambda L_t$, then the Leontief production function implies that labor is fully employed in this economy, but only a proportion of capital K_t^u is utilized where $\kappa K_t^u = \lambda L_t$. Thus, the economy employs only $K_t^u = \frac{\lambda}{\kappa} L_t$ units of capital and the remainder, $K_t - \frac{\lambda}{\kappa} L_t$, remains unused. The other possibility is that the economy has 'too much labor'. This means that $\kappa K_t < \lambda L_t$, then $L_t - \frac{\kappa}{\lambda} K_t$ units of labor are unemployed. This model may be relevant to capture growth dynamics in developing countries typically characterized by an abundance of labor but little physical capital. For our purposes, we assume that the labor force does not grow over time. The full employment level in our economy is denoted by L^f, a fixed number. The model can be expanded to include growth in L^f over time, but we use this as a simplifying assumption as it does not alter the central economic intuition behind the model.

Now, to solve the model, we re-express it in 'intensive form', meaning that all variables are expressed in units of labor. This will allow us to find a steady state and the analysis of transitional dynamics will be much more straightforward than in the case where variables are kept in aggregate form. Let lowercase letters denote 'normalization' by L_t, for example $y_t = \frac{Y_t}{L_t}$ denotes output (or income) per worker. Then, the equations characterizing the model are

$$y_t = \min\{\kappa k_t, \lambda\}, \tag{4.2}$$

$$y_t = c_t + i_t, \tag{4.3}$$

$$\overset{\bullet}{k}_t = i_t - \delta k_t, \tag{4.4}$$

$$c_t = (1 - s) y_t. \tag{4.5}$$

The second equation ($y_t = c_t + i_t$) is the national income accounting constraint – it takes this simple form since we assume that there is no government consumption and no international trade in the model. The third equation represents capital accumulation: if investment (i_t) is greater than total depreciation (δk_t), then capital will grow (i.e. $\overset{\bullet}{k}_t > 0$), or it will shrink in the opposite case. The last equation formally states the assumption that aggregate saving is some *fraction* s of national income (y_t).

Next, collapse the system in (4.2)–(4.5) into a single equation:

$$\overset{\bullet}{k}_t = s \min\{\kappa k_t, \lambda\} - \delta k_t. \tag{4.6}$$

Recall that if a variable X_t is given by $X_t = X_0 e^{g_X t}$, then the growth rate of X_t is g_X. Indeed, we have

$$\overset{\bullet}{X}_t = X_0 e^{g_X t} g_X = g_X X_t, \tag{4.7}$$

which implies that $g_X = \frac{\overset{\bullet}{X}_t}{X_t}$. So, divide both side of (4.6) by k_t to obtain the central equation describing the growth rate of capital per worker (or the capital–labor ratio) as

$$g_k = \frac{\overset{\bullet}{k}_t}{k_t} = s \min\left\{\kappa, \frac{\lambda}{k_t}\right\} - \delta. \tag{4.8}$$

We omit the time subscript on g_k to keep the notation clear, but g_k does change over time outside of steady state. Note that once we determine how capital per worker evolves over time, we can also determine the evolution of output per worker and finally overall output, or GDP, by using the production function.

Before we consider how g_k changes over time, let's see what this capital accumulation equation tells us for a given level of capital per worker k. We consider two cases: first, suppose that $\kappa > \frac{\lambda}{k}$, then equation (4.8) tells us that $g_k = s\frac{\lambda}{k} - \delta$; the rate at which capital per worker grows is inversely proportional to the level of capital k. This is expected since only high levels of capital per worker are consistent with the equation $\kappa > \frac{\lambda}{k}$. This is what we previously called the 'too much capital' scenario. In this case, because there is too much capital, a lot of it is left unused. It depreciates since the excess capital contributes nothing to the economy. For high values of k, one should expect the capital accumulation in the economy to fall.

Suppose instead that $\kappa < \frac{\lambda}{k}$: this is the case where there is 'too much labor' in the economy. Here, capital is fully utilized and contributes fully to capital accumulation for future periods. As a result, the growth rate of capital per worker in this case is $g_k = s\kappa - \delta$. Note that if κ is sufficiently small or δ is sufficiently large, it may well be that g_k is negative.

This leads us to the following consideration that will turn out to determine the evolution of g_k over time. Again, we consider two cases. Suppose that $s\kappa > \delta$, then for a low level of k_t, the gross savings per unit of capital is higher than the depreciation rate δ, and so k_t grows at a constant and positive rate. Eventually though, we reach a point where there is 'too much capital' in the economy and $g_k = s\frac{\lambda}{k} - \delta$. Capital per worker finally stabilizes at a level where $s\frac{\lambda}{k} = \delta$. The economy then reaches full employment and any further capital accumulation stops, which means output ceases to grow. If $s\kappa < \delta$, then for a low level of k_t, the gross savings per unit of capital is higher than the depreciation rate δ, and so k_t decumulates (or shrinks). The economy then converges to a zero level of capital per worker and to full unemployment. This situation happens because the rate of accumulation of capital $s\kappa$ is not sufficient to counter the rate of depreciation of existing capital. As a result, capital per worker falls, and we end up in a situation where there is 'too much labor'. In this case, most of labor goes unutilized, which of course corresponds to high levels of unemployment.

Thus, unless an economy has a savings rate that equals exactly δ/κ, there will be perpetual unemployment of labor *or* perpetual underutilization of capital. This 'knife's edge' result of Harrod and Domar held sway over researchers and policymakers for some time: if an economy did not exactly match the above savings rate, the slightest deviation would throw the economy off a growth path for a potentially long period of time. Note that neither the assumption of a fixed savings rate nor the assumption of a fixed rate of capital depreciation are innocuous. For example, the model assumes that the depreciation rate of capital is fixed regardless of whether capital is fully utilized or goes unused; also, the model assumes that the savings rate stays the same even as the rate of return on capital falls. These considerations will make us consider models with an alternate production function and where the assumption of a constant savings rate is replaced by a model where the savings rate is determined *endogenously*, according to the choice of optimizing economic agents.

4.2 The Solow Model

Given the dismal predictions of the Harrod–Domar growth model, Solow (1956) developed a model that did away with the knife-edge prediction. The main assumptions that Solow changed were as follows. First, he modeled the aggregate production function so that capital and labor were substitutable, a major departure from the Harrod–Domar case. Next, Solow dropped the assumption that labor markets were not in full employment; instead, he assumed perfectly competitive labor markets: the (implied) wages would adjust to equate labor supplied and labor demanded. The results of these changes were astounding, and the model became the foundation of modern growth theory. It is therefore instructive to study the model in some detail.

4.2.1 The nature of production

The aggregate production function is defined as

$$Y_t = F(K_t, L_t), \quad K_t > 0, \quad L_t > 0, \tag{4.9}$$

where diminishing returns to scale hold for each factor of production, so that

$$F_i > 0, \quad F_{ij} > 0, \quad \text{and} \quad F_{ii} < 0 \quad \forall\, i = K_t, L_t. \tag{4.10}$$

The production function also satisfies the so-called 'Inada' conditions:

$$\lim_{i \to 0} \quad F_i = \infty \quad \forall\, i = K_t, L_t, \tag{4.11}$$

$$\lim_{i \to \infty} \quad F_i = 0 \quad \forall\, i = K_t, L_t. \tag{4.12}$$

Finally, F has constant returns to scale (CRTS), that is,

$$zY_t = F(zK_t, zL_t) \quad \forall\, z \in \Re_{++}. \tag{4.13}$$

Recall the distinction between marginal product and returns to scale calculations. A returns to scale calculation considers the increase in output that results from increasing *all* inputs by the same scale factor. In contrast, a marginal product calculation considers the resulting increase in output if *only one* factor of production is increased, holding the quantities of other factors of production fixed. These two economic assumptions, while easily translated into mathematics, play an important role in macroeconomic growth theory. For instance, given CRTS, if one lets $z = L_t^{-1}$, then (4.9) can be written as

$$\frac{Y_t}{L_t} = F\left(\frac{K_t}{L_t}, 1\right), \tag{4.14}$$

or

$$y_t = f(k_t), \tag{4.15}$$

where $y_t = Y_t/L_t$ and $k_t = K_t/L_t$. Thus, the CRTS assumption allows the analysis of two versus three variables; this sort of 'system reduction' is often employed to ease analytical computations.

Next, Solow assumed technological progress over time (A_t). Since the objective was not to model how that progress came about but rather its effect on national output, he assumed it to be an exogenous quantity. In general, there are three ways of introducing technological progress. First, under Hicks neutrality, progress is 'neutral', in that all inputs to production, when scaled back, produce the same level of output. This happens if the ratio of marginal products of inputs remains unchanged for a given K_t/L_t ratio, yielding

$$Y_t = A_t F(K_t, L_t), \quad \dot{A}_t \geq 0. \tag{4.16}$$

Second, under Solow neutrality, progress is 'neutral', in that relative input shares (e.g. $L_t \times F_L$) remain unchanged for a given L_t/Y_t ratio, which yields

$$Y_t = F(A_t K_t, L_t), \quad \dot{A}_t \geq 0. \tag{4.17}$$

Finally, under Harrod neutrality progress is 'neutral', in that relative input shares (e.g. $L_t \times F_L$) remain unchanged for a given K_t/Y_t ratio, which yields

$$Y_t = F(K_t, A_t L_t), \quad \dot{A}_t \geq 0. \tag{4.18}$$

Recall that one of the stylized facts is that the physical capital to output ratio is constant. The only production function that is consistent with this stylized fact is one that is Harrod neutral and so we assume that functional form.

4.2.2 The nature of markets and behavioral relations

First, the allocation of output Y_t is equal to

$$Y_t = C_t + I_t, \tag{4.19}$$

with C_t as consumption and I_t as investment. This is known as the national income accounting identity. Second, if we assume that the economy saves a fraction of income, $s \in [0, 1]$, then

$$C_t = (1 - s)Y_t, \tag{4.20}$$

which becomes the assumed consumption function and the only behavioral relation in the model. Next, capital accumulates according to the following equation:

$$\dot{K}_t = I_t - \delta K_t, \tag{4.21}$$

with $\delta \in (0, 1]$ representing depreciation. Note that this capital accumulation equation says that in order to change capital in the next instant of time, investment (that is, the acquisition of new capital goods) must be balanced against economic depreciation of physical capital over time. Depreciation is not necessarily an engineering phenomenon or an accounting one; it simply reflects the fact that over time, capital goods will depreciate in *economic* value.

We consider the important example where the production function is Cobb–Douglas:

$$Y_t = K_t^{\alpha}(A_t L_t)^{1-\alpha}, \tag{4.22}$$

with the following parameters:

$$K_{(0)} = K_0, \tag{4.23}$$

$$L_{(0)} = L_0, \tag{4.24}$$

$$\alpha \in (0, 1). \tag{4.25}$$

Let

$$y_t = \frac{Y_t}{A_t L_t}, \tag{4.26}$$

$$k_t = \frac{K_t}{A_t L_t}. \tag{4.27}$$

Then, (4.22) can be transformed into the expression

$$Y_t = (A_t L_t)[K_t^{\alpha}(A_t L_t)^{-\alpha}] \tag{4.28}$$

$$\rightarrow y_t = k_t^{\alpha}. \tag{4.29}$$

We use a Cobb–Douglas specification for the production function because it is consistent with the stylized facts discussed previously. Further, the ratio of marginal products is constant, which occurs under perfect competition. Note that, at the outset, modeling choices (in this case, the choice for the functional form of the production function) are informed by data (i.e. stylized facts).

Next, let us add to the model the dynamic evolution of the exogenous processes, namely labor and technology growth:

$$\frac{\dot{L}_t}{L_t} = n \longleftrightarrow L_t = L_0 e^{nt}, \tag{4.30}$$

$$\frac{\dot{A}_t}{A_t} = g \longleftrightarrow A_t = A_0 e^{gt}. \tag{4.31}$$

We now normalize the income accounting identity by $A_t L_t$ to get

$$\frac{Y_t}{A_t L_t} = \frac{C_t}{A_t L_t} + \frac{I_t}{A_t L_t} \longleftrightarrow y_t = c_t + i_t. \tag{4.32}$$

Normalization of the consumption function yields

$$\frac{C_t}{A_t L_t} = (1-s)\frac{Y_t}{A_t L_t} \longleftrightarrow c_t = (1-s)y_t. \tag{4.33}$$

Finally, we normalize the capital accumulation equation as follows:

$$\dot{K}_t = I_t - \delta K_t \rightarrow \frac{\dot{K}_t}{K_t} = \frac{I_t}{K_t} - \delta. \tag{4.34}$$

Since

$$k_t = \frac{K_t}{A_t L_t} \rightarrow \log k_t = \log K_t - \log L_t - \log A_t \tag{4.35}$$

$$\rightarrow \frac{\dot{k}_t}{k_t} = \frac{\dot{K}_t}{K_t} - \frac{\dot{L}_t}{L_t} - \frac{\dot{A}_t}{A_t} = \frac{i_t}{k_t} - (n + \delta + g). \tag{4.36}$$

Note here that we employ the following relationships when X_t grows exponentially, meaning that $X_t = X_0 e^{g_X t}$:

$$\frac{\overset{\bullet}{X}_t}{X_t} = g_X \quad \text{as above, and} \tag{4.37}$$

$$\frac{d\log X_t}{dt} = \frac{dX_t}{dt}\frac{1}{X_t} = \frac{\overset{\bullet}{X}_t}{X_t} = g_X. \tag{4.38}$$

4.2.3 Solving and analyzing the model

The model is summarized in per capita (or more precisely, per effective worker) terms by

$$y_t = k_t^{\alpha}, \tag{4.39}$$

$$y_t = c_t + i_t, \tag{4.40}$$

$$c_t = (1-s)y_t, \tag{4.41}$$

$$\overset{\bullet}{k}_t = i_t - (n+\delta+g)k_t, \quad k_{(0)} = k_0 = \frac{K_0}{A_0 L_0}. \tag{4.42}$$

We do not need to worry about the exogenous processes for labor and technology since we normalized the equations by the number of *effective* units of labor $A_t L_t$. The first step in analyzing the model is to collapse it down to a single equation that can be analyzed.[2] To do so, substitute (4.39) and (4.41) into (4.40) to obtain

$$i_t = k_t^{\alpha} - (1-s)k_t^{\alpha} = sk_t^{\alpha}, \tag{4.43}$$

which can then be substituted into (4.42) to obtain

$$\overset{\bullet}{k}_t = sk_t^{\alpha} - (n+\delta+g)k_t = f(k_t|s,\alpha,n,\delta,g). \tag{4.44}$$

The above is a single nonlinear differential equation in k_t. Set $\overset{\bullet}{k}_t = 0$ to obtain the steady state of this equation:

$$\overline{k} = \left(\frac{s}{n+\delta+g}\right)^{\frac{1}{1-\alpha}} \tag{4.45}$$

[2] In general, very few macroeconomic models can be collapsed in this way; instead, they must be studied as systems of equations.

$$\rightarrow \bar{y} = \left(\frac{s}{n+\delta+g}\right)^{\frac{\alpha}{1-\alpha}} \quad \text{from } y_t = k_t^\alpha \tag{4.46}$$

$$\rightarrow \bar{i} = s\left(\frac{s}{n+\delta+g}\right)^{\frac{\alpha}{1-\alpha}} \quad \text{from } i_t = sk_t^\alpha \tag{4.47}$$

$$\rightarrow \bar{c} = (1-s)\left(\frac{s}{n+\delta+g}\right)^{\frac{\alpha}{1-\alpha}} \quad \text{from } c_t = y_t - i_t = (1-s)y_t \tag{4.48}$$

Given the nonlinearity, a first order Taylor series approximation (TSA1) of (4.44) around $\bar{k}$ gives

$$\overset{\bullet}{k}_t \approx f(\bar{k}) + f'(\bar{k}) \times (k_t - \bar{k}) \tag{4.49}$$

$$\approx -(1-\alpha)(n+\delta+g)(k_t - \bar{k}) \tag{4.50}$$

$$\approx -\lambda(k_t - \bar{k}). \tag{4.51}$$

This equation takes the form

$$\overset{\bullet}{x}_t = -\lambda x_t, \quad x_t = k_t - \bar{k} \rightarrow x_t = x_0 e^{-\lambda t}. \tag{4.52}$$

To study the model graphically, consider again the fundamental relation

$$\overset{\bullet}{k}_t = sk_t^\alpha - (n+\delta+g)k_t \longleftrightarrow \tag{4.53}$$

$$\overset{\bullet}{k}_t = sy_t - mk_t, \quad m = n+\delta+g \tag{4.54}$$

and plot the components of the nonlinear differential equation, illustrated in Figure 4.1.

Clearly, when $sf(k_t) > \delta k_t$, the capital stock grows ($\overset{\bullet}{k}_t > 0$) toward $\bar{k}$. When $sf(k_t) < \delta k_t$, the capital stock shrinks ($\overset{\bullet}{k}_t < 0$) toward $\bar{k}$. At the steady state, there is no growth in capital per *effective* unit of labor; however, capital per unit of labor grows at the rate g. Why? Well, realize that the growth rate of variables multiplied together is the sum of their respective growth rates. Thus, while the growth of $k_t = \frac{K_t}{A_t L_t}$ is zero in the steady state, the growth of $A_t L_t k_t$ equals the growth of A_t plus that of L_t plus that of k_t:

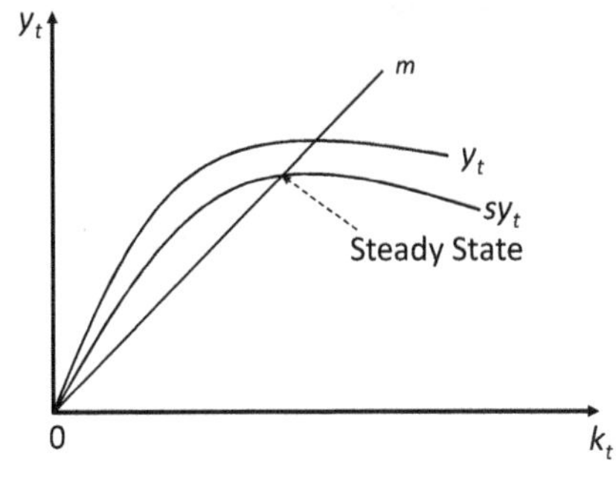

Figure 4.1. The Solow model.

$g + n + 0 = n + g$. Note that if the capital stock per worker grows over time, so does output per worker and consumption per worker. This is due to the functional form for production and the behavioral relation describing the consumption and savings behavior of a typical worker. Thus, we have a theory of growth for per capita real GDP when the economy reaches a steady state. More specifically, we have a theory of balanced growth. That is, most macroeconomic aggregates grow at the same rates in the long run. In the Solow model just described, per capita capital, output, and consumption all grow at the rate g in steady state.

Note that increasing the savings rate (s) shifts out the investment function in Figure 4.1, leading an economy to a higher steady k (implying a higher steady state y). However, if all production is devoted to investment (meaning that $s = 1$), then there would be nothing to consume. Conversely, if all production were diverted toward consumption, there would be nothing to consume *eventually* since capital accumulation would never take place. The Solow growth model can be used to find out the savings rate that maximizes consumption in the steady state. In other words, one wishes to

$$\max_{s} \quad \overline{c} = \overline{k}^{\alpha} - (n + \delta + g)\overline{k}. \tag{4.55}$$

The first-order condition is given by

$$(1 - s)\frac{\alpha}{1 - \alpha}\left(\frac{s}{n + \delta + g}\right)^{\frac{\alpha - 1}{1 - \alpha}} \frac{1}{n + \delta + g} = \left(\frac{s}{n + \delta + g}\right)^{\frac{\alpha}{1 - \alpha}} \tag{4.56}$$

$$\rightarrow s^* = \alpha. \tag{4.57}$$

So, the optimal savings rate is α. The associated level of capital is

$$k_g^* = \left(\frac{\alpha}{n+\delta+g}\right)^{\frac{1}{1-\alpha}} \tag{4.58}$$

and is referred to as the 'golden rule' level of capital accumulation. The term 'golden rule' is applied as this is the level of capital such that every generation would enjoy the same level of consumption. That is, do unto others (i.e. generations) as you would have done onto you (i.e. your generation). Now, if an economy is in the steady state and begins with a savings rate that is below α, then an increase in the savings rate toward α would have two consequences for consumption. Initially, a higher savings rate would cause consumption to fall, but as capital accumulates toward the new, higher, steady-state level, consumption would eventually rise to a level that was higher than under the old savings rate. Symmetrically, if an economy begins with a savings rate that is 'too high' relative to α, then workers in the economy would stand to consume more in both the short run and the long run if they decreased the amount of investment they make in each time period. If the savings rate fell in this economy, capital per worker would fall toward a lower steady state, but consumption per worker would increase to a permanently higher level.

The dismal prediction of the Harrod–Domar growth model, that growth will lead to a high level of unemployment of the labor force or to an underutilization of capital, is overturned in Solow's model. Growth is possible without unemployment or underutilization of factors of production. Look again at the capital accumulation equation,

$$\dot{k}_t = sk_t^{\alpha} - (n+\delta+g)k_t, \tag{4.59}$$

and plot $g_k = \frac{\dot{k}_t}{k_t}$ and $m = n + \delta + g$ against k_t, as shown in Figure 4.2.

To the left of the steady state, the growth rate is large and positive and becomes smaller until the economy reaches the steady state. To the right of the steady state, the growth rate is negative until the economy reaches steady state. Compare this to the model by Harrod and Domar: income per worker equals κ, no matter what the value of capital per worker, as long as this value is small (so that we are in the case where there are 'too many workers'). In a developing economy with a considerable number of unskilled workers, κ is relatively small

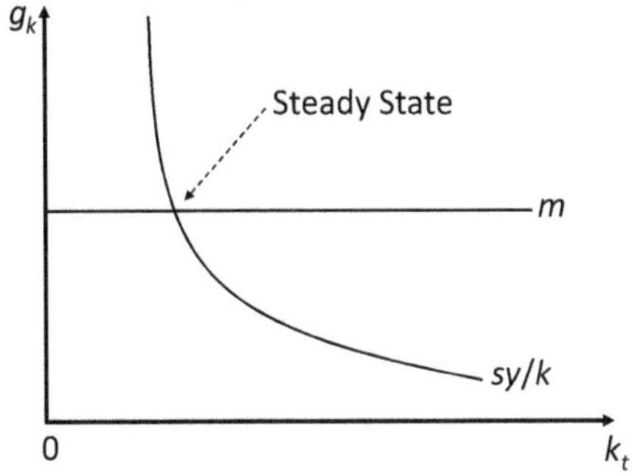

Figure 4.2. The growth rate of capital.

so that growth in income per worker (and therefore wage growth) is also small, even though overall output growth may be relatively larger. In Solow's model, growth in income per worker is very high for small values of capital per worker and gradually becomes smaller as the economy accumulates capital. This stresses the importance of choosing the appropriate model given the economy one is analyzing.

In the steady state, there is no growth in capital per worker without technological progress (g). Because this is an exogenous process, we use the term exogenous growth to describe Solow's model. While the model explains growth during the transition to the steady state, economic growth in the steady state occurs only when one assumes it. In a very real sense, one is therefore not really explaining growth but rather assuming it. A natural question to ask is whether the economic model can be modified to allow for economic growth in the steady state that is the result of actions taken by optimizing economic agents rather than simply assuming it. This is the subject covered in endogenous growth theory. Finally, we can also ask whether the savings rate in Solow's model can be endogenized. This subject is covered in optimal (exogenous) growth theory and turns out to be a rather straightforward task.

As an example, to appreciate the relative importance of the assumptions on the specification of the production function in the Solow model, consider a linear function in intensive form, $y_t = k_t$. To simplify the analysis, let us assume there is neither labor nor technology growth (i.e. $n = g = 0$). Now, the linear function has positive marginal productivity ($f'(k_t) = 1$) but fails to exhibit diminishing returns ($f''(k_t) = 0$). Moreover, the Inada conditions are both violated ($f'(k_t) = 1$ for both as k_t tends to 0 and as k_t tends to ∞). Capital accumulation will be given by

$$\overset{\bullet}{k}_t = (s - \delta)k_t$$

so that there generically exists the trivial steady state $\bar{k} = 0$ only (i.e. only in the knife-edge case $s = \delta$ will an infinity of steady states exist, meaning the solution to the accumulation equation is indeterminate). More specifically, either (i) $s > \delta$ so that $\overset{\bullet}{k}_t = (s - \delta)k_t > 0$ for all t, and the capital stock per capita experiences unbounded growth, or (ii) $s < \delta$ so that $\overset{\bullet}{k}_t = (s - \delta)k_t < 0$ for all t, and the capital stock gradually shrinks toward 0. Note that the failure of the first Inada condition allows convergence to the trivial steady state when the depreciation rate exceed the savings rate, while the failure of the second Inada condition allows the economy to diverge away from the trivial steady state toward arbitrarily large levels of capital stock. Clearly, this would overturn one of the key predictions of the Solow model – namely, that capital accumulation alone cannot sustain long-run growth.

4.3 One Sector Optimal Growth

The one sector optimal growth (also known as the Ramsey model) nicely illustrates how the savings rate, assumed to be a parameter in the Solow model, can be endogenized. The model consists of several households and a firm acting in a general equilibrium.

4.3.1 Environment

The optimal growth model has four underlying assumptions regarding households that populate the economy. First, the economy is assumed to be populated by H identical households. Second, there are L_t workers or L_t/H workers per household. Third, households are infinitely-lived; they behave like families that are not only looking out for their present interests but also their children's future. Fourth, the labor supply is assumed to be perfectly inelastic. As a result, workers are employed at a given market wage.

Every household's utility is given by

$$U = \int_0^\infty e^{-\widehat{\rho}t} u\left(\frac{C_t}{L_t}\right)\frac{L_t}{H}dt, \tag{4.60}$$

with $u' > 0$, $u'' < 0$, $u'(0) = \infty$, and $u'(\infty) = 0$. Here, $\widehat{\rho}$ is the rate of time preference: if $\widehat{\rho}$ increases, then households discount future consumption more heavily.

With respect to labor, let

$$L_t = L_0 e^{nt}, \quad n > 0, \quad L_{(0)} = L_0. \tag{4.61}$$

Plugging in (4.61) into (4.60) produces

$$U = \frac{L_0}{H}\int_0^\infty e^{-(\widehat{\rho}-n)t} u\left(\frac{C_t}{L_t}\right) dt. \tag{4.62}$$

In addition, technology can be included into the model by assuming that

$$A_t = A_0 e^{gt} \tag{4.63}$$

and then normalizing by $L_t A_t$, the effective unit of labor. In order to do so, simply set

$$c_t = \frac{C_t}{L_t A_t}. \tag{4.64}$$

Finally, the model incorporates the remaining specifications of the Solow model:

$$y_t = k_t^\alpha, \tag{4.65}$$

$$\dot{k}_t = i_t - (n + g + \delta)k_t, \tag{4.66}$$

$$y_t = c_t + i_t, \tag{4.67}$$

$$k_{(0)} = k_0. \tag{4.68}$$

4.3.2 Optimal growth and risk aversion

Suppose households have constant relative risk aversion (CRRA) preferences and we let

$$X_t = \frac{C_t}{L_t}. \tag{4.69}$$

As an example, the utility function $u(\frac{C_t}{L_t})$ may be of the form

$$u(X_t) = \frac{X_t^{1-\theta} - 1}{1-\theta}, \tag{4.70}$$

where $\theta \geq 0$. The parameter θ reflects the degree of risk aversion and measures the curvature of the utility function:

$$\text{risk neutral if} \quad \theta = 0, \tag{4.71}$$

$$\text{risk averse if} \quad \theta > 0. \tag{4.72}$$

If $\theta = 1$, then (4.70) becomes

$$u(X_t) = \log X_t. \tag{4.73}$$

Also, θ figures into the measure of the intertemporal elasticity of substitution σ. Recall that if one assumes consumption in two distinct time periods (C_1 and C_2), then σ is defined as

$$\sigma = \frac{d\left(\frac{C_1}{C_2}\right)}{d\left(\frac{P_1}{P_2}\right)} \times \frac{\frac{P_1}{P_2}}{\frac{C_1}{C_2}}, \tag{4.74}$$

or, in other words, as the absolute percentage change in the consumption ratio divided by the percentage change in the price ratio. Thus, suppose that the utility function is described by

$$u(C_1, C_2) = \frac{C_1^{1-\theta} - 1}{1-\theta} + \frac{C_2^{1-\theta} - 1}{1-\theta} \tag{4.75}$$

$$s.t.\ w = P_1C_1 + P_2C_2, \tag{4.76}$$

with w as the level of wealth. This implies that

$$\sigma = \frac{1}{\theta}. \tag{4.77}$$

Therefore, if θ is increased, then the willingness among households to wait and consume later also increases, as does the curvature of the utility function. The parameter θ therefore plays two roles: it describes both the willingness to wait for future consumption (intertemporal substitution) and risk aversion. The CRRA specification doesn't allow us to hold one fixed and vary the other. This is a weakness of this specification; on the other hand, the CRRA specification is rather straightforward to manipulate when we are trying to compute the dynamics of the model. Alternatively, households may exhibit constant absolute risk aversion (CARA). That is, the utility function may be of the form

$$u(X_t) = \frac{-e^{\alpha X_t}}{\alpha}. \tag{4.78}$$

For our purposes, assume a CRRA utility function applies:

$$u\left(\frac{C_t}{L_t}\right) = \frac{\left(\frac{C_t}{L_t}\right)^{1-\theta} - 1}{1-\theta}. \tag{4.79}$$

Normalizing by effective labor results in

$$u = \frac{(c_t A_t)^{1-\theta} - 1}{1-\theta}, \tag{4.80}$$

which, after substituting in (4.63), can be rearranged as

$$u(c_t) = \frac{A_0^{1-\theta}}{1-\theta} \times \frac{c_t^{1-\theta}}{1-\theta} e^{(1-\theta)gt}. \tag{4.81}$$

Therefore, the maximization problem involves

$$U = \frac{A_0^{1-\theta}}{1-\theta} \int_0^{\infty} e^{-(\widehat{\rho}-n)t} e^{(1-\theta)gt} \frac{c_t^{1-\theta}}{1-\theta} dt, \tag{4.82}$$

or

$$U = \int_0^{\infty} e^{-\rho t} \frac{c_t^{1-\theta}}{1-\theta} dt, \tag{4.83}$$

by ignoring the term $\frac{A_0^{1-\theta}}{1-\theta}$ and letting $\rho = \widehat{\rho} - n - (1-\theta)g$. This means that if $\theta = 0$, then $\rho = \widehat{\rho} - n - g$ and $\sigma = \infty$. As g increases, ρ decreases, so there is only an income effect. That is, as g increases, there is an increase in income and an increase in consumption.

If $\theta \in (0,1)$, then $\rho = \widehat{\rho} - n - (1-\theta)g$, and there will be both an income and a substitution effect. Lastly, if $\theta = 1$, then $\rho = \widehat{\rho} - n$, and the income and substitution effects offset one another. So, given this environment, how do we solve the problem? The fundamental theorems of welfare economics suggest two (equivalent) ways of solving the same problem: social planner methods and decentralized equilibrium methods.

4.3.3 Solution method 1: Benevolent social planner

The benevolent social planner is a dictator who makes all the choices for the economy at large. There are no markets to determine prices, wages, or interest rates; firms do not engage in competitive behavior – all economic activity is centrally planned. However, the *benevolent* social planner is always looking to further the interests of each household. The problem for the planner is to

$$\max_{\{c_t\}} \quad U = \int_0^\infty e^{-\rho t} \frac{c_t^{1-\theta}}{1-\theta} dt \tag{4.84}$$

$$s.t. \quad \overset{\bullet}{k}_t = f(k_t) - (n+g+\delta)k_t - c_t \tag{4.85}$$

$$= g(k_t, c_t), \tag{4.86}$$

$$k_{(0)} = k_0. \tag{4.87}$$

To solve this problem, set up the Hamiltonian. First, let λ_t be the time-t Lagrange multiplier (the time-t cost of relaxing the constraint). Consequently, the current value Hamiltonian (CVH) is

$$H = u(c_t) + \lambda_t g(k_t, c_t). \tag{4.88}$$

The first-order conditions for this problem are

$$\frac{\partial H}{\partial c_t} = u'(c_t) + \lambda_t \frac{dg}{dc_t} = 0 \quad \forall\ t, \tag{4.89}$$

$$\frac{\partial H}{\partial k_t} = \rho\lambda_t - \overset{\bullet}{\lambda}_t \quad \forall\ t, \tag{4.90}$$

$$\frac{\partial H}{\partial \lambda_t} = \overset{\bullet}{k}_t = g(k_t, c_t) = 0. \tag{4.91}$$

One can express (4.90) as

$$\rho\lambda_t = \overset{\bullet}{\lambda}_t + \frac{\partial H}{\partial k_t}. \tag{4.92}$$

This equation can be interpreted as the flow return of the asset ($\rho\lambda_t$) being equal to its capital appreciation ($\overset{\bullet}{\lambda}_t$) and the dividend yield of the asset ($\frac{\partial H}{\partial k_t}$). Of course, these are 'shadow prices'; this is a centrally planned economy after all. The transversality condition (TVC) is

$$\lim_{t\to\infty} e^{-\rho t}\lambda_t k_t = 0. \tag{4.93}$$

We now solve using the first-order conditions. From (4.89), one gets

$$u'(c_t) = \lambda_t \tag{4.94}$$

since $\frac{dg}{dc_t} = -1$.

Using (4.91) yields

$$\overset{\bullet}{k}_t = f(k_t) - (n+g+\delta)k_t - c_t, \tag{4.95}$$

and (4.90) produces

$$\overset{\bullet}{\lambda}_t = \rho\lambda_t - \lambda_t\left[f'(k_t) - (n+g+\delta)\right]. \tag{4.96}$$

Combining (4.94) and (4.96) results in

$$u''(c_t)\overset{\bullet}{c}_t = u'(c_t)\left[f'(k_t) - (n+g+\delta) - \rho\right]. \tag{4.97}$$

How does one interpret an equation like (4.97)? Fix the level of consumption at c_t and consider a decrease over time in consumption, meaning $\overset{\bullet}{c}_t < 0$. Then, the left-hand side of this equation is positive since $u'' < 0$. The right-hand side will therefore also be positive. And since $u' > 0$, this means that $f'(k_t) - (n+g+\delta) - \rho$, the 'net' marginal product of capital, is also positive. This term represents the additional capital accumulation that results from foregoing consumption. So, the equation can be thought of as equating the marginal cost of foregoing consumption to the marginal benefit of additional capital accumulation over time. This 'Euler equation' and others like it are a typical mathematical representation of the marginalist revolution in macroeconomics.

Now, substituting the functional forms into (4.95) and (4.97), one is left with a two-variable–two-equation system:

$$\overset{\bullet}{k}_t = k_t^{\alpha} - (n+g+\delta)k_t - c_t, \tag{4.98}$$

$$\frac{\overset{\bullet}{c}_t}{c_t} = \sigma\left[\alpha k_t^{\alpha-1} - (n+g+\delta) - \rho\right], \tag{4.99}$$

where again

$$\sigma = \frac{1}{\theta}. \tag{4.100}$$

To find the steady states, simply set $\overset{\bullet}{k}_t = 0$ and $\overset{\bullet}{c}_t = 0$. The solutions are

$$\overline{k} = \left(\frac{\alpha}{\widehat{\rho}+\delta+\theta g}\right)^{\frac{1}{1-\alpha}}, \tag{4.101}$$

$$\overline{c} = \left(\frac{\alpha}{\widehat{\rho}+\delta+\theta g}\right)^{\frac{\alpha}{1-\alpha}} - (n+g+\delta)\left(\frac{\alpha}{\widehat{\rho}+\delta+\theta g}\right)^{\frac{1}{1-\alpha}},$$

where $\rho = \widehat{\rho} - n - (1-\theta)g$. The term θg describes the tension between the income and substitution effects.

Next, given the nonlinearity of the system, take the TSA1 of both (4.98) and (4.99). This produces the expressions

$$\overset{\bullet}{k}_t = g(\overline{c},\overline{k}) + g_c'(\overline{c},\overline{k})(c_t - \overline{c}) + g_k'(\overline{c},\overline{k})(k_t - \overline{k}), \tag{4.102}$$

$$\overset{\bullet}{c}_t = f(\overline{c},\overline{k}) + f_c'(\overline{c},\overline{k})(c_t - \overline{c}) + f_k'(\overline{c},\overline{k})(k_t - \overline{k}), \tag{4.103}$$

where functions $g(\cdot)$ and $f(\cdot)$ are given by

$$g = k_t^{\alpha} - (n+g+\delta)k_t - c_t, \tag{4.104}$$

$$f = \sigma\left[\alpha k_t^{\alpha-1} - (n+g+\delta) - \rho\right] c_t. \tag{4.105}$$

Therefore, the system can be written in the form of

$$\overset{\bullet}{X}_t = AX_t, \tag{4.106}$$

with

$$\overset{\bullet}{X}_t = \begin{bmatrix} \overset{\bullet}{k}_t - \overline{k} \\ \overset{\bullet}{c}_t - \overline{c} \end{bmatrix}, \tag{4.107}$$

$$X_t = \begin{bmatrix} k_t - \overline{k} \\ c_t - \overline{c} \end{bmatrix}, \tag{4.108}$$

$$A = \begin{bmatrix} g'_k & g'_c \\ f'_k & f'_c \end{bmatrix}. \tag{4.109}$$

Here, A is simply

$$A = \begin{bmatrix} \rho & -1 \\ -\mu & 0 \end{bmatrix}, \tag{4.110}$$

where

$$\mu = \frac{(1-\alpha)(\widehat{\rho}+\delta+\theta g)}{\theta}\left(\frac{\widehat{\rho}+\delta+\theta g}{\alpha} - [n+g+\delta]\right). \tag{4.111}$$

Given the assumptions on the model, one can show that $\mu > 0$ (an exercise for the reader!). The system then becomes

$$\begin{bmatrix} \overset{\bullet}{\widetilde{k}}_t \\ \overset{\bullet}{\widetilde{c}}_t \end{bmatrix} = \begin{bmatrix} \rho & -1 \\ -\mu & 0 \end{bmatrix} \begin{bmatrix} \widetilde{k}_t \\ \widetilde{c}_t \end{bmatrix}, \tag{4.112}$$

where $\overset{\bullet}{\widetilde{x}}_t$ denotes deviations from the steady state. The solutions for $\overset{\bullet}{\widetilde{X}}_t$ can be computed by finding the eigenvalues r_1 and r_2 of A.

Recall from introductory matrix algebra that for a square matrix A, the sum of the diagonal elements is called the trace. It can be shown that the determinant of A is the multiplication of the eigenvalues of A and the sum of the eigenvalues of A is the trace of A. For a 2×2 matrix A, we then have two equations in two unknowns (the eigenvalues). The roots are given by

$$r_1, r_2 = \frac{\rho \pm \sqrt{\rho^2 + 4\mu}}{2}. \tag{4.113}$$

Since $\mu > 0$, one of the roots will be positive and the other will be negative; this produces a saddle path. To derive the saddle path, one must impose the balanced growth restriction

$$\frac{\dot{\widetilde{k}}_t}{\widetilde{k}_t} = \frac{\dot{\widetilde{c}}_t}{\widetilde{c}_t} = \gamma \tag{4.114}$$

and then solve for γ, which is the balanced growth rate, as follows.

From the system in (4.112),

$$\dot{\widetilde{c}}_t = -\mu \widetilde{k}_t, \tag{4.115}$$

which implies

$$\gamma = -\mu \frac{\widetilde{k}_t}{\widetilde{c}_t}, \tag{4.116}$$

or

$$\frac{\widetilde{c}_t}{\widetilde{k}_t} = \frac{-\mu}{\gamma}. \tag{4.117}$$

Similarly, from (4.112),

$$\dot{\widetilde{k}}_t = \rho \widetilde{k}_t - \widetilde{c}_t. \tag{4.118}$$

Dividing (4.118) and plugging in (4.117) yields the relationship

$$\frac{\dot{\widetilde{k}}_t}{\widetilde{k}_t} = \rho + \frac{\mu}{\gamma} = \gamma. \tag{4.119}$$

As a result, one finds

$$\gamma = \rho + \frac{\mu}{\gamma} \tag{4.120}$$

by solving through the quadratic equation

$$\gamma = \frac{\rho \pm \sqrt{\rho^2 + 4\mu}}{2}. \tag{4.121}$$

Due to (4.117), one finds that for all $\gamma_i > 0$ that

$$\frac{\widetilde{c}_t}{\widetilde{k}_t} < 0. \tag{4.122}$$

Let $\xi = -\gamma_i$. Then,

$$\frac{\widetilde{c}_t}{\widetilde{k}_t} = \frac{\mu}{\xi}, \tag{4.123}$$

and the formulation for the saddle path becomes

$$c_t = \overline{c} + \frac{\mu}{\xi}(k_t - \overline{k}). \tag{4.124}$$

Note that given k_0, the benevolent planner can always choose a level of consumption,

$$c_0 = \overline{c} + \frac{\mu}{\xi}(k_0 - \overline{k}), \tag{4.125}$$

to put the economy on the saddle path to the steady state. If the social planner chooses a value other than c_0, the dynamics of the system will violate the transversality condition, and the economy will not converge to the steady state.

As another example, consider an economy incorporating all the features of the one-sector optimal growth model with no technological growth ($g = 0$) and where household's utility is exponential:

$$U = \int_0^\infty e^{-(\hat{\rho}-n)t}\left(-\frac{1}{\theta}e^{-\theta c_t}\right), \ \theta > 0. \tag{4.126}$$

Note that, with exponential utility, the elasticity of intertemporal substitution is $\sigma = 1/\theta$, and thus the Euler equation reads as

$$\overset{\bullet}{c}_t = \frac{1}{\theta}\left(f'(k_t) - (n+\delta) - \rho\right), \tag{4.127}$$

whereas capital stock accumulates according to the law

$$\overset{\bullet}{k}_t = f(k_t) - (n+\delta)k_t - c_t, \tag{4.128}$$

and thus steady-state values can be derived by setting $\overset{\bullet}{c}_t = \overset{\bullet}{k}_t = 0$ to obtain

$$\bar{c} = f(\bar{k}) - (n+\delta)\bar{k}, \quad \bar{k} = f'^{-1}(n+\delta+\rho), \tag{4.129}$$

where the inverse f'^{-1} of the marginal product of capital stocks is well defined by virtue of the assumption of strict concavity.

4.3.4 Solution method 2: Decentralized equilibrium

Rather than have a planner control the economy, the decentralized method of solution involves firms choosing input levels that will maximize their profits (Π_t), taking wages (W_t), interest rates (R_t), and their production function as given. Meanwhile, households choose their level of consumption so as to maximize their utility (U), taking all prices as given. The goal is then to find prices, wages, and the interest rate which simultaneously solve the profit maximization problem (PMP) and the utility maximization problem (UMP). Note again the assumption that all markets are perfectly competitive: all actors in the economy are assumed to behave as though they cannot influence prices.

To begin, the PMP is as follows:

$$\max_{\{K_t, A_t L_t\}} \quad \Pi_t = P_t(Y_t - \delta K_t) - R_t K_t - W_t A_t L_t \tag{4.130}$$

$$s.t. \quad Y_t = A_t L_t f(k_t), \tag{4.131}$$

recalling that

$$k_t = \frac{K_t}{A_t L_t}. \tag{4.132}$$

The first-order conditions for the problem are

$$\frac{\partial \Pi_t}{\partial K_t} = P_t[A_t L_t f'(k_t) \frac{dk_t}{dK_t} - \delta] - R_t = 0, \tag{4.133}$$

$$\frac{\partial \Pi_t}{\partial A_t L_t} = P_t[f(k_t) + A_t L_t f'(k_t) \frac{dk_t}{dA_t L_t}] - W_t = 0. \tag{4.134}$$

Solving (4.133) for the rate of interest equals

$$R_t = P_t[f'(k_t) - \delta], \tag{4.135}$$

or, in terms of the real rate of interest,

$$r_t = \frac{R_t}{P_t} = f'(k_t) - \delta, \tag{4.136}$$

where the right-hand side of (4.136) is the net marginal product of capital.

Solving (4.134) for the wage rate yields

$$W_t = P_t[f(k_t) - k_t f'(k_t)], \tag{4.137}$$

or, in terms of the real wage,

$$w_t = \frac{W_t}{P_t} = f(k_t) - k_t f'(k_t), \tag{4.138}$$

where the right-hand side of (4.138) equals output less capital's share of output.

Now, recalling that the household and benevolent social planner objectives are the same, consider the households' UMP:

$$\max_{\{c_t\}} \quad U = \int_0^\infty e^{-\rho t} \frac{c_t^{1-\theta}}{1-\theta} dt \tag{4.139}$$

$$s.t. \quad c_t + \dot{a}_t + na_t = w_t + r_t a_t, \tag{4.140}$$

where a_t represents the assets owned by the households. Households cannot hold debt in steady state, so it is not included here.[3] Further, the household takes w_t and r_t as given. Assuming that households own all factors of production, we must have that $a_t = k_t$ in equilibrium. Further, assume labor growth (n) and technological growth (g) to be present in this economy. The resulting UMP (with the embedded PMP) is therefore

$$\max_{\{c_t\}} \quad U = \int_0^\infty e^{-\rho t} \frac{c_t^{1-\theta}}{1-\theta} dt \tag{4.141}$$

$$s.t. \quad \dot{k}_t = f(k_t) - (n + g + \delta)k_t - c_t \tag{4.142}$$

$$= g(k_t, c_t) \tag{4.143}$$

$$k_{(0)} = k_0. \tag{4.144}$$

[3]Perpetual holding of debt would violate the TVC. While it is possible for a given household to do that, the point behind the TVC is that an *aggregate* economy cannot do that.

This is the same as the objective of the social planner, hence the two solution methods are equivalent. Here, we see an example of the fundamental theorems of welfare economics at work. As long as production exhibits diminishing marginal product, markets are competitive and there are no externalities, public goods, or informational asymmetry issues, the solution to the social planner's problem will be the same as that of the decentralized equilibrium. If any of these conditions is broken, we can only look at the decentralized solution. With respect to our original objective, we have clearly endogenized the savings rate. In the chapter on endogenous growth, we do the same for technological growth.

4.4 Labor–Leisure Choice in the Ramsey Model

In the Ramsey model studied above, we assumed that labor supply was inelastic. That is, how much labor to supply was not a choice of households. The Cass–Koopmans version of the Ramsey model does away with this simplification of the standard Ramsey model. The model forms the basis of a number of business cycle models. These models start with a growth economy, such as that specified in the following. Then, various shocks are added that cause occasional deviations from trend, defined to be the business cycle. Therefore, given its relevance to the large business cycle literature, it is instructive to study the Cass–Koopmans model.

4.4.1 Environment and optimization

Consider a representative agent economy in continuous time in which the agent derives lifetime utility from both consumption of a composite good and leisure. That is, instantaneous utility is given by $u(C_t, L_t)$, where C denotes consumption and L denotes leisure. The agent faces the usual capital accumulation constraint in which capital depreciates at the rate δ, has a production function

$$Y_t = F(K_t, N_t) = K_t^{\alpha} N_t^{1-\alpha}, \quad \alpha \in (0,1), \tag{4.145}$$

where N denotes labor effort, and the agent can devote one unit of time to either taking leisure or exerting labor effort.

Assuming that the agent discounts time at the rate ρ, the dynamic optimization problem is

$$\max \quad \Gamma = \int_0^\infty e^{-\rho t} u(C_t, L_t)dt, \tag{4.146}$$

$$s.t. \quad C_t + \overset{\bullet}{K}_t + \delta K_t = K_t^\alpha N_t^{1-\alpha}, \tag{4.147}$$

$$N_t + L_t = 1, \tag{4.148}$$

$$K_{(0)} = K_0. \tag{4.149}$$

Clearly, the control variables are C_t and L_t and the state variable is K_t.

4.4.2 Solution

First, converting the optimization problem to a per capita problem is relatively easy since N_t is not growing. The resulting CVH is

$$H = u(c_t, l_t) + \lambda_t[F(k_t, n_t) - c_t - \delta k_t - \overset{\bullet}{k}_t] + \mu_t[1 \quad n_t - l_t]. \tag{4.150}$$

The first-order conditions are

$$c_t + \overset{\bullet}{k}_t \mid \delta k_t = F(k_t, n_t), \tag{4.151}$$

$$n_t + l_t = 1, \tag{4.152}$$

$$\lambda_t = u'_c, \tag{4.153}$$

$$\mu_t = u'_l, \tag{4.154}$$

$$\mu_t = \lambda_t F'_n, \tag{4.155}$$

$$\overset{\bullet}{\lambda}_t = \rho\lambda_t - \lambda_t(F'_k - \delta) \tag{4.156}$$

and note that the μ_t is redundant since N_t does not grow.

Combining these conditions yields

$$u'_c F'_n = u'_l \tag{4.157}$$

$$\frac{-u'_{cc}}{u'_c}\overset{\bullet}{c}_t - \frac{u'_{cl}}{u'_c}\overset{\bullet}{l}_t = F'_k - \rho - \delta. \tag{4.158}$$

Assuming that labor effort does not grow and that instantaneous utility is given by

$$\log C_t + \log L_t, \tag{4.159}$$

let us compare and contrast the model to the Ramsey model.

First, obviously, $\dot{l}_t = \dot{n}_t = 0$ since time does not grow. Imposing this yields

$$\dot{c}_t = \frac{u'_c}{u'_{cc}}(\delta - \rho - F'_k), \tag{4.160}$$

and one can show that the resulting $\frac{\dot{c}_t}{c_t}$ and $\frac{\dot{k}_t}{k_t}$ expressions are the same as in the optimal growth model except, that we will have a $-\frac{\dot{l}_t}{l_t}$ tacked on at the end. The model is therefore an extension of the Ramsey model. Even though it does not change much of the exogenous growth story, it was used as the basis of the real business cycle model that revolutionized the study of business cycles for four central macroeconomic aggregates: output, consumption, investment, and hours worked.

4.5 Conclusion

In summary, in this chapter, we have described the central Solow model of modern macroeconomics and then shown how to endogenize the savings rate in that model by using deterministic dynamic optimization. This suite of models forms the core of all of growth theory, and in the following chapter, we turn to the task of finding ways to explain the one element of exogenous growth models that is still elusive: the process of technological progress itself.

Chapter 5

Endogenous Growth

5.1 Introduction

Exogenous growth models, such as those discussed above, do not fully explain the growth process of an economy. For example, the Solow growth model displays growth in per capita income along the transitional dynamics (i.e. on the path to steady state), but once the steady state is reached, per capita income does not grow, unless one assumes that TFP grows in the steady state. So, the only way to explain that per capita income grows in this class of *exogenous* growth models is to assume it. In addition, any change to one of the parameters in the model causes only transitional changes in growth but not permanent changes. For example, an increase in the savings rate will cause per capita income growth (in effective units) to increase temporarily above zero, but eventually the growth rate will revert back to zero in the steady state. In this case, the change has caused a scale effect (an increase in per capita income) but no growth effect. More fundamentally the Solow and neo-classical models do not explain the technological progress that they use to generate long-term growth in an optimizing framework.

In this chapter, we discuss a class of growth models that will generate *endogenous* growth in per capita income, even in the long run. In particular, the models we cover will rely on changing the shape of the production function. As we shall see, once the assumption of decreasing marginal returns to capital is dropped, growth in per capita income does not necessarily taper off in the long run. In addition, changes to economic parameters (such as a preference parameter or the savings rate) cause permanent changes in the growth rate of per capita income, not just temporary ones. In this sense, these growth models are *endogenous* growth models: we do not need to assume exogenous progress in the level of technology to obtain our desired result.

5.2 AK Growth

A crucial factor explaining the lack of growth in steady state in neo-classical models is the assumption of decreasing marginal returns to factor inputs. Instead, consider a variant of the Solow growth model called the AK model, where the production function is given by $Y_t = A_t K_t$ (we ignore labor for now). As usual, we assume that a proportion δ of overall capital depreciates from one period to the next and that the representative agent saves a proportion s of her income. Capital accumulation is given by

$$\dot{K}_t = sAK_t - \delta K_t \tag{5.1}$$

if $A_t = A > 0$. Note that if $sA > \delta$, then $\dot{K}_t$ is always positive. This means that the growth of capital is bounded away from zero for all time periods. In particular, one can think of K_t as capital per worker (there is, after all, only one representative household in the economy – assuming population growth will not change the main results of the AK model). The rate of growth of capital is exactly $sA - \delta$ (which we assume to be positive). Since in general

$$\frac{\dot{Y}}{Y} = \frac{\dot{A}}{A} + \frac{\dot{K}}{K}, \tag{5.2}$$

it follows that

$$\frac{\dot{Y}}{Y} = \frac{\dot{A}}{A} + (sA - \delta) \tag{5.3}$$

in this particular case. Unlike the Solow growth model and Ramsey-type models, we have per capita output growth without the assumption of TFP growth. Indeed, even if $\frac{\dot{A}}{A} = 0$, we have

$$\frac{\dot{Y}}{Y} = sA - \delta. \tag{5.4}$$

Thus, the AK model delivers growth in the steady state. In addition, it delivers the *growth effects* of policy variables: for example, if s goes up by a bit, the rate of growth of per capita output goes up for all remaining time periods. Figures 5.1 and 5.2 reflect the intuition of the model. Compare this to the Solow model, where an increase in s causes only a temporary increase in the rate of growth of per capita output.

Unfortunately for the AK model, the assumption of constant marginal returns to physical capital is inconsistent with data, which shows that physical capital's share of output is somewhere between zero and one in the long run. But the assumption of constant marginal returns to *broader* definitions of capital will yield endogenous growth and is consistent with decreasing marginal returns to physical capital. Suppose for example that K_t in the AK model is thought of as broad capital and consists of physical, human, and

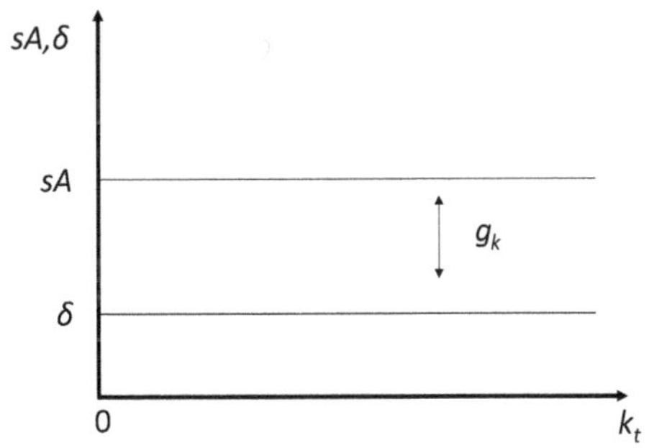

Figure 5.1. Growth in the AK model.

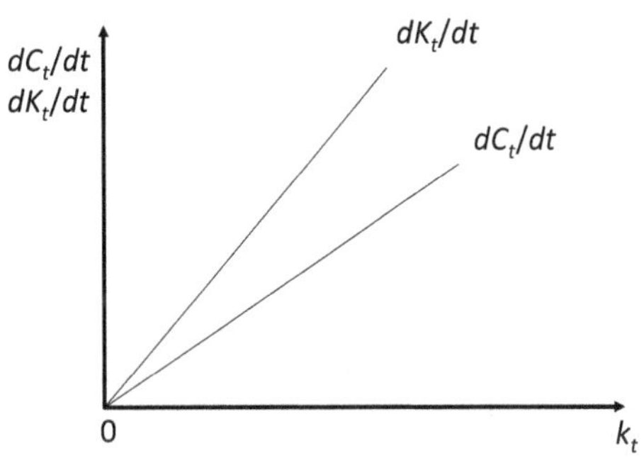

Figure 5.2. Unbounded growth.

cultural capital elements. Then,

$$K_t = K_{Pt}^{\beta} K_{Ht}^{1-\beta}, \tag{5.5}$$

which (after taking logs and differentials) implies

$$\frac{\dot{K}_t}{K_t} = \beta \frac{\dot{K}_{Pt}}{K_{Pt}} + (1-\beta) \frac{\dot{K}_{Ht}}{K_{Ht}}. \tag{5.6}$$

Suppose now that our AK economy invested proportionally in both physical and human capital, then the reduced form production function would display constant marginal product to this broad definition of capital, and the analysis above would go through as we would get endogenous growth.

As another example, consider an economy where the production function is given by $Y_t = AK_t + L_t^{1-\alpha}$, with $\alpha < 1$ and where labor increases exponentially at a rate $n > 0$, i.e. $\dot{L}_t/L_t = n$. Then, capital accumulation is given by

$$\dot{K}_t = sY_t - \delta K_t \Leftrightarrow \frac{\dot{K}_t}{K_t} = sAL_t^{1-\alpha} - \delta, \tag{5.7}$$

and thus the growth rate of output is

$$\frac{\dot{Y}_t}{Y_t} = \frac{\dot{K}_t}{K_t} + (1-\alpha)\frac{\dot{L}_t}{L_t} = sAL_t^{1-\alpha} - \delta + (1-\alpha)n, \tag{5.8}$$

that is, population growth in the standard AK model with labor entering as an input implies that the growth rate of output itself is growing at (approximately) an exponential rate.

5.3 An Optimizing AK Model

Consider now another AK growth model with optimizing agents due to Rebelo (1991). The model assumes the existence of two distinct sectors in the economy: the consumption goods sector and the investment sector. Both sectors use the existing capital stock to produce either goods or additional capital. Consumption goods cannot be used to produce further capital. The model also assumes that economic agents get utility out of the consumption good only; therefore, capital cannot be used for consumption.

The consumption goods sector employs a fixed amount of labor where the production function is assumed to be given by

$$C_t = f(\phi_t K_t) = B(\phi_t K_t)^{\alpha}. \tag{5.9}$$

We assume that $\phi_t \in [0,1]$, $\alpha \in (0,1)$, and $B > 0$. The term ϕ_t reflects the fraction of total capital that is used to produce consumption goods and is a control variable for our representative agent. Note that the production function for consumption is assumed to have decreasing marginal returns to capital. The investment goods sector on the other hand is assumed to be described by the following production function:

$$I_t = AK_t(1 - \phi_t), \tag{5.10}$$

with $A > 0$ representing the current state of the technology. Investment goods are produced by applying whatever capital is left over from the manufacture of consumption goods. As we shall see, this model also displays endogenous growth. The assumptions of the model however are not as severe as those of the simple AK model presented earlier: some sectors display decreasing marginal returns to capital, while others do not. This is an improvement over the pure AK model, as overall output in the economy (resulting from the consumption and investment sector production) displays decreasing marginal returns to capital.

Capital accumulation is assumed to be given by

$$\dot{K}_t = I_t - \delta K_t, \tag{5.11}$$

where $\delta \in (0,1)$ is the usual instantaneous depreciation of physical capital. Combining (5.10) with (5.11) produces

$$\dot{K}_t = AK_t(1 - \phi_t) - \delta K_t, \tag{5.12}$$

or

$$\frac{\dot{K}_t}{K_t} = A(1 - \phi_t) - \delta. \tag{5.13}$$

Note that the choice of ϕ_t is up to the optimizing agent. The proportion $1 - \phi_t$ is simply the proportion of capital used for investment. If this proportion was constant over time, we would be back to the AK model in terms of the dynamics of capital and output. When optimizing, the planner seeks to obtain balanced growth in the steady state. This corresponds to a situation where $\frac{\dot{K}_t}{K_t}$ and $\frac{\dot{C}_t}{C_t}$ are constant. In the steady state, it has to be that the proportion invested by the social planner ϕ_t is constant, otherwise $\dot{K}_t$ would not exhibit constant growth. Given these assumptions, we aim to solve the following social planner's problem:

$$\max_{\{\phi_t\}} \quad U = \int_0^\infty e^{-\rho t} U(C_t) dt \tag{5.14}$$

$$s.t. \quad C_t = B\phi_t^\alpha K_t^\alpha, \quad \alpha \in (0,1), \quad B > 0 \tag{5.15}$$

$$\dot{K}_t = AK_t(1-\phi_t) - \delta K_t, \quad \delta \in (0,1) \tag{5.16}$$

$$K_{(0)} = K_0 > 0 \tag{5.17}$$

We realize that we are solving a social planner's problem because the economy that Rebelo (1991) describes satisfies all of the assumptions of the first welfare theorem. Alternatively, we could consider directly the competitive equilibrium. By checking that Rebelo's solution is identical to the one presented as follows, one can verify that the first welfare theorem does in fact apply here.

Going back to the problem, note that the variable ϕ_t is the control variable; for a given level of capital, this is as if the social planner was choosing directly the level of consumption C_t. The CVH for this problem is

$$H = U(B\phi_t^\alpha K_t^\alpha) + \lambda_t[AK_t(1-\phi_t) - \delta K_t]. \tag{5.18}$$

The corresponding first-order conditions are

$$\frac{\partial H}{\partial \phi_t} = U'\alpha B\phi_t^{\alpha-1}K_t^\alpha - \lambda_t AK_t = 0, \tag{5.19}$$

$$\frac{\partial H}{\partial K_t} = \rho\lambda_t - \dot{\lambda}_t \tag{5.20}$$

$$= U'\alpha B\phi_t^\alpha K_t^{\alpha-1} + \lambda_t[A(1-\phi_t) - \delta], \tag{5.21}$$

$$\frac{\partial H}{\partial \lambda_t} = \dot{K}_t = AK_t(1-\phi_t) - \delta K_t. \tag{5.22}$$

From equation (5.19), we have

$$U'\alpha B\phi_t^{\alpha-1}K_t^{\alpha} = \lambda_t AK_t, \tag{5.23}$$

$$U'\alpha B\phi_t^{\alpha-1}K_t^{\alpha-1} = \lambda_t A. \tag{5.24}$$

To make sense out of this equation, first note that the marginal product of investing an additional unit of capital (MP_I) is $A(1-\phi_t)$, whereas the marginal product of using a unit of capital to produce additional consumption (MP_C) is $B\alpha\phi_t^{\alpha}K_t^{\alpha-1}$. So, the above equation can be rewritten as $U'MP_C/\phi_t = \lambda_t MP_I/(1-\phi_t)$, or

$$(1-\phi_t)\frac{U'MP_C}{\lambda_t} = \phi_t MP_I. \tag{5.25}$$

An optimal choice of ϕ_t therefore involves equating the (normalized) marginal utility of consumption times the marginal product of consumption to the marginal product of additional investment. In particular, suppose that $\frac{U'MP_C}{\lambda_t} = MP_I$, then the optimal choice of ϕ_t is 1/2. If $\frac{U'MP_C}{\lambda_t} > MP_I$, then the representative agent is not consuming 'enough', so the optimal ϕ_t in this case should be greater than 1/2, which would make the term $(1-\phi_t)\frac{U'MP_C}{\lambda_t}$ smaller and the term $\phi_t MP_I$ bigger, ensuring equality. Note that as capital is accumulated in this economy, the term MP_C will become eventually smaller than MP_I because of decreasing marginal returns in the consumption goods sector. So, the marginal cost of producing one unit of the consumption good eventually exceeds the marginal cost of producing an additional unit of physical capital. The model therefore predicts that as time passes, the relative price of consumption goods to investment goods increases; this turns out to be at odds with the data.

We now solve for the balanced growth path. Recall that, from the equation above, we have

$$U'\alpha B\phi_t^{\alpha-1}K_t^{\alpha-1} = \lambda_t A. \tag{5.26}$$

Now, taking the time derivative of $U'\alpha B\phi_t^{\alpha-1}K_t^{\alpha-1} = \lambda_t A$ gives

$$\begin{aligned} &U''(C)\dot{C}_t\alpha B\phi_t^{\alpha-1}K_t^{\alpha-1} + U'(C)\left[\alpha(\alpha-1)B\phi_t^{\alpha-2}K_t^{\alpha-1}\dot{\phi}_t\right. \\ &\quad \left.+\alpha(\alpha-1)B\phi_t^{\alpha-1}K_t^{\alpha-2}\dot{K}_t\right] = \dot{\lambda}_t A + \dot{A}\lambda_t. \end{aligned} \tag{5.27}$$

For simplicity, we assume that $\overset{\bullet}{A}_t = 0$. Also, along the balanced growth path, we have that $\overset{\bullet}{\phi}_t = 0$, so the above becomes

$$U''(C)\overset{\bullet}{C}_t \alpha B \phi_t^{\alpha-1} K_t^{\alpha-1} + U'(C)\alpha(\alpha-1) B \phi_t^{\alpha-1} K_t^{\alpha-2} \overset{\bullet}{K}_t = \overset{\bullet}{\lambda}_t A.$$

Substituting this expression into (5.20) gives

$$\rho\lambda_t - \frac{U''(C)\overset{\bullet}{C}_t \alpha B \phi_t^{\alpha-1} K_t^{\alpha-1} + U'(C)\alpha(\alpha-1) B \phi_t^{\alpha-1} K_t^{\alpha-2} \overset{\bullet}{K}_t}{A}$$
$$= U'\alpha B \phi_t^{\alpha} K_t^{\alpha-1} + \lambda_t[A(1-\phi_t) - \delta]. \tag{5.28}$$

Replace

$$\lambda_t = \frac{U'\alpha B \phi_t^{\alpha-1} K_t^{\alpha-1}}{A} \tag{5.29}$$

to get

$$\rho\frac{U'\alpha B \phi_t^{\alpha-1} K_t^{\alpha-1}}{A}$$
$$- \frac{U''(C)\overset{\bullet}{C}_t \alpha B \phi_t^{\alpha-1} K_t^{\alpha-1} + U'(C)\alpha(\alpha-1) B \phi_t^{\alpha-1} K_t^{\alpha-2} \overset{\bullet}{K}_t}{A}$$
$$= U'\alpha B \phi_t^{\alpha} K_t^{\alpha-1} + \frac{U'\alpha B \phi_t^{\alpha-1} K_t^{\alpha-1}}{A}[A(1-\phi_t) - \delta]. \tag{5.30}$$

For simplicity of exposition, let $\xi = \alpha B \phi_t^{\alpha-1} K_t^{\alpha-1}$. Then,

$$-\frac{U''\xi}{A}\overset{\bullet}{C}_t - \frac{U'(\alpha-1)\xi}{AK}\overset{\bullet}{K}_t = U'\xi\phi + \frac{U'\xi}{A}[A(1-\phi_t) - \delta - \rho]. \tag{5.31}$$

Multiplying through by A yields

$$-U''\xi\overset{\bullet}{C}_t - U'(\alpha-1)\xi\frac{\overset{\bullet}{K}_t}{K_t} = AU'\xi\phi + U'\xi[A(1-\phi_t) - \delta - \rho]. \tag{5.32}$$

Note that the left-hand side of (5.32) is the decrease in marginal utility and marginal product of capital, while the right-hand side is the sum of the indirect and direct wealth effects.

Next, let

$$U(C_t) = \frac{C_t^{1-\theta}}{1-\theta}. \tag{5.33}$$

Then, $U' = C_t^{-\theta}$ and $U'' = -\theta C_t^{-\theta-1}$. Replace this into equation (5.32) to get

$$\theta C_t^{-\theta-1}\xi\overset{\bullet}{C}_t - \frac{C_t^{-\theta}(\alpha-1)\xi}{K}\overset{\bullet}{K}_t$$
$$= AC_t^{-\theta}\xi\phi + C_t^{-\theta}\xi[A(1-\phi_t)-\delta-\rho].$$

In rates of growth,

$$\theta C_t^{-\theta}\xi\frac{\overset{\bullet}{C}_t}{C_t} - C_t^{-\theta}(\alpha-1)\xi\frac{\overset{\bullet}{K}_t}{K_t} = AC_t^{-\theta}\xi\phi + C_t^{-\theta}\xi[A(1-\phi_t)-\delta-\rho].$$

Divide both sides by $C_t^{-\theta}\xi$ to get

$$\theta\frac{\overset{\bullet}{C}_t}{C_t} + (1-\alpha)\frac{\overset{\bullet}{K}_t}{K_t} = A\phi + [A(1-\phi_t)-\delta-\rho],$$

or

$$\theta\frac{\overset{\bullet}{C}_t}{C_t} + (1-\alpha)\frac{\overset{\bullet}{K}_t}{K_t} = A-(\rho+\delta). \tag{5.34}$$

Now, from the capital accumulation equation (5.22), we infer that

$$\frac{\overset{\bullet}{K}_t}{K_t} = A(1-\phi_t)-\delta. \tag{5.35}$$

This in turn allows us to obtain the rate of growth of consumption by inserting the above into (5.34). This gives

$$\theta\frac{\overset{\bullet}{C}_t}{C_t} + (1-\alpha)[A(1-\phi_t)-\delta] = A-(\rho+\delta). \tag{5.36}$$

Finally, using the production function in the consumption goods sector (5.15), one finds that

$$\frac{\overset{\bullet}{C}_t}{C_t} = \alpha\frac{\overset{\bullet}{K}_t}{K_t}, \tag{5.37}$$

which is *not* balanced growth. Nevertheless, to get an expression for the growth rate of capital, plug in (5.37) into (5.34) to get

$$\frac{\overset{\bullet}{K}_t}{K_t} = \frac{A-(\rho+\delta)}{1+\alpha(\theta-1)}, \tag{5.38}$$

and so

$$\frac{\overset{\bullet}{C}_t}{C_t} = \frac{\alpha A - \alpha(\rho + \delta)}{1 + \alpha(\theta - 1)}. \tag{5.39}$$

The above two expressions tell us the rates of growth of consumption and capital along a growth path where they are constant. Along these paths, ϕ_t is also a constant. We now go about computing it. The social planner needs to choose ϕ_t optimally. Along the growth path, it would be equal to a constant ϕ^*. First, let

$$\nu = [1 + \alpha(\theta - 1)]^{-1} \tag{5.40}$$

and put into (5.38) to give

$$\frac{\overset{\bullet}{K}_t}{K_t} = \nu[A - (\rho + \delta)], \tag{5.41}$$

or

$$\overset{\bullet}{K}_t = \nu\,[A - (\rho + \delta)]\,K_t. \tag{5.42}$$

Substitute (5.42) into the budget constraint (5.22),

$$\nu\,[A - (\rho + \delta)] = A(1 - \phi_t) - \delta, \tag{5.43}$$

and solve for ϕ^*:

$$\phi^* = 1 - \nu(1 - \frac{\rho}{A}) - \frac{\delta}{A}(1 - \nu). \tag{5.44}$$

This means that C_t and K_t will grow infinitely into the future and will exhibit long-term sustainable growth. Note that upon examination of (5.41), it is clear that it is necessary for $A > \rho + \delta$ in order for $\frac{\overset{\bullet}{K}_t}{K_t}$ to be positive: if the current level of technology is not sufficiently large relative to the sum of the rate of impatience of the representative agent and the rate of depreciation of capital, the level of consumption demanded by the representative agent will cause capital to depreciate faster than it accumulates. Eventually, the agent will have nothing to consume.

Finally, note that this is an endogenous growth model: a one-time increase in the level of technology causes output growth (the sum of the consumption and investment sector) to increase permanently to a new level. This *growth effect* is absent from traditional neo-classical models. It suggests that government policy can have permanent effects not just on the level of per capita income but also on the growth rates of per capita income. If the government can pass a policy that causes people to save more (for example by taxing current consumption), the rate of growth of the economy will jump to a new level. There is no room for this kind of rationale in neo-classical growth models or in Solow's model. There, an increase in the savings rate causes only a scale effect but not a growth effect. We can now use the results obtained thus far to analyze dynamics around the balanced growth path. We have

$$\frac{\dot{K}_t}{K_t} = A(1-\phi_t) - \delta, \tag{5.45}$$

$$\phi_t^* = 1 - \nu(1 - \frac{\rho}{A}) - \frac{\delta}{A}(1-\nu), \tag{5.46}$$

$$\dot{\phi}_t = 0, \tag{5.47}$$

which can be expressed as

$$\frac{\dot{K}_t}{K_t} = A(1-\phi_t) - \delta = g^K(\phi_t, K_t), \tag{5.48}$$

$$\frac{\dot{\phi}_t}{\phi_t} = 0 = g^C(\phi_t, K_t). \tag{5.49}$$

To find the stability of the system, one needs to first linearize these relationships. This results in obtaining the system

$$\begin{matrix} \frac{\dot{K}_t}{K_t} \\ \frac{\dot{\phi}_t}{\phi_t} \end{matrix} = \begin{bmatrix} 0 & -A \\ 0 & 0 \end{bmatrix} \begin{bmatrix} \frac{\dot{K}_t}{K_t} - \frac{\dot{K}_t^*}{K_t^*} \\ \frac{\dot{\phi}_t}{\phi_t} - \frac{\dot{\phi}^*_t}{\phi_t^*} \end{bmatrix}. \tag{5.50}$$

In this case, the eigenvalues are both zero. As a result, the system is only stable if one begins at the steady state already; otherwise, the system explodes. There is no possibility to adjust to get back onto the saddle path if an initial deviation has been made. A possible fix to this problem is to let

$$\overset{\bullet}{\phi}_t = -w(\phi_t - \phi_t^*), \tag{5.51}$$

with w arbitrary and strictly greater than zero. Then,

$$\begin{matrix} \dfrac{\overset{\bullet}{K}_t}{K_t} \\ \overset{\bullet}{\phi}_t \end{matrix} = \begin{bmatrix} 0 & -A \\ 0 & -w \end{bmatrix} \begin{bmatrix} \dfrac{\overset{\bullet}{K}_t}{K_t} - \dfrac{\overset{\bullet}{K}{}_t^*}{K_t^*} \\ \phi_t - \phi_t^* \end{bmatrix}. \tag{5.52}$$

In this modified system, the eigenvalues are $\lambda_1 = 0$ and $\lambda_2 = -w$, which implies a stable saddle path is obtainable. In actuality, Rebelo (1991) and others provide a way to endogenize the w term, and we refer the reader to the literature covered by Acemoglu (2009) and other excellent texts covering endogenous growth theory in detail.

5.4 Knowledge and Growth

We have seen in the previous section that the assumption of constant returns to a factor of production is a sure way to get endogenous growth. We justified this assumption by saying that capital could be thought of as 'broad' capital, comprising both physical and human capital. In this section, we consider a typical firm i with a production function of the type

$$Y_{it} = F(K_{it}, A_{it}L_{it}), \tag{5.53}$$

which is subject to the Inada conditions, as given in the Solow model. In particular, we assume a Cobb–Douglas production function, given as $Y_{it} = K_{it}^{\alpha} \times (A_{it}L_{it})^{1-\alpha}$. If we assumed that A_{it}, the labor augmenting technology, was growing exogenously, we would be back to a neo-classical model. Instead, we assume that A_{it} somehow reflects knowledge spillovers, as proxied by the level of existing capital $\bar{K}_t$. We assume that

$$A_{it} = \gamma \bar{K}_t = \gamma \sum_{i}^{H} K_{it}, \quad \text{where } \gamma \in (0, 1]. \tag{5.54}$$

If one thinks of A_{it} as total knowledge in society, then the rate of growth of knowledge equals the rate of growth of capital:

$$\frac{\overset{\bullet}{A}_{it}}{A_{it}} = \sum_{i}^{H} \frac{\overset{\bullet}{K}_{it}}{K_{it}}. \tag{5.55}$$

Plugging equation (5.54) into the production function gives

$$Y_{it} = F(K_{it}, \gamma \bar{K}_t L_{it}) \tag{5.56}$$

$$Y_{it} = K_{it}^{\alpha} \times (\gamma \bar{K}_t L_{it})^{1-\alpha}. \tag{5.57}$$

We can normalize this production function by L_{it}; this is because we assume that labor is supplied inelastically:

$$Y_{it} = k_{it}^{\alpha} \times (\gamma \bar{k}_t)^{1-\alpha}. \tag{5.58}$$

This simple R&D-based model will turn out to generate endogenous growth. It can be analyzed either as a decentralized problem or as a social planner's problem. Observe, however, that the presence of knowledge spillovers means that the social planner's solution and the decentralized solution are not the same. The difference arises because there is an externality that a social planner could mitigate. Here, when an individual firm is choosing how much capital to produce to maximize its profits, it takes $\bar{k}_t$ as a given. So, a typical firm is facing decreasing marginal returns to its own capital. In the decentralized problem, all firms behave this way. Note however that by symmetry, the production function for the whole of society is linear in capital. It equals $Y_t = \sum_i Y_{it} = \gamma \bar{k}_t$. So, from the social planner's point of view, the level of production of capital is too low; if society internalized this productive externality, overall output would rise, which of course gives rise to a motivation regarding policy interventions that accentuate the effects of positive spillovers.

5.4.1 The decentralized equilibrium

In the decentralized method of solution, firms maximize their profits by choosing the level of inputs, while households maximize their utility through their choice of consumption. Households own both capital and labor, and they sell (or rent) these to the firms at prices R_t and W_t, respectively. First, consider the ith firm's PMP, which is

$$\max_{\{L_t,K_t\}} \quad \Pi_t = Y_t - R_tK_t - W_tL_t, \tag{5.59}$$

$$s.t. \quad Y_t = K_t^{\alpha} \times (\gamma\bar{K}_tL_t)^{1-\alpha}, \tag{5.60}$$

with $P_t = 1$. The associated first-order conditions are

$$\frac{\partial \Pi_t}{\partial K_t} = \alpha K_t^{\alpha-1}(\gamma\bar{K}_tL_t)^{1-\alpha} - R_t = 0, \tag{5.61}$$

$$\frac{\partial \Pi_t}{\partial L_t} = (1-\alpha)K_t^{\alpha} \times (\gamma\bar{K}_tL_t)^{-\alpha}\gamma\bar{K}_t - W_t = 0. \tag{5.62}$$

Note here that the firm takes as a given the level of capital $\bar{K}_t$ in the economy. Rewriting these conditions yields

$$\alpha K_t^{\alpha-1}(\gamma\bar{K}_tL_t)^{1-\alpha} = R_t, \tag{5.63}$$

$$(1-\alpha)K_t^{\alpha} \times (\gamma\bar{K}_tL_t)^{-\alpha}\gamma\bar{K}_t = W_t, \tag{5.64}$$

or more simply,

$$\frac{\alpha Y_t}{K_t} = R_t, \tag{5.65}$$

$$\frac{(1-\alpha)Y_t}{L_t} = W_t. \tag{5.66}$$

Second, consider the UMP faced by households:

$$\max_{\{C_t\}} \quad U = \int_0^{\infty} e^{-\rho t}U(C_t)dt \tag{5.67}$$

$$s.t. \quad C_t + \dot{K}_t + \delta K_t = R_tK_t + W_tL_t \tag{5.68}$$

$$K_{(0)} = K_0 > 0, \tag{5.69}$$

where

$$U(C_t) = \frac{C_t^{1-\theta}}{1-\theta}, \tag{5.70}$$

as well as R_t and W_t given by (5.65) and (5.66), respectively. Substituting these into (5.68) gives

$$C_t + \overset{\bullet}{K}_t + \delta K_t = \frac{\gamma Y_t}{K_t} K_t + \frac{(1-\gamma)Y_t}{L_t} L_t, \tag{5.71}$$

which can be simplified to

$$C_t + \overset{\bullet}{K}_t + \delta K_t = Y_t, \tag{5.72}$$

$$C_t + \overset{\bullet}{K}_t + \delta K_t = K_t^{\alpha}(\gamma \bar{K}_t L_t)^{1-\alpha}. \tag{5.73}$$

The CVH for the UMP is thus

$$H = \frac{C_t^{1-\theta}}{1-\theta} + \lambda_t[K_t^{\alpha}(\gamma \bar{K}_t L_t)^{1-\alpha} - C_t - \delta K_t]. \tag{5.74}$$

The first-order conditions are

$$\frac{\partial H}{\partial C_t} = C_t^{-\theta} - \lambda_t = 0, \tag{5.75}$$

$$\frac{\partial H}{\partial K_t} = \lambda_t[\alpha K_t^{\alpha-1}(\gamma \bar{K}_t L_t)^{1-\alpha} - \delta] = \rho\lambda_t - \overset{\bullet}{\lambda}_t, \tag{5.76}$$

$$\frac{\partial H}{\partial \lambda_t} = K_t^{\alpha}(\gamma \bar{K}_t L_t)^{1-\alpha} - C_t - \delta K_t = \overset{\bullet}{K}_t. \tag{5.77}$$

From (5.76), one obtains

$$\overset{\bullet}{\lambda}_t = \lambda_t[\rho + \delta - \alpha K_t^{\alpha-1}(\gamma \bar{K}_t L_t)^{1-\alpha}], \tag{5.78}$$

and via (5.77), one obtains

$$\frac{\overset{\bullet}{K}_t}{K_t} = K_t^{\alpha-1}(\gamma \bar{K}_t L_t)^{1-\alpha} - \frac{C_t}{K_t} - \delta. \tag{5.79}$$

Taking the derivative of (5.75) results in the relationship

$$\frac{\overset{\bullet}{C}_t}{C_t} = -\theta^{-1}\frac{\overset{\bullet}{\lambda}_t}{\lambda_t}, \tag{5.80}$$

or

$$\frac{\overset{\bullet}{C}_t}{C_t} = \theta^{-1}[\alpha K_t^{\alpha-1}(\gamma K_t L_t)^{1-\alpha} - \rho - \delta], \tag{5.81}$$

by inserting (5.78) and simplifying. Next, since all firms are identical, symmetry dictates that

$$K_{it} = K_t \quad \forall\, t, \tag{5.82}$$

which implies that

$$\bar{K}_t = \sum_{i=1}^{H} K_{it} = HK_t. \tag{5.83}$$

Applying (5.83) to (5.79) and (5.81) yields

$$\frac{\overset{\bullet}{K}_t}{K_t} = K_t^{\alpha-1}(\gamma HK_tL_t)^{1-\alpha} - \frac{C_t}{K_t} - \delta \tag{5.84}$$

$$= (\gamma HL_t)^{1-\alpha} - \frac{C_t}{K_t} - \delta, \tag{5.85}$$

$$\frac{\overset{\bullet}{C}_t}{C_t} = \theta^{-1}[\alpha K_t^{\alpha-1}(\gamma HK_tL_t)^{1-\alpha} - \rho - \delta] \tag{5.86}$$

$$= \theta^{-1}[\alpha(\gamma HL_t)^{1-\alpha} - \rho - \delta], \tag{5.87}$$

and for regularity, assume $\alpha(\gamma HL_t)^{1-\alpha} - \rho - \delta > 0$. This assumption is needed to ensure that variables of interest grow positively over time. It is not required for endogenous growth, for which we simply need that $\alpha(\gamma HL_t)^{1-\alpha} - \rho - \delta \neq 0$. At this point, impose the restriction of balanced growth,

$$\frac{\overset{\bullet}{K}_t}{K_t} = \frac{\overset{\bullet}{C}_t}{C_t}, \tag{5.88}$$

and solve for conditions under which it is true.

Equate (5.84) with (5.86) and solve for $\frac{C_t}{K_t}$. If one lets

$$\eta = \frac{C_t}{K_t}, \tag{5.89}$$

then

$$\eta = (1 - \frac{\alpha}{\theta})(\gamma HL_t)^{1-\alpha} + \frac{\rho}{\theta} - (1 - \theta^{-1})\delta \tag{5.90}$$

$$= (\gamma HL_t)^{1-\alpha} - \delta - \theta^{-1}[\alpha(\gamma HL_t)^{1-\alpha} - \rho - \delta] \tag{5.91}$$

$$= (\gamma HL_t)^{1-\alpha} - \delta - g, \tag{5.92}$$

where the rate of technology growth is given by

$$g = \theta^{-1}[\alpha(\gamma H L_t)^{1-\alpha} - \rho - \delta]. \tag{5.93}$$

It follows from (5.81) and (5.93) that

$$\frac{\overset{\bullet}{K}_t}{K_t} = \frac{\overset{\bullet}{C}_t}{C_t} = g. \tag{5.94}$$

Observe in (5.93) that the size of the spillover effect, as measured by γ, affects growth, and so does the number of households H in the economy. This is a very different result from Solow's growth model since here, more households imply greater capital accumulation and therefore greater spillovers. In Solow's model, more population growth simply shrinks per capita income because of decreasing marginal returns to capital. Recall that in the AK model, more population growth simply slows down and, only temporarily, the rate of growth of per capita income. As in the AK model, preference parameters also have growth effects, not just scale effects. Specifically, when θ or ρ become larger, households prefer to consume sooner rather than later and the rate of growth g becomes smaller.

5.4.2 The benevolent social planner

In this section, we consider how a social planner would go about allocating resources in the economy. Since the social planner does not take as a given the productive externality, he can 'force' a typical household or firm to invest more than it would have on its own. This additional investment, with its corresponding knowledge spillovers, causes output to rise in a manner that is linear with overall capital. We should expect that growth in this economy is higher than in the competitive equilibrium, as discussed in the previous section. The planner's problem is

$$\max_{\{C_t\}} \quad U = \int_0^\infty e^{-\rho t} U(C_t) dt \tag{5.95}$$

$$s.t. \quad C_t + \overset{\bullet}{K}_t + \delta K_t = K_t^\alpha(\gamma \bar{K}_t L_t)^{1-\alpha} \tag{5.96}$$

$$U(C_t) = \frac{C_t^{1-\theta}}{1-\theta}. \tag{5.97}$$

Applying (5.83), the constraint (5.96) becomes

$$C_t + \dot{K}_t + \delta K_t = K_t^{\alpha}(\gamma H K_t L_t)^{1-\alpha} \quad (5.98)$$
$$= K_t(\gamma H L_t)^{1-\alpha}. \quad (5.99)$$

The CVH is

$$H = \frac{C_t^{1-\theta}}{1-\theta} + \lambda_t[K_t(\gamma H L_t)^{1-\alpha} - C_t - \delta K_t], \quad (5.100)$$

with the first-order conditions

$$\frac{\partial H}{\partial C_t} = C_t^{-\theta} - \lambda_t = 0, \quad (5.101)$$

$$\frac{\partial H}{\partial K_t} = \lambda_t[(\gamma H L_t)^{1-\alpha} - \delta] = \rho\lambda_t - \dot{\lambda}_t, \quad (5.102)$$

$$\frac{\partial H}{\partial \lambda_t} = K_t(\gamma H L_t)^{1-\alpha} - C_t - \delta K_t = \dot{K}_t. \quad (5.103)$$

Note that the social planner chooses capital by internalizing the productive externality. He does not take as a given what other households produce when he is choosing the level of capital for a given household. From (5.103), one can get the expression

$$\frac{\dot{K}_t}{K_t} = (\gamma H L_t)^{1-\alpha} - \frac{C_t}{K_t} - \delta. \quad (5.104)$$

Similarly, from (5.101),

$$\frac{\dot{C}_t}{C_t} = \theta^{-1}[(\gamma H L_t)^{1-\alpha} - \rho - \delta], \quad (5.105)$$

and let

$$\theta^{-1}[(\gamma H L_t)^{1-\alpha} - \rho - \delta] = g^{sp}. \quad (5.106)$$

This allows us to distinguish the rate of technological growth in the social planner environment from that of the decentralized equilibrium. Comparing g with g^{sp}, one obtains

$$g^{sp} - g = \theta^{-1}\left[(1-\alpha)(\gamma H L_t)^{1-\alpha}\right]. \quad (5.107)$$

This term is positive since $\alpha < 1$. As the number of households H or the knowledge spillover parameter γ increases, so does the difference between g^{sp} and g. This is because the externality that the social planner is internalizing becomes more important. On the other hand, note that as θ increases, the social planner and decentralized growth rates converge. This reflects the fact that as agents become more impatient, savings fall to zero and so do corresponding growth rates. Thus, the social planner's problem yields a Pareto optimal allocation of consumption and savings over time. This results in growth rates along the balanced growth path that are higher than those found when analyzing the competitive equilibrium. As a final note, observe that the solution described when analyzing the decentralized problem is the correct one to consider from a descriptive point of view, as it represents what is actually happening in the economy. The outcome of this problem, as has been already mentioned, is not Pareto optimal. On the other hand, one can obtain the same solution as in the decentralized problem by analyzing a 'constrained' version of the social planner's problem. This involves assuming the following production function when obtaining the optimality conditions,

$$K_t^{\alpha}(\gamma \bar{K}_t L_t)^{1-\alpha},$$

and then imposing the condition that $K_t = \bar{K}_t$. The resulting solution to this constrained problem will be the same as the decentralized problem.

5.5 Exogenous vs. Endogenous Growth Models

As we have seen above, neo-classical growth does not provide any explanation for why per capita income grows in the steady state. Instead, neo-classical growth assumes growth in TFP (for example), which in turn directly implies that per capita income will grow for all time periods. This is unsatisfactory because growth in TFP is a process that economic agents presumably have control over, so there should be growth in TFP only if it is the result of individuals in a 'decentralized' optimizing setting. So far in this chapter, we have seen that modifying the production function can overcome the results of neo-classical growth. One assumption that can give a production function that is linear in overall capital is to assume that overall capital comprises different forms of capital (physical and human capital, for example). In this case and if society saves a constant proportion of its income toward accumulating each type of capital, a modified

Solow growth model can yield per capita income growth in the steady state.

The model by Rebelo (1991) shows that a model can display decreasing returns to scale in some sectors and constant returns to scale in others and still give rise to endogenous growth. In his model, as in the original AK model, policy variables not only have transitory effects, they also cause the growth rate of per capita income to change permanently. Finally, we have also considered an economic model where the production function is a standard CRTS Cobb–Douglas function but where labor was assumed to be a linear proportion of capital. We justified this on the grounds of knowledge spillovers. By making this assumption, the reduced-form production function still displayed decreasing private marginal returns while displaying constant social marginal returns to capital. By analyzing both the decentralized competitive equilibrium and the social planner's problem, we obtained endogenous growth; this growth however was higher in the case of the social planner's solution. This is because in a competitive equilibrium, individual firms take the positive externality (in this case, an average of overall capital in the economy) as a given. The social planner knows that the positive externality is underprovided and will make sure that consumers invest more than they would have under the competitive equilibrium case. The model shows that economies can display decreasing marginal returns at the private level and still produce endogenous growth. The model of course also has policy implications; in this case, it suggests that a government policy that encourages savings will produce higher rates of growth if society's production function displays constant marginal returns to its factor inputs.

Note that the reason that we have obtained endogenous growth in the models presented so far is that we got rid of the assumption of decreasing marginal returns to capital. In the AK and Rebelo (1991) models, we assumed it, while in the knowledge spillover model, we assumed that labor was proportional to capital. In the latter, the assumption is far from innocuous: as capital K grows, so does A at the same rate. This ensures a 'virtuous circle', whereby capital per worker will never slow down due to decreasing marginal returns. While we are not directly assuming exogenous technological progress, the assumption is a cousin, or 'once removed'; and while casual empiricism makes it very clear that technological progress is not exogenous (it does not fall from the sky; instead, it is the result of arduous work by many in the research and development sector), we have not presented any evidence either in favor or against the notion that knowledge is proportional to physical capital (does owning 1,000 computers make you any smarter or more knowledgeable than owning your laptop computer?).

As a final note, let us revert back to a simple modification of Solow's growth model and uncover further relationships between the production function, other aspects of the economy, and how they generate endogenous growth. Instead of assuming a CRTS technology as in Solow, let us consider the following production function:

$$Y_t = AK_t^{\beta} L_t^{\alpha}. \tag{5.108}$$

Here, no restriction is made on the coefficients α and β. As in Solow's model, we assume that the population saves a constant proportion of gross income for the future. The capital accumulation equation then takes the following familiar form:

$$\dot{K}_t = sAK_t^{\beta} L_t^{\alpha} - \delta K_t. \tag{5.109}$$

We also assume that population grows at a rate n:

$$\frac{\dot{L}_t}{L_t} = n. \tag{5.110}$$

Using the fact that $\frac{\dot{k}_t}{k_t} = \frac{\dot{K}_t}{K_t} - \frac{\dot{L}_t}{L_t}$, where $k_t = \frac{K_t}{L_t}$, the capital accumulation equation in per capita form can be rewritten in the following form:

$$\frac{\dot{k}_t}{k_t} = sAk_t^{\beta-1} L_t^{\alpha+\beta-1} - (\delta + n). \tag{5.111}$$

If there is a steady-state growth rate, then

$$\frac{\dot{k}_t}{k_t} = \gamma \tag{5.112}$$

must hold for some constant γ. From (5.111),

$$\gamma = sAk_t^{\beta-1}L_t^{\alpha+\beta-1} - (\delta + n). \tag{5.113}$$

Taking logs and derivatives, we get

$$\frac{\overset{\bullet}{\gamma}}{\gamma} = (\beta - 1)\frac{\dot{k}}{k} + (\alpha + \beta - 1)\frac{\dot{L}}{L}. \tag{5.114}$$

Recall that $\frac{\overset{\bullet}{L_t}}{L_t} = n$ and $\frac{\overset{\bullet}{k_t}}{k_t} = \gamma$. Replacing this in the above equation gives

$$\frac{\overset{\bullet}{\gamma}}{\gamma} = (\beta - 1)\gamma + (\alpha + \beta - 1)n. \tag{5.115}$$

Let's now consider the different cases and how they impact growth rates of per capita income. First, if $\alpha + \beta = 1$. where $\alpha \in (0, 1)$ and $\beta \in (0, 1)$. then there exists a constant γ such that the above equation is satisfied. If γ is constant, then $\frac{\overset{\bullet}{\gamma}}{\gamma} = 0$ and

$$\gamma = \frac{(1 - \alpha - \beta)\,n}{\beta - 1}. \tag{5.116}$$

Here, with $\alpha + \beta = 1$, we have that $\gamma = 0$. This is the case for example in the Solow growth model.

Next, continue to assume $\alpha + \beta = 1$ except where $\alpha = 0$ and $\beta = 1$. Note now that we cannot solve for γ as in the above formula. Instead, we go back to equation (5.115), where we get $\frac{\overset{\bullet}{\gamma}}{\gamma} = 0$. From equation (5.111), we have $\gamma = sA - (\delta + n)$. If the state of technology or the savings rate is sufficiently high, then $\gamma > 0$. This case corresponds to the AK model and is the exogenous savings rate version of Rebelo's (1991) model.

Now, assume instead that $\alpha + \beta < 1$, where $\alpha \in (0, 1)$ and $\beta \in (0, 1)$, that is, decreasing returns to scale. This yields a value of γ which is negative as long as $n > 0$; the expression for γ is given by equation (5.116). The economy converges to a steady state, where per capita income is zero. If $n = 0$, then $\gamma = 0$ in the steady state. Indeed, using equation (5.113), we have

$$sAk_t^{\beta-1}L_t^{\alpha+\beta-1} = \delta.$$

So, the steady-state value of capital is given by

$$(k^*)^{\beta-1} = \left(\frac{\delta}{sA\,(L^*)^{\alpha+\beta-1}}\right)^{\frac{1}{\beta-1}},$$

where L^* is the constant level of the population.

Assuming instead that $\alpha + \beta > 1$, if $\beta < 1$, then $\gamma > 0$ as long as $n > 0$. When $n = 0$, $\gamma = 0$. This seems a bit odd since increasing returns to scale with a stable population should yield more growth per person than a growing population. But the factors of production happen to be both capital *and* labor. If labor does not grow, then the production function is really just a function of capital, displaying decreasing marginal returns. Finally, if $\alpha + \beta > 1$ but with $\beta > 1$, then there is no constant γ that satisfies (5.115). Instead, we can say that $\gamma_t > 0$ for all time periods. In addition, an analysis of equation (5.115) reveals that $\frac{\dot{\gamma}}{\gamma} > 0$, so γ_t is positive and diverges to infinity as $t \to +\infty$.

Thus, one can generate endogenous growth of different kinds with this simple modified Solow model. In the case where $\alpha + \beta = \beta = 1$, we end up with a balanced growth path where per capita income grows at a steady rate from one period to the next. In the case where $\alpha + \beta > 1$, population growth matters if $\beta < 1$. A positive growth rate of population ensures that productive synergies with capital will yield higher levels of per capita income. Without this growth, existing capital cannot generate sufficient growth to increase per capita income from one period to the next: unlike the Solow growth model, where population growth always has a negative effect on the level of per capita income (though not on per capita income growth – this is after all an *exogenous* growth model!), a model displaying increasing returns to scale *requires* growth in population to generate per capita income growth if individual factors of production display decreasing marginal returns.

5.6 Conclusion

This chapter has focused on changing certain characteristics of the production function; we have seen that once one drops the assumption of decreasing marginal returns to production, one can generate growth endogenously. But much remains to be explored. In particular, we initially criticized exogenous growth models for not explaining the growth process of TFP. We know that TFP growth results in part from the process of research and development, which involves the discovery of ideas and the marketing of resulting products; these in turn involve large opportunity costs but also potentially substantial rewards that need to be modeled if they are to be understood. The class of models discussed in this chapter fall short of modeling these processes; the interested reader however can now consult books such as that by Aghion and Howitt (1997) that explore precisely this topic.

Chapter 6

Real Business Cycles

6.1 Introduction

Up until the time of Keynes, macroeconomic theory was thought to be an aggregation of classical microeconomic theory. With the publication of Keynes's *General Theory* and the onset of the Great Depression, macroeconomic theory came into its own in two main areas: growth and cycles. With respect to growth, the previous chapters demonstrate how the theory of macroeconomic growth progressed from Harrod–Domar to endogenous growth explanations. With respect to cycles, Keynes's *General Theory* was interpreted by Hicks and others and made operational or translated into the (in)famous IS-LM model augmented with the Phillips curve. This model was thought usable for short-run policy purposes and considered to be accurate enough to employ on a frequent basis. And it was so employed. Policymakers of the monetary and fiscal variety took the model as a tool they could use to fine-tune an economy; the Cowles commission approach of a system of equations describing an economy took hold in research and policy circles.

In the 1960s and 1970s, two major economic events took place, particularly in the U.S., that the IS-LM model could not account for satisfactorily. The first challenge was stagflation, a macroeconomic situation in which both inflation and unemployment were high, contrary to the inverse relation predicted by the Phillips curve. The second challenge was, in a sense, most damaging, namely, 'policy invariance', a situation in which policy stimuli, as dictated by the

IS-LM model, did not lead the economy to respond in a predictable manner.

Milton Friedman and others then devised the monetarist framework that relied more than the IS-LM model on classical economic assumptions. Unlike the IS-LM framework, the monetarist framework could account for certain data but had difficulty in explaining involuntary unemployment. Eventually, with the advent of rational expectations, the conventional IS-LM model started to die out, as Lucas (1972) demonstrated how, by combining the microeconomic rigor of a Samelson (1958) style OLG model with the rational expectations assumption of Muth (1961), the Phillips curve had shifted and why policy stimuli were ineffective.[1] However, the interest in a monetary-policy-induced cycle remained. Robert E. Lucas Jr. and others tried to model such cycles by introducing the possibility that there was an inability to distinguish between relative and absolute price changes or a cash in advance constraint could lead to cycles; ultimately, these explanations were not terribly satisfactory even though they heralded the advent of rational expectations in stochastic macroeconomic models.

Thus, to model cycles, Kydland and Prescott (1982) eschewed such explanations and went back to the basic neo-classical growth model and augmented it with stochastic shocks. They found that a vast majority of cyclical fluctuations could be accounted for using a stochastic Solow residual. This was the beginning of real business cycle theory in particular and modern business cycle methodology in general. Their assumptions and some predictions (such as no unemployment) could not be squared with data however, but rational expectations was still very much the paradigm. Eventually, neo-Keynesian models were developed that incorporated rational expectations but deviated from neo-classical economic assumptions. Given this temporal evolution of modern business cycle theory, we will study the neo-classical real business cycle model, followed by a typical neo-Keynesian business cycle model in the following chapter.

[1]The earlier chapters in Sargent (1987) provide a description of the conventional IS-LM model.

6.2 A Stochastic Ramsey Model

Can the optimal growth model, a 'workhorse' model in growth theory, do a good job in explaining business cycles as well? Kydland and Prescott (1982) answered this question in the affirmative. We first show that a stochastic technology shock that is not correlated (i.e. white noise) can cause output to be serially correlated (i.e. display fluctuations over time). We therefore demonstrate that such a shock can cause business cycles; this is the stochastic version of Ramsey's model. The intuition behind the serial correlation is straightforward: a positive shock to technology causes household to increase their investment in capital since it is more productive. As the shock dissipates, the increased capital continues to contribute to output – but this contribution diminishes over time as capital depreciates. During these time periods however, consumption can increase above its steady-state value.

Second, we show that a classical two-sector optimal growth model akin to the Cass–Koopmans framework can characterize the cyclical behavior of output, consumption, investment, and hours. This is the real business cycle model with indivisible labor. Just as in the stochastic version of the Ramsey model, output, consumption, and investment increase shortly following a technology shock. Because of capital accumulation, the increase in output is serially correlated. In this case, we also observe a (serially correlated) increase in the number of hours worked. This is because of substitutability between capital and labor. As more capital is used in the production of output, the marginal rate of technical substitution (MRTS) between capital and labor falls below the relative price of capital to labor. Firms will then increase the number of hours worked to ensure equality of relative prices and the MRTS. This process is also temporary since depreciation ensures that all variables return to their steady-state values.

6.2.1 Environment

The model is written in discrete time and features a representative household that acts as both a consumer and a producer and lives forever. We assume that there is perfect competition in all markets, so the household takes factor and output prices as given. We can solve the social planner's problem since we make all of the assumptions needed to make the first fundamental welfare theorem hold. The two methods of solving for equilibrium outcomes yield the same solution.

The household has period utility given by $u(C_t)$ and discounts the future at a rate of $\beta \in (0,1)$. The household can produce output Y_t using capital K_t according to the following production function: $Y_t = A_t K_t^{\alpha}$ ($\alpha \in (0,1)$), where A_t represents stochastic technological progress given by

$$\log A_{t+1} = \rho \log A_t + \varepsilon_{t+1}, \quad |\rho| < 1, \quad \varepsilon_t \sim WN(0, \sigma^2). \tag{6.1}$$

The household is also subject to a capital accumulation constraint,

$$K_{t+1} = I_t, \tag{6.2}$$

where we are assuming complete depreciation ($\delta = 1$). This is only an expositional assumption so that we may analytically derive a solution for the model. The output can only be used either for consumption or for investment, thus the aggregate resource constraint takes the form $Y_t = C_t + I_t$.

6.2.2 Optimization and the model representation

The social planner solves

$$\max_{\{C_t\}_{t=0}^{\infty}} \quad \Gamma = E_0 \sum_{t=0}^{\infty} \beta^t u(C_t), \quad \beta \in (0,1) \tag{6.3}$$

$$s.t. \quad Y_t = A_t K_t^{\alpha}, \quad \alpha \in (0,1), \tag{6.4}$$

$$Y_t = C_t + I_t, \tag{6.5}$$

$$K_{t+1} = I_t, \tag{6.6}$$

$$\log A_{t+1} = \rho \log A_t + \varepsilon_{t+1}, \quad |\rho| < 1, \quad \varepsilon_t \sim WN(0, \sigma^2). \tag{6.7}$$

Ignoring the exogenous stochastic process for A_t for now, the problem can be collapsed into

$$\max_{\{C_t\}_{t=0}^{\infty}} \quad \Gamma = E_0 \sum_{t=0}^{\infty} \beta^t u(C_t) \tag{6.8}$$

$$s.t. \quad K_{t+1} = A_t K_t^{\alpha} - C_t. \tag{6.9}$$

Substituting the constraint in $u(C_t)$ turns the problem into an unconstrained optimization albeit with the choice variable now being K_{t+1}:

$$\max_{\{K_{t+1}\}_{t=0}^{\infty}} \quad \Gamma = E_0 \sum_{t=0}^{\infty} \beta^t u(A_t K_t^{\alpha} - K_{t+1}), \tag{6.10}$$

with the associated first-order condition now being

$$E_0 \left\{ \beta^t u'(C_t)(-1) + \beta^{t+1} u'(C_{t+1}) \alpha A_{t+1} K_{t+1}^{\alpha-1} = 0 \right\}. \tag{6.11}$$

The problem is 'unconstrained' because we assume that $u'(0) = +\infty$, so the household will never choose K_{t+1} in a way that gives non-positive consumption. At this point, we need a functional form for utility; assuming $u(C_t) = \log C_t$, we obtain

$$E_0 \left\{ \frac{1}{C_t} = \frac{1}{C_{t+1}} \alpha \beta A_{t+1} K_{t+1}^{\alpha-1} \right\}, \tag{6.12}$$

and pulling in the expectations operator E_0 (while recalling the LIE) yields

$$\frac{1}{C_t} = \alpha \beta E_t \left\{ \frac{A_{t+1} K_{t+1}^{\alpha-1}}{C_{t+1}} \right\}. \tag{6.13}$$

This equation states that the household will keep on investing in capital until the (expected and discounted) marginal utility of con sumption next period, multiplied by the marginal product of capital, equals the marginal utility of consumption this period. Effectively, the agent is equating the marginal benefit from increasing consumption today to the discounted expected marginal benefit from doing so in period $t+1$.

We now have a system of nonlinear stochastic expectational difference equations that represents the stochastic equilibrium

$$\frac{1}{C_t} = \alpha \beta E_t \left\{ \frac{A_{t+1} K_{t+1}^{\alpha-1}}{C_{t+1}} \right\}, \tag{6.14}$$

$$Y_t = A_t K_t^{\alpha}, \tag{6.15}$$

$$Y_t = C_t + I_t, \tag{6.16}$$

$$K_{t+1} = I_t, \tag{6.17}$$

$$\log A_{t+1} = \rho \log A_t + \varepsilon_t. \tag{6.18}$$

In order to solve the system analytically, we collapse the system as follows. First, note that using the production function and the capital accumulation constraint, the first-order condition for optimal consumption can be written as

$$\frac{1}{C_t} = \alpha\beta E_t \left\{ \frac{Y_{t+1}/I_t}{C_{t+1}} \right\}. \tag{6.19}$$

Next, substituting the national income accounting constraint into the above equation yields

$$\frac{I_t}{C_t} = \alpha\beta E_t \left\{ \frac{C_{t+1} + I_{t+1}}{C_{t+1}} \right\}, \tag{6.20}$$

where we have also multiplied both sides by I_t. The equation now reads as

$$\frac{I_t}{C_t} = \alpha\beta E_t \left\{ 1 + \frac{I_{t+1}}{C_{t+1}} \right\} = \alpha\beta + \alpha\beta E_t \frac{I_{t+1}}{C_{t+1}} \tag{6.21}$$

and is a linear expectational difference of the following variety:

$$x_t = \xi + \xi E_t x_{t+1}, \quad \xi = \alpha\beta. \tag{6.22}$$

The solution of this equation in x_t, using the method of recursive substitution and assuming that $x_t = \frac{I_{t+1}}{C_{t+1}}$ is bounded (note that $|\alpha\beta| < 1$), is given by

$$x_t = \frac{\xi}{1 - \xi}. \tag{6.23}$$

Thus, substituting in $x_t = \frac{I_{t+1}}{C_{t+1}}$ yields the solution

$$\frac{I_{t+1}}{C_{t+1}} = \frac{\alpha\beta}{1 - \alpha\beta}. \tag{6.24}$$

Now, using the national income accounting identity again yields the consumption rule of our stochastic Ramsey model,

$$C_t = (1 - \alpha\beta) Y_t, \tag{6.25}$$

and we further note that our capital accumulation equation with complete depreciation implies that

$$I_t = K_{t+1} = \alpha\beta Y_t. \tag{6.26}$$

Thus, in order to show that output does indeed display fluctuations, we use the remaining equation, the production function, to show that

$$Y_t = A_t K_t^{\alpha} \tag{6.27}$$

$$\rightarrow Y_t = A_t(\alpha\beta Y_{t-1})^{\alpha}. \tag{6.28}$$

Now, apply logarithms to both sides of the above equation to obtain

$$\log Y_t = \log A_t + \alpha \log(\alpha\beta Y_{t-1}) \tag{6.29}$$

$$= \log A_t + \alpha(\log \alpha\beta + \log Y_{t-1}) \tag{6.30}$$

$$\rightarrow \log Y_t = \alpha \log \alpha\beta + \alpha \log Y_{t-1} + \log A_t. \tag{6.31}$$

Clearly, since $\log A_{t+1} = \rho \log A_t + \varepsilon_{t+1}$, we have now shown that equilibrium output follows a CSSP; that is, there are 'wiggles' (i.e. business cycles) in the output, possible due to exogenous shocks to technology (ε_t). Note that since Y_t is a function of Y_{t-1}, any shock (in the form of a change in A_t) will 'propagate' both to the current and future periods; so business cycles in this economy do not reflect contemporaneous, one-for-one, shocks to technology. However, in the absence of technology shocks, the economy will converge to a steady state and remain there. There are no relationships in this model that cause it to display fluctuations endogenously – business cycles are entirely driven by exogenous shocks to technology.

6.3 A Real Business Cycle Model with Indivisible Labor

Our exposition here is taken from Ireland (2004). The model is a now-standard version of the seminal contribution by Kydland and Prescott (1982). Dr. Peter Ireland has done a huge service to the field by placing his Matlab code and model derivations on his web-page. By doing so, he has demonstrated that he is one of the best macroeconomists to learn from, provided the reader is willing to work through his influential papers along with their attendant model derivations and code.

6.3.1 Environment

Utility for the representative agent is given by

$$E_0 \sum_{t=0}^{\infty} \beta^t [\log C_t - \gamma H_t], \tag{6.32}$$

where C_t is consumption, H_t is hours worked, $\beta \in (0,1)$ is the discount factor, and $\gamma > 0$ is the parameter that governs the linearity of utility in hours worked. Since instantaneous utility is logarithmic, the intertemporal marginal rate of substitution between present and future consumption is unitary. Hansen (1985) and Rogerson (1988) show that an appropriate modeling of an economy populated by many identical individuals, each of whom either works full time or remains unemployed, is to assume that the marginal disutility of work is linear in the number of hours worked; one need only deduct γH_t from the instantaneous utility specification.

Production is given by

$$Y_t = A_t K_t^{\theta} (\eta^t H_t)^{1-\theta}, \tag{6.33}$$

where Y_t is output, A_t is neutral technological progress, K_t is capital, $\eta > 1$ is the gross rate of labor augmenting technological progress, and $\theta \in (0,1)$ is the elasticity of output with respect to capital. This is a constant returns to scale production function which incorporates both Hicks-neutral and labor-augmenting technological progress. The neutral technological progress A_t is assumed to follow

$$A_t = A^{(1-\rho)} A_{t-1}^{\rho} \exp(\varepsilon_t) \tag{6.34}$$

$$A > 0, \quad |\rho| < 1, \quad \varepsilon_t \sim N(0, \sigma^2) \tag{6.35}$$

$$\to \log A_t = (1-\rho)\log A + \rho \log A_{t-1} + \varepsilon_t \tag{6.36}$$

Capital accumulation is given by

$$K_{t+1} = (1-\delta)K_t + I_t, \quad \delta \in (0,1), \tag{6.37}$$

and the national income accounting constraint is given by

$$Y_t = C_t + I_t. \tag{6.38}$$

The endogenous variables are therefore

$$\{Y_t \ C_t \ I_t \ H_t \ K_t \ A_t\}, \tag{6.39}$$

where the predetermined variables are K_t and A_t and the rest are non-predetermined. The only exogenous variable is ε_t, and the deep or structural parameters are given by

$$\mu = [\beta\ \gamma\ \eta\ \theta\ A\ \delta\ \rho\ \sigma]'. \tag{6.40}$$

6.3.2 Optimization and the nonlinear representation

Since this is a representative agent perfectly competitive framework, the split consumer-producer/social planner solves

$$\max_{\{Y_t,C_t,I_t,H_t,K_{t+1}\}_{t=0}^{\infty}} \quad E_0\sum_{t=0}^{\infty}\beta^t\left[\log C_t - \gamma H_t\right] \tag{6.41}$$

$$s.t. \quad Y_t = A_t K_t^{\theta}(\eta^t H_t)^{1-\theta}, \tag{6.42}$$

$$K_{t+1} = (1-\delta)K_t + I_t, \tag{6.43}$$

$$Y_t = C_t + I_t. \tag{6.44}$$

The constraints can be collapsed into

$$K_{t+1} = (1-\delta)K_t + A_t K_t^{\theta}(\eta^t H_t)^{1-\theta} - C_t. \tag{6.45}$$

The following Lagrangian is therefore maximized with respect to C_t, H_t, and K_{t+1}:

$$\begin{aligned}\mathcal{L} = E_0\sum_{t=0}^{\infty}&\{\beta^t\left[\log C_t - \gamma H_t\right]\\ &+ \beta^t\lambda_t\left[(1-\delta)K_t + A_t K_t^{\theta}(\eta^t H_t)^{1-\theta} - C_t - K_{t+1}\right]\Big\}.\end{aligned} \tag{6.46}$$

The FONC are

$$\frac{\beta^t}{C_t} - \beta^t\lambda_t = 0 \tag{6.47}$$

$$-\beta^t\gamma + \beta^t\lambda_t\left[A_t K_t^{\theta}\frac{(1-\theta)(\eta^t H_t)^{1-\theta}}{H_t}\right] = 0 \tag{6.48}$$

$$-\beta^t\lambda_t + E_t\beta^{t+1}\lambda_{t+1}\left[(1-\delta) + A_{t+1}\theta K_{t+1}^{\theta-1}(\eta^{t+1}H_{t+1})^{1-\theta}\right] = 0. \tag{6.49}$$

From equation (6.47), we see that λ_t should be interpreted as the marginal utility of consumption. Using the specification of the production function (that is, $Y_t = A_t K_t^{\theta}(\eta^t H_t)^{1-\theta}$), these FONC can be collapsed into

$$\gamma C_t H_t = (1-\theta)Y_t \tag{6.50}$$

$$\frac{1}{C_t} = \beta E_t\left\{\left(\frac{1}{C_{t+1}}\right)\left[\theta\frac{Y_{t+1}}{K_{t+1}}\right]+1-\delta\right\}. \tag{6.51}$$

The full nonlinear system of equations that describes this model is therefore

$$Y_t = A_t K_t^{\theta}(\eta^t H_t)^{1-\theta} \tag{6.52}$$

$$\log A_t = (1-\rho)\log A + \rho\log A_{t-1} + \varepsilon_t, \tag{6.53}$$

$$Y_t = C_t + I_t, \tag{6.54}$$

$$K_{t+1} = (1-\delta)K_t + I_t, \tag{6.55}$$

$$\gamma C_t H_t = (1-\theta)Y_t, \tag{6.56}$$

$$\frac{1}{C_t} = \beta E_t\left\{\left(\frac{1}{C_{t+1}}\right)\left[\theta\frac{Y_{t+1}}{K_{t+1}}+1-\delta\right]\right\}. \tag{6.57}$$

In addition to the equation describing the intertemporal consumption trade-off equation (6.57), we have equation (6.56) which pins down the number of hours worked in period t. It can be rewritten as $\gamma C_t = (1-\theta)\frac{Y_t}{H_t}$, or $\frac{\gamma}{\lambda_t} = (1-\theta)\frac{Y_t}{H_t}$. This equates the marginal rate of substitution of hours worked and consumption to the marginal product of labor. By comparison, equation (6.57) can be rewritten in a similar way. Ignoring uncertainty and setting depreciation equal to unity, it is equivalent to $\frac{\lambda_t}{\lambda_{t+1}} = \beta\theta\frac{Y_{t+1}}{K_{t+1}}$. This equates the marginal rate of substitution of present and future consumption to the discounted marginal product of capital.

6.3.3 The stationary form of the model

Note that the source of deterministic growth in this model is from the Hicks neutral portion of the production function (η^t). This induces a trend that we need to remove to make the model 'stationary' (i.e. variables fluctuating around a trend). Let

$$y_t = \frac{Y_t}{\eta^t}, \quad c_t = \frac{C_t}{\eta^t}, \quad i_t = \frac{I_t}{\eta^t}, \quad k_t = \frac{K_t}{\eta^t}, \tag{6.58}$$

$$h_t = H_t, \quad a_t = A_t, \tag{6.59}$$

$$\eta k_{t+1} = \eta \frac{K_{t+1}}{\eta^{t+1}} = \frac{K_{t+1}}{\eta^t}, \tag{6.60}$$

and employ these definitions throughout the nonlinear model. This is often called normalizing the model with respect to the deterministic growth factor. The system, when made stationary through this normalization, yields the new system

$$y_t = a_t k_t^\theta h_t^{1-\theta} \tag{6.61}$$

$$\log a_t = (1-\rho)\log A + \rho \log a_{t-1} + \varepsilon_t, \tag{6.62}$$

$$y_t = c_t + i_t, \tag{6.63}$$

$$\eta k_{t+1} = (1-\delta)k_t + i_t, \tag{6.64}$$

$$\gamma c_t h_t = (1-\theta)y_t, \tag{6.65}$$

$$\frac{\eta}{c_t} = \beta E_t\left\{\left(\frac{1}{c_{t+1}}\right)\left[\theta\frac{y_{t+1}}{k_{t+1}} + 1 - \delta\right]\right\}. \tag{6.66}$$

The next steps are to compute the non-stochastic steady states, linearize around them, and solve the resulting system under rational expectations. Then, the model will also be in a form such that it can be evaluated for empirical validity using any number of structural econometric methods (see DeJong and Dave (2011)).

6.3.4 The non-stochastic steady state

In order to linearize the system around non-stochastic steady states, we need to analytically compute them. Non-stochastic steady states occur when random stochastic processes are set to zero and the resulting system solved for steady state values. Here, we know that if $\varepsilon_t = 0$ for all t, then we are looking for the following steady-state values: y, c, i, h, k, and a.

For (6.62), take the exponential of both sides to obtain

$$\exp[\log a] = \exp[(1-\rho)\log A + \rho \log a], \tag{6.67}$$

$$\rightarrow a = A^{1-\rho}a^\rho, \tag{6.68}$$

$$\rightarrow a^{1-\rho} = A^{1-\rho}, \tag{6.69}$$

$$\rightarrow a = A. \tag{6.70}$$

Next, suppose we know the steady-state value of y_t, which we have denoted as y. Then, use (6.66) to solve for k as follows:

$$\frac{\eta}{c} = \beta\left[\frac{1}{c}\frac{\theta y}{k} + \frac{1}{c}(1-\delta)\right], \tag{6.71}$$

$$\frac{\eta}{\beta} = \frac{\theta y}{k} + 1 - \delta, \tag{6.72}$$

$$k = \left(\frac{\theta}{\frac{\eta}{\beta} - 1 + \delta}\right) y. \tag{6.73}$$

Now, use (6.64) and (6.73) to solve for i as follows:

$$\eta k = (1-\delta)k + i, \tag{6.74}$$

$$i = \eta\left(\frac{\theta}{\frac{\eta}{\beta} - 1 + \delta}\right) y - (1-\delta)\left(\frac{\theta}{\frac{\eta}{\beta} - 1 + \delta}\right) y, \tag{6.75}$$

$$= \left(\frac{\theta(\eta - 1 + \delta)}{\frac{\eta}{\beta} - 1 + \delta}\right) y, \tag{6.76}$$

and use the solution for i in (6.76) along with (6.63) to get c

$$c = \left[1 - \left(\frac{\theta(\eta - 1 + \delta)}{\frac{\eta}{\beta} - 1 + \delta}\right)\right] y. \tag{6.77}$$

For computing h, use (6.65) along with the expression for c to get

$$h = \left(\frac{1-\theta}{\gamma}\right)\left[1 - \left(\frac{\theta(\eta - 1 + \delta)}{\frac{\eta}{\beta} - 1 + \delta}\right)\right]^{-1}. \tag{6.78}$$

Finally, to compute y, use (6.73) and (6.78) in (6.61) to get

$$y = a^{\frac{1}{1-\theta}}\left(\frac{\theta}{\frac{\eta}{\beta} - 1 + \delta}\right)^{\frac{\theta}{1-\theta}}\left(\frac{1-\theta}{\gamma}\right)\left[1 - \left(\frac{\theta(\eta - 1 + \delta)}{\frac{\eta}{\beta} - 1 + \delta}\right)\right]^{-1}. \tag{6.79}$$

Note that none of the steady-state values depend on ρ or σ^2, which are the stochastic parameters – this should be expected since we are looking for a non-stochastic steady state.

6.3.5 Linearization

The model can be log-linearized around the steady state by using a TSA_1 on each equation in the nonlinear system. Here, we only do so for one equation; the rest are left to readers as an exercise to practice. Consider the stochastic Euler equation given in (6.66):

$$\frac{\eta}{c_t} = \beta E_t \left\{ \left(\frac{1}{c_{t+1}} \right) \left[\theta \frac{y_{t+1}}{k_{t+1}} + 1 - \delta \right] \right\}. \tag{6.80}$$

Rewrite it as

$$\frac{\eta}{c \exp(\widehat{c}_t)} = \beta E_t \left\{ \left(\frac{1}{c \exp(\widehat{c}_{t+1})} \right) \left[\begin{matrix} \theta \left(\dfrac{y \exp(\widehat{y}_{t+1})}{k \exp(\widehat{k}_{t+1})} \right) \\ +1 - \delta \end{matrix} \right] \right\} \tag{6.81}$$

$$\frac{\eta}{c} \exp(-\widehat{c}_t) = \beta E_t \left\{ \frac{1}{c} \exp(-\widehat{c}_{t+1}) \left[\begin{matrix} \theta \left(\frac{y}{k} \exp(\widehat{y}_{t+1} - \widehat{k}_{t+1}) \right) \\ +1 - \delta \end{matrix} \right] \right\}. \tag{6.82}$$

Here, 'hats' denote detrended logarithmic deviations from steady state, e.g. for $x_t = \frac{X_t}{\eta^t}$, $\widehat{x}_t = \log(x_t) - \log(x)$. where x is the non-stochastic steady-state value of x_t. Then, take the TSA_1 around the previously computed steady states:

$$\frac{\eta}{c}(1 - \widehat{c}_t) = \beta E_t \left\{ \frac{1}{c}(1 - \widehat{c}_{t+1}) \left[\theta \left(\frac{y}{k}(1 + \widehat{y}_{t+1} - \widehat{k}_{t+1}) \right) + 1 - \delta \right] \right\}. \tag{6.83}$$

We know that $\frac{y}{k} = \left(\frac{\frac{\eta}{\beta} - 1 + \delta}{\theta} \right)$ from the steady states, so rewrite (6.83) as

$$\begin{aligned} \eta(1 - \widehat{c}_t) = \beta E_t &\left\{ (1 - \widehat{c}_{t+1}) \left[\frac{\eta}{\beta} + \left(\frac{\eta}{\beta} - 1 + \delta \right) \right. \right. \\ &\times \left. \left. \left(\widehat{y}_{t+1} - \widehat{k}_{t+1} \right) \right] \right\} \end{aligned} \tag{6.84}$$

$$\vdots$$

$$\frac{\eta}{\beta} \widehat{c}_t = \frac{\eta}{\beta} E_t \widehat{c}_{t+1} + \left(\frac{\eta}{\beta} - 1 + \delta \right) (E_t \widehat{y}_{t+1} - \widehat{k}_{t+1}). \tag{6.85}$$

The final linearized system is then given by the following. The production $y_t = a_t k_t^\theta h_t^{1-\theta}$ becomes

$$\widehat{y}_t = \widehat{a}_t + \theta\widehat{k}_t + (1-\theta)\widehat{h}_t, \tag{6.86}$$

whereas $\log a_t = (1-\rho)\log A + \rho \log a_{t-1} + \varepsilon_t$ becomes

$$\widehat{a}_t = \rho\widehat{a}_{t-1} + \varepsilon_t, \quad \text{where } d\varepsilon_t \approx \log\left(\frac{\exp(\varepsilon_t)}{\exp(\varepsilon)}\right) = \varepsilon_t - \varepsilon = \varepsilon_t. \tag{6.87}$$

National income accounting ($y_t = c_t + i_t$) becomes

$$\begin{aligned}\left(\frac{\eta}{\beta} - 1 + \delta\right)\widehat{y}_t = &\left[\left(\frac{\eta}{\beta} - 1 + \delta\right) - \theta(\eta - 1 + \delta)\right]\widehat{c}_t \\ &+ \theta(\eta - 1 + \delta)\widehat{i}_t,\end{aligned} \tag{6.88}$$

while capital accumulation $\eta k_{t+1} = (1-\delta)k_t + i_t$ becomes

$$\eta\widehat{k}_{t+1} = (1-\delta)\widehat{k}_t + (\eta - 1 + \delta)\widehat{i}_t, \tag{6.89}$$

and the optimality condition determining hours worked ($\gamma c_t h_t = (1-\theta)y_t$) becomes

$$\widehat{y}_t = \widehat{c}_t + \widehat{h}_t. \tag{6.90}$$

The Euler equation $\frac{\eta}{c_t} = \beta E_t\{(\frac{1}{c_{t+1}})[\theta\frac{y_{t+1}}{k_{t+1}} + 1 - \delta]\}$ becomes

$$\frac{-\eta}{\beta}\widehat{c}_t = \frac{-\eta}{\beta}E_t\widehat{c}_{t+1} + \left(\frac{\eta}{\beta} - 1 + \delta\right)E_t\widehat{y}_{t+1} - \left(\frac{\eta}{\beta} - 1 + \delta\right)\widehat{k}_{t+1}. \tag{6.91}$$

So, we have six linear expectational difference equations for the six variables ($\widehat{y}_t, \widehat{c}_t, \widehat{i}_t, \widehat{h}_t, \widehat{k}_t$, and $\widehat{a}_t$) with eight parameters: $(\beta, \gamma, \eta, \theta, A, \delta, \rho, \sigma)$.

6.3.6 Model solution under rational expectations

Rewrite the linearized model as

$$\widehat{y}_t - \widehat{a}_t - \theta\widehat{k}_t - (1-\theta)\widehat{h}_t = 0, \tag{6.92}$$

$$\kappa\widehat{y}_t - [\kappa - \theta\lambda]\,\widehat{c}_t - \theta\lambda\widehat{i}_t = 0, \tag{6.93}$$

$$\frac{\eta}{\beta}\widehat{c}_t - \frac{\eta}{\beta}E_t\widehat{c}_{t+1} + \kappa E_t\widehat{y}_{t+1} - \kappa\widehat{k}_{t+1} = 0, \tag{6.94}$$

$$\eta\widehat{k}_{t+1} - (1-\delta)\widehat{k}_t - \lambda\widehat{i}_t = 0, \tag{6.95}$$

$$\widehat{c}_t + \widehat{h}_t - \widehat{y}_t = 0, \tag{6.96}$$

$$\widehat{a}_t - \rho\widehat{a}_{t-1} = \varepsilon_t, \tag{6.97}$$

$$\kappa = \frac{\eta}{\beta} - 1 + \delta, \tag{6.98}$$

$$\lambda = \eta - 1 + \delta. \tag{6.99}$$

Next, define

$$x_t = [\widehat{y}_t \quad \widehat{c}_t \quad \widehat{i}_t \quad \widehat{h}_t \quad \widehat{k}_t \quad \widehat{a}_t]', \tag{6.100}$$

$$A = \begin{bmatrix} 1 & 0 & 0 & -(1-\theta) & -\theta & -1 \\ \kappa & -[\kappa-\theta\lambda] & -\theta\lambda & 0 & 0 & 0 \\ \kappa & \frac{-\eta}{\beta} & 0 & 0 & -\kappa & 0 \\ 0 & 0 & 0 & 0 & \eta & 0 \\ -1 & 1 & 0 & 1 & 0 & 0 \\ 0 & 0 & 0 & 0 & 0 & 1 \end{bmatrix}, \tag{6.101}$$

and

$$B = \begin{bmatrix} 0 & 0 & 0 & 0 & 0 & 0 \\ 0 & 0 & 0 & 0 & 0 & 0 \\ 0 & \frac{-\eta}{\beta} & 0 & 0 & 0 & 0 \\ 0 & 0 & \lambda & 0 & 1-\delta & 0 \\ 0 & 0 & 0 & 0 & 0 & 0 \\ 0 & 0 & 0 & 0 & 0 & \rho \end{bmatrix} \tag{6.102}$$

$$C = \begin{bmatrix} 0 \\ 0 \\ 1 \\ 0 \\ 0 \\ 0 \end{bmatrix}, \quad D = \begin{bmatrix} 0 \\ 0 \\ 0 \\ 0 \\ 0 \\ 1 \end{bmatrix}. \tag{6.103}$$

Next, let υ_t be the rational expectations error. Then, the model can be written as

$$A(\mu)x_{t+1} = B(\mu)x_t + C(\mu)\upsilon_{t+1} + D(\mu)\varepsilon_{t+1}, \tag{6.104}$$

where μ contains all of the structural parameters of the model. With the model written in this manner, it can be solved using the methods given by Sims (2001), which leads to a model representation of the form

$$x_{t+1} = F(\mu)x_t + e_{t+1}, \quad e_t = G(\mu)\varepsilon_t, \quad E(e_t e_t') = Q(\mu). \tag{6.105}$$

Given numeric values for the parameter vector μ, equation (6.105) is a $VAR(1)$ representation, which means we can get impulse responses, that is, the response of $\widehat{y}_t$, $\widehat{c}_t$, $\widehat{i}_t$, $\widehat{h}_t$, and $\widehat{k}_t$ to a time t shock of ε_t. The remaining question is: how do we get numbers for μ? DeJong and Dave (2011) provide a description of several econometric methods to obtain numerical values for parameters; we now discuss the method of calibration given its central place in the modern theory of business cycles.

6.3.7 Calibration

Kydland and Prescott (1996) outline a five-step procedure to calibrate a model. The first step is to decide whether the purpose of the simulation is (a) to assess theoretical implications of changes in policy (e.g. potential welfare gains associated with a given tax reform) or (b) to assess the ability of a model to mimic features of the actual economy. The second step is to use 'well-tested theory' to address the question. However, a caveat applies: every model is, at best, approximate and flawed on some dimensions. The point is that the chosen model must be suitable to the empirical question at hand. Kydland and Prescott (1996) state that 'In the case of neoclassical growth theory [...] it fails spectacularly when used to address economic development issues. [...] This does not preclude its usefulness in evaluating tax policies and in business cycle research'. The third step is to construct the model; the more detailed and complex the model, the harder it is to analyze. So, the model being analyzed should be sufficiently rich to address the research question but shouldn't include unnecessary complexities. A targeted model has an additional advantage: it helps in highlighting the important mechanisms at work in generating a particular result.

The fourth step is the calibration of model parameters. The idea is to employ data to obtain value for model parameters so that the model has a chance of mimicking the real world along clear dimensions. This process places no restriction on specific data used to specify parameter values and certain data have come to be applied rather extensively in a wide range of applications: long-run averages such as the share of output paid to labor and the fraction of available hours worked per household. In addition, empirical results obtained in micro studies conducted at the individual or household level are often employed as well. The fifth step is to run the simulation given the calibrated parameter values $\overline{\mu}$. Just how this is done depends upon the question at hand, but at a minimum this involves the solution of the model under rational expectations. The solution is of course written as

$$x_{t+1} = F(\overline{\mu})x_t + G(\overline{\mu})\varepsilon_{t+1}, \tag{6.106}$$

which is the 'state' equation describing the model dynamics. With the model in this form, we can conduct any of the empirical exercises discussed, in broad terms, by Hamilton (1994).

The model solution also yields a 'state-space representation' of the form

$$x_{t+1} = F(\mu)x_t + G(\mu)\varepsilon_{t+1} = F(\mu)x_t + e_{t+1}, \tag{6.107}$$

$$X_t = H(\mu)'x_t, \tag{6.108}$$

$$E(e_t e_t') = G(\mu)E\left(\varepsilon_t \varepsilon_t'\right)G(\mu)' \equiv Q(\mu). \tag{6.109}$$

Recall that x_t represents the full set of variables included in the model, represented as deviations from steady-state values, and μ contains the structural parameters of the model. The vector X_t represents the collection of associated observable variables, that is, those elements of the vector x_t for which one can obtain data. For example, in the RBC model outlined above, $x_t = [\widehat{y}_t \; \widehat{c}_t \; \widehat{i}_t \; \widehat{h}_t \; \widehat{k}_t \; \widehat{a}_t]'$, but typically we can only obtain the variables $X_t = [\widehat{y}_t \; \widehat{c}_t \; \widehat{i}_t \; \widehat{h}_t]'$ from NIPA data. The matrix $H(\mu)$ then is a selection matrix that picks the observed variables out of the state vector (x_t). Once a state-space representation is obtained, we can estimate the value of μ directly using NIPA data. This is particularly useful since calibrated values of μ rarely if ever come with any uncertainty (i.e. standard errors) associated with them. The particular topic of how to estimate μ using NIPA data is the topic dealt by DeJong and Dave (2011), who cover the entire range of techniques available to researchers.

6.3.8 Model evaluation

For the RBC model at hand, suppose the parameter values are

$$\begin{aligned} \beta &= \overline{\beta} = 0.99, \\ \gamma &= \overline{\gamma} = 0.0045, \\ \eta &= \overline{\eta} = 1.0042, \\ \theta &= \overline{\theta} = 0.20, \\ A &= \overline{A} = 6, \\ \delta &= \overline{\delta} = 0.0250, \\ \rho &= \overline{\rho} = 0.95, \\ \sigma^2 &= \overline{\sigma}^2 = 0.007. \end{aligned} \tag{6.110}$$

Then, the model after solving under rational expectations is

$$x_{t+1} = F(\overline{\mu})x_t + G(\overline{\mu})\varepsilon_{t+1}. \tag{6.111}$$

For impulse responses, start from the non-stochastic steady state in which $\varepsilon_t = 0$ and assume that at time t, there is a temporary shock to ε_t. That is, ε increases by σ in time t and then returns to 0 thereafter. Thus, at time t,

$$x_t = G\sigma, \tag{6.112}$$

and in period $t+1$ after the shock,

$$x_{t+1} = Fx_t, \tag{6.113}$$

and so on for $t+2, \ldots, t+T$. The result is provided in Figures 6.1 and 6.2 (for different parameter values).

The impulse responses clearly indicate that the intuition of Kydland and Prescott (1982) that shocks to total factor productivity can deliver business cycles is valid since output, consumption,

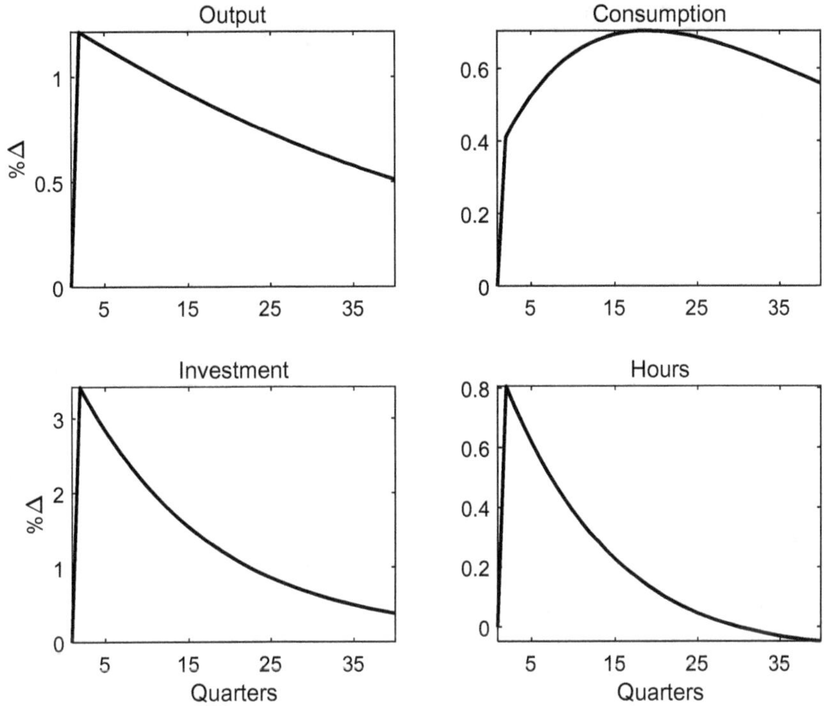

Figure 6.1. RBC model impulse responses I.

investment, and hours worked all increase temporarily in response to such a shock, as the theory would predict. Note that this simple business cycle model captures salient features of the U.S. economy. Consumption is smoother than output, and output is smoother than investment. This economic model provides a simple rationale for this: since the technology shock is temporary and provides the greatest benefit now, the household decides (rationally) to invest as much as possible and generate higher (technology-driven) output. The resulting increase in output is then used to increase consumption (at a later date) along the transitional dynamics. As the shock dissipates, consumption and other variables return to their steady states. Because of factor substitutability, hours worked also increase temporarily but since the marginal disutility of hours is constant (as opposed to increasing), the rise and fall in hours worked is more abrupt: the household is minimizing a discounted sum of disutility from labor – how this disutility is spread out over time does not

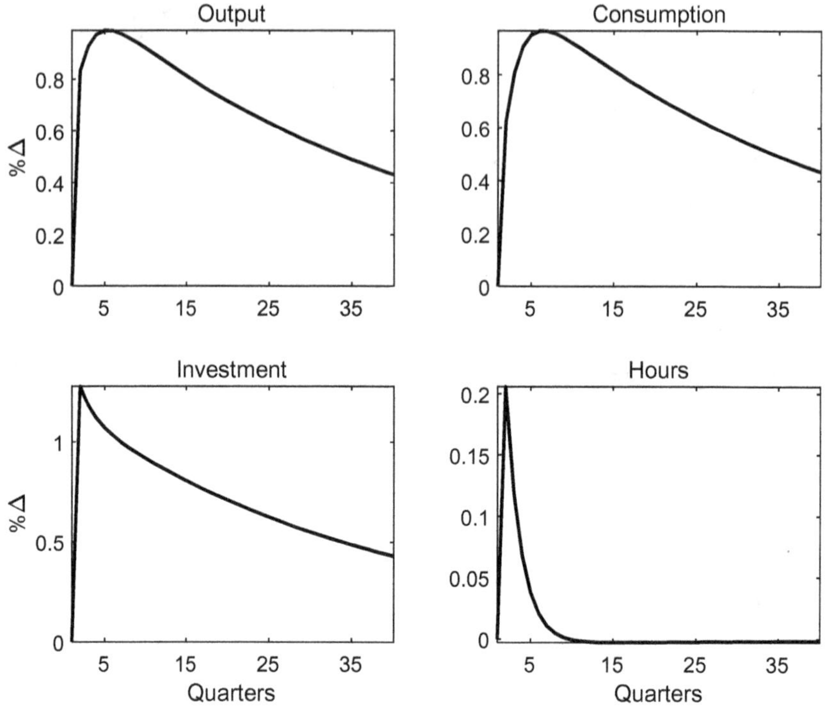

Figure 6.2. RBC model impulse responses II.

matter. In this case, the household is willing to supply labor soon after the shock takes place to take full advantage of the (temporary) increase in productivity.

6.4 Conclusion

In this chapter, we take growth models and adapt them to explain fluctuations in the short run. First, a modified Ramsey model is considered. We show that technology shocks can be used to generate business cycles in the form of persistent fluctuations in output, consumption, and investment. A one-time shock to technology affects output directly in one period. The household knows that the shock is temporary and converts the 'additional' output into capital. By doing this, it ensures that the benefits of a one-time technology shock persist in future periods. The reason that a one-time shock to technology generates persistence in output and other variables is because of increased capital accumulation. As depreciation takes hold, all variables revert back to their steady states.

We also consider a modified version of the Cass–Koopmans growth model – specifically we assume that the marginal disutility of labor is constant. This is not necessary for the qualitative features of the dynamics but is done to ensure that the model fits certain facts from the labor market. We show how to linearize the model and generate impulse response functions – graphical representations of how variables react over time to a one-time shock in technology.

While RBC models are a useful methodological advance over the Keynesian IS-LM model, they explain all fluctuations in the economy through the prism of technology shocks – a major drawback since it is unclear how various potential causes for business cycles would necessarily translate into random fluctuations in total factor productivity. Much like the Solow growth model, they provide some insights into understanding business cycles but do not explain ultimately how technology shocks are generated in the economy. In addition, the classical dichotomy obviates the need to model the monetary side of the economy, and so money-induced cycles are not present; yet data do suggest nominal-real relationships yet to be modeled.

Chapter 7

New Keynesian Models

7.1 Introduction

The economic environment of the real business cycle (RBC) model introduces the concept of a rational expectations equilibrium in a macroeconomic setting. In addition, the RBC model allows for business cycles emanating from a TFP shock. While the model – despite its simplicity – is surprisingly good at capturing important stylized facts of business cycles, it fails in other important ways. In particular, it has proved unable to account satisfactorily for movements in hours worked at the quarterly frequency. Additionally, because all of the conditions of a Pareto optimum are met (perfect competition, etc.), there is no room for government intervention – at least not if the objective is to generate gains in efficiency. In reality, while the assumption of perfect competition may well be accurate for a long-run modeling exercise, in the short run it appears to be less defensible an assumption given that industry-wide markups over marginal costs exhibit particular patterns that are hard to reconcile with the assumption of perfect competition. Thus, there are potential gains in efficiency if government intervention were to mitigate the negative effects of imperfect competition. Additionally, the classical dichotomy of an RBC model ensures that nominal variables only act as 'window-dressing'. Because nominal variables do not influence real outcomes, they need not be included in the economic model.

In reality of course, nominal variables such as inflation and money supply may influence (and are potentially influenced by) real variables in complicated ways. Keynes recognized this and developed a number of ideas that were summarized by Hicks in the IS-LM model. While the model was static and lacked micro-foundations, it captured salient features of actual economies and contained important and useful economic intuition about the linkages between various 'demand-side' aspects of the economy. In this chapter, we focus on bringing Keynesian features into modern macroeconomic theory. First, we cover a model by Lucas (1972), who shows that only 'unexpected' shocks to money supply can have real effects on the economy. In contrast, expected policy announcements will result in little to no changes in output (and employment). The importance of this model is that it nicely illustrates the so-called 'Lucas Critique of Econometric Policy Evaluation', namely that the government (and in this case, the monetary authority) cannot exploit statistical relationships in the data because these relationships are themselves a function of policy. Presumably, one should not read into this Lucas model that the monetary authority should conduct policy in a way that is 'unexpected' for two reasons. First, because a policy that has real effects (for example, reducing unemployment) has to be unexpected, the real effects of such a policy are necessarily limited in time, and second, the model does not model any negative effects of unexpected (or unannounced) policy – perhaps the additional uncertainty is bad for the investment climate. As a result, one might conclude that the best monetary policy is to 'do no harm': by following an expected and anticipated policy, the monetary authority ensures that money fulfills its various roles (store of value, etc.) but keeps 'nominal disturbances' to a minimum.

Second, we cover a more standard neo-Keynesian model due to Ireland (2003). In this model, we allow for capital accumulation. We saw that this was an important element in generating business cycles in the RBC model. In addition, we introduce real and nominal rigidities. This in turn ensures that there is room for government intervention to ensure that economic outcomes can be improved upon by intervention that mitigates the negative effects of the rigidities (frictions). One way to allow for government intervention is fiscal policy. In his model, Ireland considers the role of monetary policy instead. Since one cannot introduce fiat money unless households consider it to be valuable, the model allows for this by assuming that households get utility out of holding real money balances. In reality, of course, individuals (typically) do not derive pleasure out of holding money;

instead, the assumption should be viewed as a modeling shortcut: we know that people use money to transact, and by including it in the utility function, we ensure that money is held by households. The way that it is introduced is broadly in agreement with a 'transactions demand' for money; greater output (and consumption) imply greater demand for money, *ceteris paribus*. We then go on to solve the model and see how well it performs in explaining additional features of the business cycle.

7.2 Money and Output in Competitive Equilibrium

We saw with RBC models that technology shocks are able to generate cycles in aggregate real GDP. The environment was 'real'; there was no role for money. Preceding the neo-Keynesian model, the question was whether one can have a 'monetary business cycle model' in a competitive equilibrium-flexible price environment. One answer, following Lucas (1972), was *Yes, but*.... We therefore study the Lucas (1972) model as exposited by Benassy (2001). (In fact, the published research papers and books by Dr. Jean-Pascal Benassy are an excellent way to learn about modern business cycle theory among other topics.) We need to introduce heterogeneity into the model to ensure that there is demand for money. One way of doing so is to assume that at time t, there are two generations: one young and one old. Households work when they are young, and they consume when they are old. The fact that the goods are perishable ensures that there is a positive demand for money balances. Finally, to allow for an 'effective' monetary policy, we introduce a stochastic element into the model. The resulting stochastic overlapping generations model is explained as follows.

7.2.1 Environment

The economy consists of $j \in [0, 1]$ sectors, or 'islands'. Firms are competitive and produce specific intermediate goods, as given by

$$Q_{jt} = Z_{jt} L_{jt}, \tag{7.1}$$

where Z_{jt} is a sector-specific shock and L_{jt} is the amount of labor. Note that there is no capital accumulation in this environment.

Households consume a unique consumption good produced by a competitive firm as per

$$\log Y_t = \int_0^1 \theta_{jt}(\log Q_{jt})d_j \tag{7.2}$$

subject to

$$\int_0^1 \theta_{jt}d_j = 1, \tag{7.3}$$

where Y_t is the total amount of output consumed and θ_{jt} is the island-specific demand shock. Each island has households with mass equal to one, all identical. In addition, each island has an overlapping generations (OLG) structure. Therefore,

$$U_{jt} = C_{jt+1} - \frac{L_{jt}^{\beta}}{\beta}, \tag{7.4}$$

where C_{jt+1} is consumption when old and $\beta > 1$ is the degree of disutility of work when young.

Households transfer wealth using money M_t, and the government provides

$$M_t = X_t M_{t-1,}, \tag{7.5}$$

where

$$X_t \sim N(\mu_X, \sigma_X^2). \tag{7.6}$$

That is, money changes are carried out by lump-sum taxes (transfers) to the old who hold all the money. Thus, the budget constraint is

$$P_t C_{jt} = W_{jt-1}L_{jt-1} + T_{jt}, \tag{7.7}$$

where P_t is the aggregate price level, W_{jt-1} is the level of savings (equal to the wage), and T_{jt} is the amount of tax transfers, subject to

$$T_{jt} = X_{t-1}M_{t-1}, \tag{7.8}$$

which assumes that transfers are identical across all households. To clarify matters, suppose that at the beginning of period t, $M_t = 1$

and $X_s = 1$ for all $s \geq t$. This means that government takes a passive approach to monetary policy. One unit of the currency is in circulation and is given to the initial (period t) old. Note that the utility function does not involve money, so that money is intrinsically valueless (a related reason is that fiat money is not like commodity money – backed by a precious metal such as gold – and therefore does not enter the utility function). The way that money achieves value is whether the current young are willing to accept it from the current old in exchange for the consumption good. The current young are willing to accept it only if they think that they will receive the consumption good when they become old (in period $t+1$). Suppose for example that the 'world ended' in period T, where $T > t$, then money would not have value because the last generation of young people would not accept it since they would have no one to trade with when they become old. So, the penultimate generation would also not want to carry money. By backward induction, money would be valueless. As a result, no one would produce anything since there is no consumption when old to compensate for work effort when young.

Going back to this model, money will have value and people will be willing to hold it because they know that the next generation is willing to hold it. As a result, although money is intrinsically valueless, it achieves social value by allowing successive generations to trade with each other. Note that money is also the so-called 'numeraire good', meaning that its nominal price is unity (from equation (7.7)). Its price relative to the consumption good is $\frac{1}{P_t}$. So, one can trade one unit of money for $\frac{1}{P_t}$ units of the consumption good: if the price P_t is high, then money buys little consumption. When P_t is infinite, money is valueless. The question that we aim to address is whether shocks to money supply have real effects, in particular whether the government can alter production and consumption by manipulating the amount of money available.

7.2.2 Stochastics

Let

$$Z_{jt} = Z_t A_{jt}. \tag{7.9}$$

Then, taking natural logarithms gives

$$\log Z_{jt} = \log Z_t + \log A_{jt}, \tag{7.10}$$

or

$$z_{jt} = z_t + a_{jt}, \tag{7.11}$$

where lowercase represents the natural logarithm of a given variable (this convention will be used throughout). As shown, z_{jt} has two components: a global component z_t that affects everyone and a local component a_{jt} that affects only a certain island. Assume that

$$z_t \sim N(0, \sigma_z^2), \tag{7.12}$$

$$a_{jt} \sim N(0, \sigma_a^2), \tag{7.13}$$

$$\theta_{jt} \sim N(\mu_\theta, \sigma_\theta^2). \tag{7.14}$$

From (7.3),

$$E(\theta_{jt}) = \exp\left(\mu_\theta + \frac{\sigma_\theta^2}{2}\right) = 1, \tag{7.15}$$

which implies that

$$\mu_\theta = -\frac{\sigma_\theta^2}{2}. \tag{7.16}$$

Also, integrating across all islands,

$$\int_0^1 \theta_{jt}(\log Q_{jt})d_j = \log\left[\exp\left(\frac{\sigma_\theta^2}{2}\right)\right] \tag{7.17}$$

$$= \log \xi. \tag{7.18}$$

The information set Ξ_{jt} is given by

$$\Xi_{jt} = (M_{t-1}, P_{jt}, Q_{jt}, W_{jt}, L_{jt}), \tag{7.19}$$

meaning that one does not know P_t, X_t or Y_t. Therefore, the utility maximization problem is based on what one expects transfers (which are a function of x_t) and prices will be and is given by

$$\max_{\{L_{jt}\}} \quad E_{jt}\left[C_{jt+1} - \frac{L_{jt}^\beta}{\beta}\right] \tag{7.20}$$

subject to

$$C_{jt+1} = \frac{W_{jt}L_{jt} + T_{jt+1}}{P_{t+1}}. \tag{7.21}$$

The first-order condition is

$$L_{jt}^{\beta-1} = W_{jt}E_{jt}\left(\frac{1}{P_{t+1}}\right). \tag{7.22}$$

7.2.3 Equilibrium conditions and profit maximization implications

Assume that the intermediate goods markets are competitive, with wages equal to the marginal product of labor,

$$W_{jt} = Z_{jt}P_{jt}, \tag{7.23}$$

and that the consumption goods markets are also competitive so that the relative price of j is equal to the marginal productivity of j,

$$\frac{P_{jt}}{P_t} = \frac{\theta_{jt}Y_t}{Q_{jt}}. \tag{7.24}$$

From the quantity of money equation, the aggregate goods market equilibrium is

$$Y_t = \frac{M_t}{P_t}, \tag{7.25}$$

where the velocity of money is equal to one. This equation equates money supply, (M_t), to demand for money, (P_tY_t) . If money loses value, then as P_t tends to $+\infty$ (keeping M_t fixed), Y_t tends to 0. There is no point in producing the consumption good if the current young think that money is not worth holding.

7.2.4 An undetermined coefficients rational expectation solution

To understand the effects of monetary policy on relative prices (in particular P_t), we will make an assumption about how households form their expectations of P_t. Their expectation of the price P_t has to be correct for some parameter values. This means that the 'true' price has to be in the range of prices that they think might turn out to be true. Intuitively, we expect this price to be an increasing function of M_t since higher money supply means that it money is not worth as much. This corresponds to a higher value of P_t (or, equivalently, to a lower relative price of money $\frac{1}{P_t}$). Since $M_t = X_t M_{t-1}$, our last comment implies that P_t has to be an increasing function of M_{t-1} and X_t (the money supply shock from the government). Finally, the relative price will also be a function of the supply shock Z_t. We summarize this using a so-called *price theory function* adopted by each household:

$$P_t = \varsigma M_{t-1} X_t^{\gamma} Z_t^{\delta}, \tag{7.26}$$

which implies that

$$P_{t+1} = \varsigma M_t X_{t+1}^{\gamma} Z_{t+1}^{\delta}. \tag{7.27}$$

That is price will be a function of the money in circulation, the change in money supply, and some technology shock (productivity change). This is akin to conjecturing a rational expectations solution to the model in an undetermined coefficients approach to solving expectational difference equations.

Taking the inverse of (7.27), substituting (7.5), and then taking expectations yields

$$E_{jt}\left(\frac{1}{P_{t+1}}\right) = (\varsigma M_{t-1})^{-1} E_{jt}(X_t^{-1}) E_{jt}(X_{t+1}^{-\gamma}) E_{jt}(Z_{t+1}^{-\delta}). \tag{7.28}$$

For now, let

$$E_{jt}(X_{t+1}^{-\gamma}) = \exp\left(-\gamma\mu_x + \frac{\gamma^2\sigma_X^2}{2}\right) \tag{7.29}$$

$$E_{jt}(Z_{t+1}^{-\delta}) = \exp\left(\frac{\delta^2\sigma_z^2}{2}\right), \tag{7.30}$$

and we use signal extraction to determine $E_{jt}(X_t^{-1})$ as follows.

The household is assumed to observe a signal about the aggregate economy that will inform their expectations of the price of the consumption good. The signal $\theta_{jt} X_t$ is positively related to a demand shock and to a monetary shock. This captures the idea that the household has difficulty observing whether changes in prices are indicative of changes in relative prices (meaning, a demand shock) that would imply that it should produce more or a change in the price level (a monetary shock) that would imply that production should remain the same. What the household observes is summarized in the following equation, where S_t is the observed signal about the economy:

$$S_t = \theta_{jt} X_t, \tag{7.31}$$

or, in logarithms,

$$s_t = \log \theta_{jt} + x_t, \tag{7.32}$$

and then households compute $E(X_t^{-1} \mid S_t)$. In logs, the conditional distribution is given by

$$x_t \mid s_t \sim N(\mu_{x|s}, \sigma^2_{x|s}). \tag{7.33}$$

In other words, since X_t is unobservable, one can use another variable which is observable in order to help estimate it.

By rational expectations, if

$$A_t \sim N(\mu_A, \sigma^2_A), \tag{7.34}$$

$$B_t \sim N(\mu_B, \sigma^2_B), \tag{7.35}$$

$$\sigma_{AB} > 0, \tag{7.36}$$

then

$$\mu_{A|B} = \mu_A + \frac{\sigma^2_{AB}}{\sigma^2_B}(B_t - \mu_B) \tag{7.37}$$

$$\sigma^2_{A|B} = \sigma^2_A \left(1 - \frac{\sigma^2_{AB}}{\sigma^2_A \sigma^2_B}\right). \tag{7.38}$$

As a result, by (7.37),

$$E(x_t \mid s_t) = \mu_x + \frac{\sigma^2_{xs}}{\sigma^2_s}(s_t - \mu_s), \tag{7.39}$$

which can be rewritten as

$$\mu_{x|x+\log\theta} = \mu_x + \rho(x_t + \log\theta_{jt} - \mu_{x} - \mu_{\log\theta}), \tag{7.40}$$

where

$$\rho = \frac{\sigma^2_{x,x+\log\theta}}{\sigma^2_{x+\log\theta}}. \tag{7.41}$$

Also, by the definition of variance,

$$\begin{aligned} \sigma_{xs} &= E\left[x_t(\log\theta_{jt} + x_t)\right] - E(x_t)E(\log\theta_{jt} + x_t) && (7.42)\\ &= \sigma^2_x + \sigma^2_{\log\theta,x} && (7.43)\\ &= \sigma^2_x && (7.44) \end{aligned}$$

since the covariance between x_t and $\log\theta_{jt}$ is zero by definition. Likewise,

$$\sigma^2_s = \sigma^2_x + \sigma^2_{\log\theta}. \tag{7.45}$$

Equation (7.37) also implies that by (7.38),

$$\begin{aligned} \sigma^2_{x|s} &= \sigma^2_x\left(1 - \frac{\sigma^2_{xs}}{\sigma^2_x\sigma^2_s}\right) && (7.46)\\ &= \sigma^2_x\left(1 - \frac{\left(\sigma^2_x\right)^2}{\sigma^2_x[\sigma^2_x + \sigma^2_{\log\theta}]}\right) && (7.47)\\ &= \sigma^2_x\left(\frac{\sigma^2_x + \sigma^2_{\log\theta} - \sigma^2_x}{\sigma^2_x + \sigma^2_{\log\theta}}\right) && (7.48)\\ &= \left(\frac{\sigma^2_x}{\sigma^2_x + \sigma^2_{\log\theta}}\right)\sigma^2_{\log\theta} && (7.49)\\ &= \rho\sigma^2_{\log\theta}. && (7.50) \end{aligned}$$

Now, recall that

$$\log X_t \sim N(\mu_x, \sigma^2_x) \tag{7.51}$$

so X_t has a log normal distribution

$$\exp\left[-\mu_x + (-1)^2\frac{\sigma^2_x}{2}\right]. \tag{7.52}$$

Therefore,

$$E(x_t^{-1}|s_t) = \exp\left(\mu_{x|s} + \frac{\sigma_{x|s}^2}{2}\right) \tag{7.53}$$

$$= \exp(\rho(x_t + \log\theta_{jt})) \times \exp\left(\rho\mu_{\log\theta_{jt}} - (1-\rho)\mu_x + \rho\frac{\sigma_x^2}{2}\right) \tag{7.54}$$

$$= \left[\frac{1}{x_{t\log\theta_{jt}}}\right]^\rho \exp[-(1-\rho)\mu_x]. \tag{7.55}$$

Inserting (7.55), (7.29), and (7.30) into (7.28) produces

$$E\left(\frac{1}{P_{t+1}}\right) = (\varsigma M_{t-1})^{-1}\left[\frac{1}{x_{t\log\theta_{jt}}}\right]^\rho \times \exp\left[-(1-\rho)\mu_x - \gamma\mu_x + \frac{\gamma^2\sigma_X^2}{2} + \frac{\delta^2\sigma_z^2}{2}\right] \tag{7.56}$$

$$= \frac{\Lambda}{\varsigma}M_{t-1}^{-1}\left[\frac{1}{x_{t\log\theta_{jt}}}\right]^\rho, \tag{7.57}$$

where

$$\Lambda = \exp\left[-(1-\rho)\mu_x - \gamma\mu_x + \frac{\gamma^2\sigma_X^2}{2} + \frac{\delta^2\sigma_z^2}{2}\right]. \tag{7.58}$$

7.2.5 Model solution

Rewrite (7.22) as

$$W_{jt}L_{jt} = L_{jt}^\beta E_{jt}\left(\frac{1}{P_{t+1}}\right)^{-1} \tag{7.59}$$

so that total wage is set equal to the total product. Using (7.1), (7.5), (7.23), (7.24), and (7.25), one finds that

$$P_{jt}Q_{jt} = W_{jt}L_{jt} \tag{7.60}$$

$$= \theta_{jt}M_t \tag{7.61}$$

$$= \theta_{jt}X_tM_{t-1}. \tag{7.62}$$

Substituting (7.59) into (7.62) yields

$$L_{jt}^{\beta} E_{jt} \left(\frac{1}{P_{t+1}} \right)^{-1} = \theta_{jt} X_t M_{t-1}, \tag{7.63}$$

and plugging in (7.57),

$$L_{jt}^{\beta} \left(\frac{\Lambda}{\varsigma} M_{t-1}^{-1} \left[\frac{1}{x_{t \log \theta_{jt}}} \right]^{\rho} \right)^{-1} = \theta_{jt} X_t M_{t-1}, \tag{7.64}$$

which gives

$$L_{jt}^{*} = \left(\frac{\Lambda}{\varsigma} \right)^{\frac{1}{\beta}} (\theta_{jt} X_t)^{\frac{1-\rho}{\beta}}. \tag{7.65}$$

Inserting (7.65) into (7.1),

$$Q_{jt} = Z_{jt} L_{jt}^{*} \tag{7.66}$$

$$= Z_{jt} \left(\frac{\Lambda}{\varsigma} \right)^{\frac{1}{\beta}} (\theta_{jt} X_t)^{\frac{1-\rho}{\beta}}, \tag{7.67}$$

and taking logarithms,

$$\log Q_{jt} = \log Z_{jt} + \frac{1}{\beta} \log \left(\frac{\Lambda}{\varsigma} \right) + \frac{1-\rho}{\beta} \log(\theta_{jt} X_t). \tag{7.68}$$

Substituting (7.68) into (7.2) and using equations (7.18) and (7.3),

$$\log Y_t = \int_0^1 \theta_{jt} \left[\log Z_{jt} + \frac{1}{\beta} \log \left(\frac{\Lambda}{\varsigma} \right) \right.$$

$$\left. + \frac{1-\rho}{\beta} \log(\theta_{jt} X_t) \right] d_j \tag{7.69}$$

$$= \int_0^1 \theta_{jt} \log Z_{jt} d_j + \int_0^1 \theta_{jt} \frac{1}{\beta} \log \left(\frac{\Lambda}{\varsigma} \right) d_j$$

$$+\int_0^1 \theta_{jt}\left(\frac{1-\rho}{\beta}\right)\log(\theta_{jt}X_t)d_j \tag{7.70}$$

$$= \log Z_t + \frac{1}{\beta}\log\left(\frac{\Lambda}{\varsigma}\right)$$

$$+\left(\frac{1-\rho}{\beta}\right)\log X_t + \left(\frac{1-\rho}{\beta}\right)\log\xi, \tag{7.71}$$

or, taking the logs away by exponentiating both sides yields

$$Y_t^* = Z_t\left(\frac{\Lambda}{\varsigma}\right)^{\frac{1}{\beta}} X_t^{\left(\frac{1-\rho}{\beta}\right)}\xi^{\left(\frac{1-\rho}{\beta}\right)}. \tag{7.72}$$

Together, equations (7.5), (7.25), and (7.72) imply that

$$P_t = M_t Y_{t-1} \tag{7.73}$$

$$= X_t M_{t-1} Y_{t-1} \tag{7.74}$$

$$= \frac{(\frac{\Lambda}{\varsigma})^{-\frac{1}{\beta}} M_{t-1} X_t^{1-\left(\frac{1-\rho}{\beta}\right)}\xi^{-\left(\frac{1-\rho}{\beta}\right)}}{Z_t}. \tag{7.75}$$

Let

$$1-\left(\frac{1-\rho}{\beta}\right) = \gamma \tag{7.76}$$

$$-1 = \delta, \tag{7.77}$$

so

$$P_t = \left(\frac{\Lambda}{\varsigma}\right)^{-\frac{1}{\beta}} M_{t-1} X_t^{\gamma} Z_t^{\delta}\xi^{-\left(\frac{1-\rho}{\beta}\right)}. \tag{7.78}$$

From (7.26), one knows that

$$P_t = \varsigma M_{t-1} X_t^{\gamma} Z_t^{\delta}; \tag{7.79}$$

therefore,

$$\varsigma = \left(\frac{\Lambda}{\varsigma}\right)^{-\frac{1}{\beta}}\xi^{-\left(\frac{1-\rho}{\beta}\right)}, \tag{7.80}$$

or

$$\varsigma = \Lambda^{-\frac{1}{\beta-1}} \xi^{-\left(\frac{1-\rho}{\beta-1}\right)}. \tag{7.81}$$

From (7.58), using (7.76) and (7.77),

$$\Lambda = \exp\left[\left\{-1+\rho-1+\left(\frac{1-\rho}{\beta}\right)\right\}\mu_x + \frac{\left[1-\left(\frac{1-\rho}{\beta}\right)\right]^2 \sigma_X^2}{2} + \frac{\sigma_z^2}{2}\right]. \tag{7.82}$$

Plugging (7.81) into (7.65),

$$L_{jt}^* = \left(\frac{\Lambda}{\Lambda^{-\frac{1}{\beta-1}} \xi^{-\left(\frac{1-\rho}{\beta-1}\right)}}\right)^{\frac{1}{\beta}} (\theta_{jt} X_t)^{\frac{1-\rho}{\beta}} \tag{7.83}$$

$$= \Lambda^{\frac{1}{\beta}+\frac{1}{\beta}\left(\frac{1}{\beta-1}\right)} \xi^{\frac{1}{\beta}\left(\frac{1-\rho}{\beta-1}\right)} (\theta_{jt} X_t)^{\frac{1-\rho}{\beta}} \tag{7.84}$$

$$= \Lambda^{\frac{1}{\beta-1}} \xi^{\frac{1}{\beta}\left(\frac{1-\rho}{\beta-1}\right)} (\theta_{jt} X_t)^{\frac{1-\rho}{\beta}}. \tag{7.85}$$

Similarly, from (7.72),

$$Y_t^* = Z_t^{\frac{1}{\beta}} \left(\frac{\Lambda}{\varsigma}\right) X_t^{\frac{1-\rho}{\beta}} \xi^{\frac{1-\rho}{\beta}} \tag{7.86}$$

$$= Z_t X_t^{\frac{1-\rho}{\beta}} \Lambda^{\frac{1}{\beta-1}} \xi^{\frac{1-\rho}{\beta}} \xi^{\frac{1}{\beta}\left(\frac{1-\rho}{\beta-1}\right)} \tag{7.87}$$

$$= Z_t X_t^{\frac{1-\rho}{\beta}} \Lambda^{\frac{1}{\beta-1}} \xi^{\frac{1-\rho}{\beta-1}}. \tag{7.88}$$

Taking logs,

$$\log Y_t = \log Z_t + \frac{1-\rho}{\beta} \log X_t + \frac{1}{\beta-1} \log \Lambda + \frac{1-\rho}{\beta-1} \log \xi, \tag{7.89}$$

which can be written as

$$\log Y_t = \beta_0 + \frac{1-\rho}{\beta} \log X_t + \log Z_t, \tag{7.90}$$

where

$$\beta_0 = \frac{1}{\beta-1} \log \Lambda + \frac{1-\rho}{\beta-1} \log \xi. \tag{7.91}$$

Note that using (7.41), one finds that

$$\frac{1-\rho}{\beta} = \frac{1}{\beta}\left(\frac{\sigma^2_{\log\theta}}{\sigma^2_x + \sigma^2_{\log\theta}}\right). \tag{7.92}$$

Equation (7.90) kind of looks like a regular regression and that it is a function of β, which is entirely in the control of the private sector. Therefore, policymakers can't control output. This is precisely what Lucas (1973) had in mind with his critique of econometric policy evaluation.

Finally, note that the Phillips curve in logs is given by

$$\mathrm{Cov}(Y_t, \Pi_t) = \frac{\rho(\beta - 1 + \rho)}{\beta^2}\sigma^2_{\log\theta} - \sigma^2_z, \tag{7.93}$$

where

$$\Pi_t = P_t - P_{t-1}. \tag{7.94}$$

This covariance can be positive or negative and that the coefficient in front of $\log X_t$ indicates that the response of money to output is greater than zero.

7.2.6 Conclusions

The importance of the Lucas model lies in showing that the economy responds more to unexpected monetary shocks than to expected shocks (i.e. lagged money supply). This is one instance of the famous Lucas critique of econometric policy: the estimated (positive) relationship between output and inflation cannot be used to permanently lower unemployment. In this particular model, this means that an (expected) monetary policy expansion will not increase output permanently and therefore will not permanently lower unemployment. Only 'unexpected' policies will produce results, but these results will be temporary since, by definition, they are unexpected and therefore cannot have permanent policy effects. The implication for the conduct of monetary policy is straightforward: policy should be stable and expected and so it doesn't affect the 'real' side of the economy. Why not exploit the real effects of unexpected shocks? They should perhaps not be exploited because many negative effects of 'unexpected' policies have not been modeled (for example, nominal uncertainty in making investment decisions, etc.).

However, there is some statistical evidence that in the short run, both types of monetary policy (expected and unexpected) influence output. The idea that money does not affect the long-run level of output is widely believed. Unless monetary policy is conducted in a very irresponsible way (and say, generates hyperinflation – such as in Zimbabwe), then money should not influence long-run (real) outcomes in the economy. There is some empirical support for the idea that the long run is not affected by the nominal side of the economy.

The Lucas model is not seen as a good model of the cycle because output fluctuates in response to white-noise shocks, whereas in reality output fluctuations are serially correlated. The model does not generate any persistence in output. Further, the model not only does not increase the persistence of shocks assumed as the impulse to the model, but it also serves to dampen down their effect. Money supply shocks influence output by less than one-for-one. Finally, the Lucas model, as described above, does not allow for capital accumulation. As we saw in the RBC chapter, TFP shocks create serial correlation in output because capital accumulation initially increases, and as it slowly depreciates, increased capital cause output to rise. Thus, we now turn to a model with capital accumulation; in addition, we introduce money into the model by assuming that individuals have utility for money. This way, we can analyze the short-run (or business cycle) effects of monetary shocks on the real side of the economy.

7.3 Introduction to a New Keynesian Model

The RBC model extended the Cass–Koopmans exogenous growth model by incorporating a stochastic technology shock in order to account for cyclical fluctuations in real GDP, consumption, investment, and hours worked. It did not allow for any nominal variables (such as inflation and nominal interest rates) and was silent on the effects of policy (versus technology) shocks on the macroeconomy. But nominal variables do correlate with real variables, and policy does matter based on reduced form statistical time series analyses.

Keynes thought about these things in some detail, specifically imperfect market structures, nominally sticky prices, adjustment costs, shocks to the marginal efficiency of investment with endogenous capital utilization, and policy shocks from a monetary authority that can set the base nominal interest rate (on bonds). His model was translated by Hicks and others into the (in)famous IS-LM model. It performed well but failed in the 1970s, which led to the neo-classical rational expectations revolution. The rational expectations revolution required microfoundations for any model. Lucas and Stokey (1987) tried, through cash-in-advance models, to get nominal variables to move together with real ones, but the attempt did not meet with success. Microfoundations have only recently been developed for neo-Keynesian models. So, we turn to a typical neo-Keynesian environment by Ireland (2003).

7.3.1 Economic environment

We consider a discrete time economy with a representative household $i \in [0, 1]$ that consumes a final good and produces an intermediate and differentiated good, denoted i. The final good is produced using all of the intermediate goods in the continuum $i \in [0, 1]$ by a representative final goods producing firm. The model imposes enough symmetry on tastes and technologies to permit the analysis to focus on the behavior of a representative intermediate goods-producing firm, identified by the generic index i. The representative household has preferences defined over consumption of the finished good, leisure, and real cash balances, giving rise to a conventional specification for money demand as a function of a scale variable, aggregate consumption, and an opportunity cost variable (the nominal interest rate). Intermediate good i is produced with capital and labor provided competitively from household i. Since intermediate goods substitute imperfectly for one another in the representative finished goods-producing firm's production function, the representative intermediate goods-producing firm sells its output in a monopolistically competitive market. Hence, intermediate firm i acts as a price-setter in the market for good i.

The model introduces two kinds of adjustment costs: (a) a 'real rigidity' in the form of adjustment costs to capital, one possible interpretation of which is to think of this as a 'learning by doing' cost – when household i wishes to expand its capital, it will have to learn how to use the new capital (machinery, technology, etc.) that is now available; and (b) a 'nominal rigidity' in the form of adjustment costs to the price of the intermediate good by household i – this price stickiness may be due to menu costs or other real-world phenomena that cause price setting to be staggered rather than instantaneous.

The reason that these rigidities are introduced in the model is to allow a role for monetary policy. The model also introduces two additional things: (a) money in the utility function and (b) a monetary authority that sets the interest rate according to a so-called Taylor rule. Assumption (a) ensures that households will hold money balances – in the absence of this, fiat money has no purpose in the economy and will have a relative price of zero in equilibrium. Now that households hold money balances, assumption (b) ensures that the government can manipulate the interest rate to influence real economic outcomes. In particular, the monetary authority can change investment behavior: if investment is too low and is not adjusting quickly enough because of the real rigidities, the monetary authority can lower interest rates and stimulate investment: this would lead the economy back to the steady state faster. The monetary authority can also manipulate interest rates to adjust prices and in particular inflation. In light of the money in the utility specification and the rigidities that we introduced, it should be no surprise that nominal variables will bear an influence on real economic outcomes.

So far, we have discussed two different financial instruments: physical capital (that earns the owner a rate of return) and money whose rate of return is an opportunity cost of holding other financial instruments. The latter could of course be physical capital, but the model also introduces a third financial instrument called a bond. The rate of return on the bond is equal to the opportunity cost of holding money.

Strictly, bonds are purely cosmetic in this economy, but they do provide a Keynesian flavor to the model: money holdings are a stand-in for monetary assets (currency, time deposits, etc.) and bonds are a stand-in for non-monetary assets (longer-term deposits and stocks in financial markets). The introduction of bonds is cosmetic because they are not held in equilibrium – all agents are identical and a 'zero net trade' assumption on bond holdings ensures that equilibrium purchases of bonds are zero. Their price however is positive and is determined through a no-arbitrage condition that ensures that the rate of return of capital equals the interest rate. The modeling of bonds, and in general financial markets, is therefore somewhat unsatisfactory: causal empiricism suggests that financial markets have important wealth effects and have a (complicated) influence on the real side of the economy.

7.3.2 The representative household

The representative household carries M_{t-1} units of money, B_{t-1} bonds, and K_t units of capital into period t. At the beginning of the period, the household receives a lump-sum nominal transfer T_t from the monetary authority. This nominal transfer is one way that the government can alter money supply in the economy and (indirectly) other variables that affect real outcomes (such as the real interest rate). Next, the household's bonds mature, providing B_{t-1} additional units of money. The household uses some of this money to purchase B_t new bonds at the cost of $1/r_t$ units of money per bond, where r_t denotes the gross nominal interest rate between periods t and $t+1$. During period t, the household supplies $h_t(i)$ units of labor at the nominal wage rate W_t and $K_t(i)$ units of capital at the nominal rental rate Q_t to each intermediate goods-producing firm $i \in [0, 1]$. The household's choices of $h_t(i)$ and $K_t(i)$ must satisfy

$$h_t = \int_0^1 h_t(i)di, \tag{7.95}$$

where h_t denotes total hours worked and

$$K_t = \int_0^1 K_t(i)di \tag{7.96}$$

for all t.

The household, therefore, receives total nominal factor payments $W_t h_t + Q_t K_t$ during period t. In addition, the household receives total nominal profits $D_t(i)$ from each firm $i \in [0, 1]$ for a total of

$$D_t = \int_0^1 D_t(i)di \tag{7.97}$$

during period t. The household uses its funds to purchase output at the nominal price P_t from the finished goods-producing firm, which it divides between consumption C_t and investment I_t. In order to transform invested units of the finished good into new units of productive capital, the household must pay a *real* adjustment cost, measured in terms of the finished good and given by

$$\frac{\phi_K}{2}\left(\frac{K_{t+1}}{gK_t}-1\right)^2 K_t, \tag{7.98}$$

where g is the rate of labor-augmenting technological progress. The rate g turns out to be the steady-state growth rate of the capital stock per household. Finally,

$$K_{t+1} = (1-\delta)K_t + x_t I_t. \tag{7.99}$$

The adjustment cost specification implies that the cost is zero in the model's steady state. In (7.99), x_t is a shock to the marginal efficiency of investment; it follows the autoregressive process

$$\log x_t = \rho_x \log x_{t-1} + \varepsilon_{xt}, \quad \varepsilon_{xt} \sim N(0, \sigma_x^2). \tag{7.100}$$

The household then carries M_t units of money, B_t bonds, and K_{t+1} units of capital into period $t+1$; these quantities must satisfy the budget constraint

$$\frac{M_{t-1}+T_t+B_{t-1}+W_t h_t+Q_t K_t+D_t}{P_t} = C_t + I_t + \frac{\phi_K}{2}\left(\frac{K_{t+1}}{gK_t}-1\right)^2 K_t + \frac{B_t/r_t+M_t}{P_t}. \tag{7.101}$$

The household's preferences are described by the expected utility function

$$E_0\sum_{t=0}^{\infty}\beta^t u(C_t, M_t/P_t, h_t), \tag{7.102}$$

where

$$u(C_t, M_t/P_t, h_t) = a_t\left[\frac{\gamma}{\gamma-1}\right]\log\left[C_t^{\frac{\gamma}{\gamma-1}} + e_t^{\frac{1}{\gamma}}\left(\frac{M_t}{P_t}\right)^{\frac{\gamma}{\gamma-1}}\right] + \eta\log(1-h_t). \tag{7.103}$$

Because $\frac{M}{P}$, real money balances, are part of the utility function, the preference shock a_t mimics a shock to both the IS and LM curves in the traditional Keynesian IS-LM model: on the one hand, a shock to a_t increases demand for the consumption good and therefore decreased savings for a fixed level of output – this causes the IS curve to shift up (why?), but it also increases demand for money, which causes the LM curve to shift down. In equilibrium, demand for real money balances are a function of consumption (and the interest rate), so a_t may be viewed as a shock to consumption only.

We assume that a_t follows the autoregressive process

$$\log a_t = \rho_a \log a_{t-1} + \varepsilon_{at}, \quad \varepsilon_{at} \sim N(0, \sigma_a^2). \tag{7.104}$$

The preference shock e_t translates into a disturbance to the model's money demand curve; it follows the autoregressive process

$$\log e_t = (1 - \rho_e)\log e + \rho_e \log e_{t-1} + \varepsilon_{et}, \quad \varepsilon_{et} \sim N(0, \sigma_e^2). \tag{7.105}$$

The household, therefore, chooses C_t, h_t, M_t, B_t, I_t, and K_{t+1} for all $t = 0, 1, 2, \ldots$ to maximize its utility function subject to the constraints (7.99) and (7.101). The first-order conditions for this problem are

$$a_t = \Lambda_t C_t^{\frac{1}{\gamma}} \left[C_t^{\frac{\gamma-1}{\gamma}} + e_t^{\frac{1}{\gamma}} \left(\frac{M_t}{P_t} \right)^{\frac{\gamma}{\gamma-1}} \right] \tag{7.106}$$

$$\eta - \Lambda_t \left(\frac{W_t}{P_t} \right)(1 - h_t), \tag{7.107}$$

$$a_t e_t^{\frac{1}{\gamma}} = \left(\frac{M_t}{P_t} \right)^{\frac{1}{\gamma}} \left[C_t^{\frac{\gamma-1}{\gamma}} + e_t^{\frac{1}{\gamma}} \left(\frac{M_t}{P_t} \right)^{\frac{\gamma-1}{\gamma}} \right] \times \left[\Lambda_t - \beta E_t \left(\frac{\Lambda_{t+1} P_t}{P_{t+1}} \right) \right], \tag{7.108}$$

$$\Lambda_t = \beta r_t E_t \left(\frac{\Lambda_{t+1} P_t}{P_{t+1}} \right) \tag{7.109}$$

$$\Lambda_t \left[\frac{1}{x_t} + \left(\frac{\phi_K}{g} \right) \left(\frac{K_{t+1}}{g K_t} - 1 \right) \right] - \beta E_t \left[\Lambda_{t+1} \left(\frac{Q_{t+1}}{P_{t+1}} + \frac{1 - \delta}{x_{t+1}} \right) \right]$$

$$-\left(\frac{\beta\phi_K}{2}\right)E_t\left[\Lambda_{t+1}\left(\frac{K_{t+2}}{gK_{t+1}}-1\right)^2\right]$$
$$+\beta\phi_K E_t\left[\Lambda_{t+1}\left(\frac{K_{t+2}}{gK_{t+1}}-1\right)\frac{K_{t+2}}{gK_{t+1}}\right], \qquad (7.110)$$

where Λ_t is the multiplier on the constraint (7.101).

7.3.3 The representative final goods-producing firm

The representative finished goods-producing firm uses $Y_t(i)$ units of each intermediate good $i \in [0,1]$ to produce Y_t units of the finished good according to the constant returns to scale technology described by

$$\left[\int_0^1 Y_t(i)^{\frac{\theta-1}{\theta}}di\right]^{\frac{\theta}{\theta-1}} = Y_t. \qquad (7.111)$$

Intermediate good i sells at the nominal price $P_t(i)$, while the finished good sells at the nominal price P_t; given these prices, the finished goods-producing firm chooses Y_t and $Y_t(i)$ for all $i \in [0,1]$ to maximize its profits,

$$P_tY_t - \int_0^1 P_t(i)Y_t(i)di, \qquad (7.112)$$

subject to the constraint imposed by the production function.

The first-order conditions for this problem imply that

$$Y_t(i) = \left[\frac{P_t(i)}{P_t}\right]^{-\theta} Y_t \qquad (7.113)$$

for all $i \in [0,1]$ and t. This condition implies that if the final goods firm needed to produce an amount Y_t of the final good, it would require $Y_t(i)$ units of good i to produce it in a way that minimizes costs. When θ tends to 0, goods are highly differentiated so that even if the price $P_t(i)$ of good i is high, the firm's price elasticity of demand for this intermediate good converges to zero. On the other hand, when θ tends to $+\infty$, good i is much less 'important' for the production of the final good: if the price $P_t(i)$ increases, the demand $Y_t(i)$ for good i falls rather quickly.

Competition in the market for the finished good requires that the representative firm earn zero profits in equilibrium. This zero-profit condition determines P_t as

$$P_t = \left[\int_0^1 P_t(i)^{1-\theta} di\right]^{\frac{1}{1-\theta}}. \tag{7.114}$$

7.3.4 The representative intermediate goods-producing firm

The representative intermediate goods-producing firm hires $h_t(i)$ units of labor and rents $K_t(i)$ units of capital from the representative household during period t in order to produce $Y_t(i)$ units of intermediate good i according to the constant returns to scale technology described by

$$K_t(i)^{\alpha}[g^t z_t h_t(i)]^{1-\alpha} = Y_t(i), \tag{7.115}$$

where g denotes the gross rate of labor-augmenting technological progress. The technology shock z_t follows the autoregressive process

$$\log z_t = (1-\rho_z)\log z + \rho_z \log z_{t-1} + \varepsilon_{zt}, \quad \varepsilon_{zt} \sim N(0, \sigma_z^2). \tag{7.116}$$

Since intermediate goods substitute imperfectly for one another as inputs to producing the finished good, the representative intermediate goods-producing firm sells its output in a monopolistically competitive market; during each period t, it sets a nominal price $P_t(i)$, subject to the requirement that it satisfy the representative finished goods-producing firm's demand, taking P_t and Y_t as given.

In addition, the representative intermediate goods-producing firm faces a cost of adjusting its nominal price, measured in units of the finished good and given by

$$\frac{\phi_P}{2}\left[\frac{P_t(i)}{\pi P_{t-1}(i)} - 1\right]^2 Y_t, \tag{7.117}$$

where π is the gross steady-state rate of inflation (note that π tracks changes in the price P_t, not $P_t(i)$ – this will not make a difference because in equilibrium, all prices equate).

In general, the cost of price adjustment makes the firm's problem dynamic; it chooses $h_t(i)$, $K_t(i)$, $Y_t(i)$, and $P_t(i)$ to maximize its total market value subject to the constraint offered by the production function:

$$\max \quad E_0 \sum_{t=0}^{\infty} \beta^t \Lambda_t \left[\frac{D_t(i)}{P_t}\right] \tag{7.118}$$

$$s.t. \quad \frac{D_t(i)}{P_t} = \left[\frac{P_t(i)}{P_t}\right]^{1-\theta} Y_t - \frac{W_t h_t(i) + Q_t K_t(i)}{P_t} - \frac{\phi_P}{2}\left[\frac{P_t}{\pi P_{t-1}(i)} - 1\right]^2 Y_t \tag{7.119}$$

$$K_t(i)^{\alpha}[g^t z_t h_t(i)]^{1-\alpha} = \left[\frac{P_t(i)}{P_t}\right]^{-\theta} Y_t, \tag{7.120}$$

Which yields the FONC

$$\frac{\Lambda_t W_t h_t(i)}{P_t} = (1-\alpha)\Xi_t K_t(i)^{\alpha}[g^t z_t h_t(i)]^{1-\alpha} \tag{7.121}$$

$$\frac{\Lambda_t Q_t K_t(i)}{P_t} = \alpha \Xi_t K_t(i)^{\alpha}[g^t z_t h_t(i)]^{1-\alpha} \tag{7.122}$$

and

$$\begin{aligned} &\phi_P \Lambda_t \left[\frac{P_t(i)}{\pi P_{t-1}(i)} - 1\right]\left[\frac{P_t(i)}{\pi P_{t-1}(i)}\right] \\ &= (1-\theta)\Lambda_t \left[\frac{P_t(i)}{P_t}\right]^{-\theta} + \theta \Xi_t \left[\frac{P_t(i)}{P_t}\right]^{-\theta-1} \\ &+ \beta \phi_P E_t \left\{ \begin{array}{c} \Lambda_{t+1}\left[\frac{P_{t+1}(i)}{\pi P_t(i)} - 1\right] \\ \times \left[\frac{P_{t+1}(i) P_t}{\pi P_t(i)^2}\right] \frac{Y_{t+1}}{Y_t} \end{array} \right\}, \end{aligned} \tag{7.123}$$

where $\beta^t \Lambda_t / P_t$ measures the marginal utility to the representative household provided by an additional dollar of profits during period t and where Ξ_t denotes the multiplier on (7.120). We do not prove this here, but the reader should convince themselves that maximizing a different objective (such as $E_0 \sum_{t=0}^{\infty} \beta^t [\frac{D_t(i)}{P_t}]$) is not utility maximizing but only, in this case, wealth maximizing.

7.3.5 The monetary authority

The monetary authority conducts monetary policy by adjusting a linear combination of the short-term nominal interest rate r_t and the money growth rate $\mu_t = M_t/M_{t-1}$ in response to deviations of inflation $\pi_t = P_t/P_{t-1}$ and detrended output $y_t = Y_t/g^t$ from their steady-state values. It uses the policy rule

$$\begin{aligned}\omega_r \log(r_t/r) = \omega_\mu \log(\mu_t/\mu) + \omega_\pi \log(\pi_t/\pi)\\ + \omega_y \log(y_t/y) + \log(v_t),\end{aligned} \tag{7.124}$$

which nests as special cases a money growth rule (when $\omega_r = 0$) and an interest rate rule (when $\omega_\mu = 0$). In (7.124), r, μ, π, and y are the steady-state values of r_t, μ_t, π_t, and y_t, respectively.

The policy shock v_t follows the autoregressive process

$$\log(v_t) = \rho_v \log(v_{t-1}) + \varepsilon_{vt}, \quad \varepsilon_{vt} \sim N(0, \sigma_v^2). \tag{7.125}$$

Since it is useful to allow for the possibility that any of the ω parameters in (7.124) equals zero, the standard deviation of ε_{vt} must be normalized; a convenient choice is $\sigma_v - 0.01$.

7.3.6 Equilibrium and the linearized system

Let

$$N_t = Y_t/h_t \tag{7.126}$$

denote the average product of labor and add it to the system of equations (equations (7.99)–(7.125)) thus far.

We look for a symmetric equilibrium which requires that we impose upon the system (7.99)–(7.126) that

$$P_t(i) = P_t, \quad Y_t(i) = Y_t, \quad h_t(i) = h_t, \quad K_t(i) = K_t, \tag{7.127}$$

$$D_t(i) = D_t \quad \forall\, i \in [0, 1]. \tag{7.128}$$

We impose market clearing, implying that

$$M_t = M_{t-1} + T_t, \tag{7.129}$$

$$B_t = B_{t-1} = 0 \tag{7.130}$$

are imposed upon (7.99)–(7.126).

Next, we normalize the system to remove the source of growth (g^t) requiring the following definitions to be imposed upon (7.99)–(7.126):

$$\mu_t = M_t/M_{t-1}, \quad y_t = Y_t/g^t, \quad \pi_t = P_t/P_{t-1}, \tag{7.131}$$

$$c_t = C_t/g^t, \quad i_t = I_t/g^t, \tag{7.132}$$

$$n_t = N_t/g^t, \quad m_t = (M_t/P_t)/g^t, \tag{7.133}$$

$$w_t = (W_t/P_t)/g^t, \quad q_t = Q_t/P_t, \tag{7.134}$$

$$d_t = (D_t/P_t)/g^t, \quad k_t = K_t/g^t \tag{7.135}$$

$$\lambda_t = g^t \Lambda_t, \quad \xi_t = g^t \Xi_t. \tag{7.136}$$

This procedure yields 20 equations in the following 20 stationary variables: y_t, c_t, i_t, h_t, n_t, m_t, μ_t, w_t, q_t, d_t, π_t, r_t, k_t, λ_t, ξ_t, a_t, e_t, z_t, x_t, and v_t

The equations are first

$$gk_{t+1} = (1-\delta)k_t + x_t i_t \tag{7.137}$$

$$\log x_t = \rho_x \log x_{t-1} + \varepsilon_{xt} \tag{7.138}$$

$$\begin{aligned} y_t = c_t + i_t &+ \left(\frac{\phi_K}{2}\right)\left(\frac{k_{t+1}}{k_t} - 1\right)^2 k_t \\ &+ \left(\frac{\phi_P}{2}\right)\left(\frac{\pi_{t+1}}{\pi} - 1\right)^2 y_t \end{aligned} \tag{7.139}$$

$$\log a_t = \rho_a \log a_{t-1} + \varepsilon_{at} \tag{7.140}$$

$$\log e_t = (1-\rho_e)\log e + \rho_e \log e_{t-1} + \varepsilon_{et} \tag{7.141}$$

and

$$a_t = \lambda_t c_t^{\frac{1}{\gamma}} \left[c_t^{\frac{\gamma-1}{\gamma}} + e_t^{\frac{1}{\gamma}} m_t^{\frac{\gamma-1}{\gamma}} \right] \tag{7.142}$$

$$\eta = \lambda_t w_t (1 - h_t) \tag{7.143}$$

$$e_t c_t = m_t \left(1 - \frac{1}{r_t}\right)^{\gamma} \tag{7.144}$$

$$g\lambda_t = \beta r_t E_t\left(\frac{\lambda_{t+1}}{\pi_{t+1}}\right), \tag{7.145}$$

in addition

$$\begin{aligned} g\left(\frac{\lambda_t}{x_t}\right) &+ \phi_K\lambda_t\left(\frac{k_{t+1}}{k_t}-1\right) \\ &= \beta E_t\left\{\lambda_{t+1}\left[q_{t+1}+\frac{1-\delta}{x_{t+1}}\right]\right\} \\ &\quad -\beta\left(\frac{\phi_K}{2}\right)E_t\left\{\lambda_{t+1}\left[\frac{k_{t+2}}{k_{t+1}}-1\right]^2\right\} \\ &\quad +\beta\phi_K E_t\left\{\lambda_{t+1}\left[\frac{k_{t+2}}{k_{t+1}}-1\right]\frac{k_{t+2}}{k_{t+1}}\right\} \end{aligned} \tag{7.146}$$

$$\log z_t = (1-\rho_z)\log z + \rho_z \log z_{t-1} + \varepsilon_{zt} \tag{7.147}$$

$$d_t = y_t - w_t h_t - q_t k_t - \left(\frac{\phi_P}{2}\right)\left(\frac{\pi_t}{\pi}-1\right)^2 y_t \tag{7.148}$$

$$y_t = k_t^{\alpha}(z_t h_t)^{1-\alpha} \tag{7.149}$$

$$\lambda_t w_t h_t = (1-\alpha)\xi_t y_t \tag{7.150}$$

$$\lambda_t q_t k_t = \alpha\xi_t y_t \tag{7.151}$$

$$\begin{aligned} \phi_P\lambda_t\left(\frac{\pi_t}{\pi}-1\right)\frac{\pi_t}{\pi} &= (1-\theta)\lambda_t + \theta\xi_t + \beta\phi_P E_t \\ &\quad \times\left\{\lambda_{t+1}\left(\frac{\pi_{t+1}}{\pi}-1\right)\frac{\pi_{t+1}}{\pi}\frac{y_{t+1}}{y_t}\right\} \end{aligned} \tag{7.152}$$

$$\begin{aligned} \omega_r\log(r_t/r) &= \omega_\mu\log(\mu_t/\mu) + \omega_\pi\log(\pi_t/\pi) \\ &\quad + \omega_y\log(y_t/y) + \log(v_t) \end{aligned} \tag{7.153}$$

$$\log(v_t) = \rho_v\log(v_{t-1}) + \varepsilon_{vt} \tag{7.154}$$

$$n_t = \frac{y_t}{h_t}, \quad \mu_t = g\left(\frac{m_t}{m_{t-1}}\right)\pi_t \tag{7.155}$$

The non-stochastic steady state can be calculated (by hand) for this system, as follows. Use (7.100), (7.104), (7.105), (7.116), and (7.125) to solve for (note that the steady-state values for e_t and z_t are e and z, respectively)

$$x = 1, \quad a = 1, \quad v = 1. \tag{7.156}$$

Let the steady-state growth rate of money, μ, be determined by the policymaker. Then, use (7.109) and (7.155) to get

$$\pi = \mu/g, \quad r = \mu/\beta. \tag{7.157}$$

Next, use (7.110) and (7.123) to solve for

$$q = g/\beta - 1 + \delta, \quad \xi = [(\theta - 1)/\theta]\lambda. \tag{7.158}$$

Use (7.106) and (7.108) to solve for

$$c = \left[1 + e\left(\frac{r}{r-1}\right)^{\gamma-1}\right]^{-1}\left(\frac{1}{\lambda}\right), \quad m = e\left(\frac{r}{r-1}\right)^{\gamma} c. \tag{7.159}$$

Next, use (7.99), (7.101), (7.119)–(7.122), and (7.126) to obtain

$$y = \left[1 - (g - 1 + \delta)\left(\frac{\theta - 1}{\theta}\right)\left(\frac{\alpha}{q}\right)\right]^{-1} c, \tag{7.160}$$

$$k = \left(\frac{\theta - 1}{\theta}\right)\left(\frac{\alpha y}{q}\right), \tag{7.161}$$

$$i = (g - 1 + \delta)k, \tag{7.162}$$

$$h = \frac{1}{z}\left(\frac{y}{k^{\alpha}}\right)^{\frac{1}{1-\alpha}}, \tag{7.163}$$

$$w = (1 - \alpha)\left(\frac{\theta - 1}{\theta}\right)\left(\frac{y}{h}\right), \tag{7.164}$$

$$d = y - wh - qk, \tag{7.165}$$

$$n = y/h. \tag{7.166}$$

Finally, use (7.107) to obtain

$$\lambda = \frac{\eta + (1 - \alpha)\left[1 + e\left(\frac{r}{r-1}\right)^{\gamma-1}\right]^{-1}\left[\left(\frac{\theta-1}{\theta}\right) - (g - 1 + \delta)\left(\frac{\alpha}{q}\right)\right]^{-1}}{(1 - \alpha)z\left(\frac{\theta-1}{\theta}\right)^{\frac{1}{1-\alpha}}\left(\frac{\alpha}{q}\right)^{\frac{\alpha}{1-\alpha}}}. \tag{7.167}$$

Having calculated the steady-state values, the system can be log-linearized around these steady-state values, yielding 20 linear expectational difference equations in the following 20 variables: $\widehat{y}_t$, $\widehat{c}_t$, $\widehat{i}_t$, $\widehat{h}_t$, $\widehat{n}_t$, $\widehat{m}_t$, $\widehat{\mu}_t$, $\widehat{w}_t$, $\widehat{q}_t$, $\widehat{d}_t$, $\widehat{\pi}_t$, $\widehat{r}_t$, $\widehat{k}_t$, $\widehat{\lambda}_t$, $\widehat{\xi}_t$, $\widehat{a}_t$, $\widehat{e}_t$, $\widehat{z}_t$, $\widehat{x}_t$, and $\widehat{v}_t$. The system can be written in the form required for solution by Sims (2001):

$$A(\psi)\zeta_{t+1} = B(\psi)\zeta_t + C(\psi)v_{t+1} + D(\psi)\varepsilon_{t+1}, \tag{7.168}$$

where ψ represents the deep parameters and ζ_t are the variables etc. The Sims (2001) procedure then yields a solution of the form

$$\zeta_{t+1} = F(\psi)\zeta_t + e_{t+1}, \quad e_t = G(\psi)\varepsilon_t, \quad E(e_t e_t') = Q(\psi). \tag{7.169}$$

Thus, given numeric values for ψ, we can compute the impulse response of any one of the shocks to any one of the variables, e.g. the effect of a one standard deviation technology shock on output, the effect of a one standard deviation money demand shock to investment, etc.

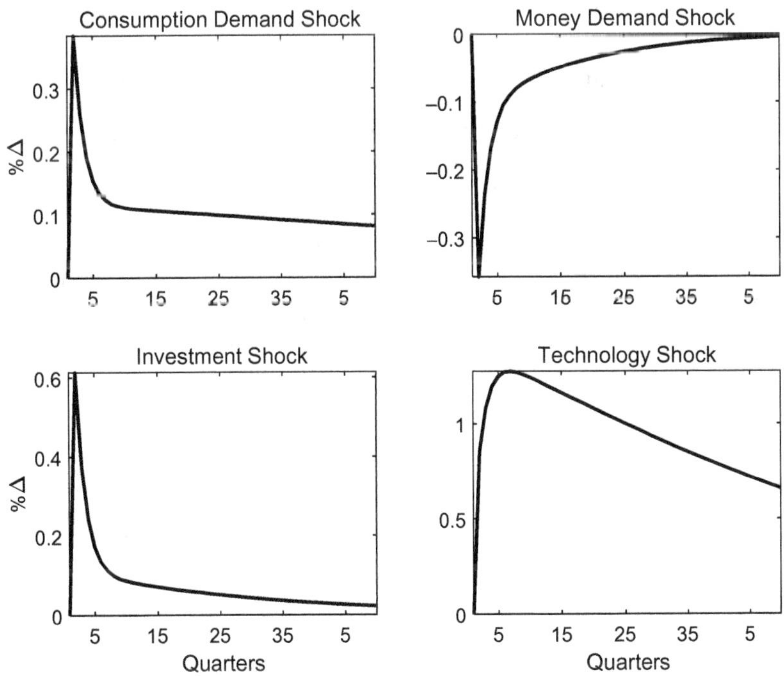

Figure 7.1. Output IRFs $\phi_P > 0$.

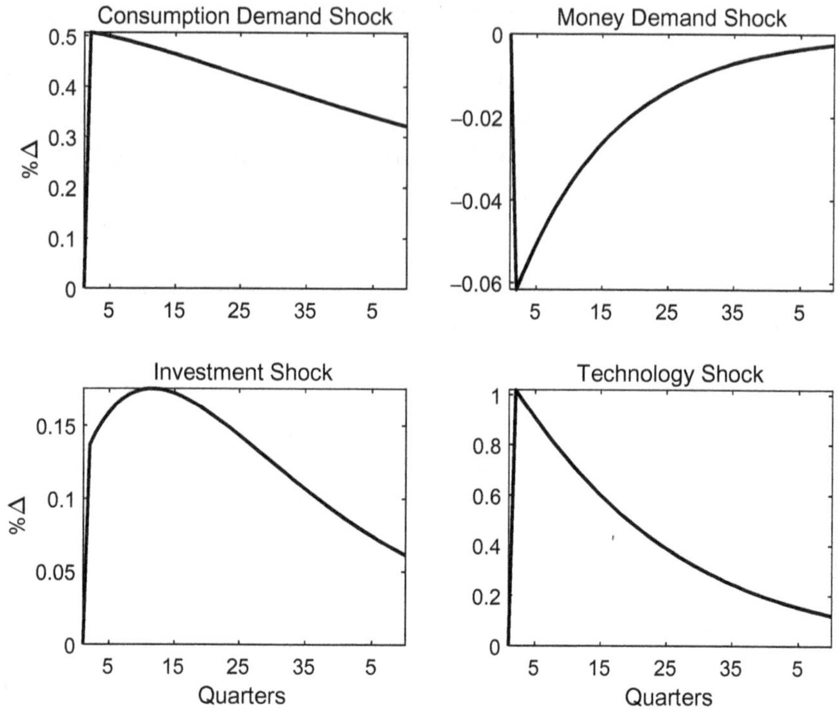

Figure 7.2. Output IRFs $\phi_P = 0$.

In the above model, note that the parameter ϕ_P governs whether prices are flexible or not (see Ireland (2003)). So, as an example, we plot two sets of impulse responses as follows. In each set, we provide the IRF for output as a function of four different shocks ($\widehat{a}_t$, $\widehat{e}_t$, $\widehat{z}_t$, and $\widehat{x}_t$). In Figure 7.1 the IRF for output for the four shocks are plotted under the assumption that $\phi_P > 0$ and Figure 7.2 is the flexible price specification of the model when $\phi_P = 0$; all parameter values are the same as those given by Ireland (2003). The two figures clearly show the difference across sticky price and flexible price versions of the model in terms of the response of output to the four shocks.

7.4 Conclusion

Modern neo-Keynesian models incorporate into the basic RBC model several frictions, market imperfections, and other relevant features thought to induce a role for fiscal and monetary policy. Unlike its IS-LM predecessors, these models are micro-founded and can compete with neo-classical models on the same rational expectations playing field in providing descriptions of macroeconomic data. This chapter has described briefly the evolution of thought in this area and described some basic models that fall within this category.

Chapter 8

Asset Pricing

8.1 Introduction

A major research agenda in modern macroeconomic theory concerns the pricing of assets, other than physical and human capital, in an aggregate economy. Having determined the price of such assets, and how they may exhibit what are commonly known as 'bubbles', another related research issue lies in linking those assets to the real macroeconomy. In the real macroeconomy, financial assets assist consumers in making intertemporal consumption decisions and assist firms in making intertemporal investment decisions. The main theoretical difficulty is that, for example, partial equilibrium models of consumption behavior in a macroeconomy typically treat financial asset prices as exogenous in order to focus on the main stylized fact regarding real consumption, namely that aggregate consumption is smooth relative to aggregate income (real GDP). Current general equilibrium models of asset prices on the other hand treat variables such as aggregate consumption as exogenous. The main empirical object of analysis is of course the pricing of risky assets like stocks. An excellent data source is the website of Dr. Robert Shiller that provides data on the S&P 500 on a monthly basis since 1871; Figure 8.1 plots the quarterly-averaged version of the data in real (i.e. inflation adjusted) terms.

Thus, in this chapter, we focus on seminal models of asset prices, bubbles, and related empirical issues, to the exclusion of the second major portion of the research agenda (linking financial sectors to the rest of the macroeconomy) given the rapidly developing nature of the

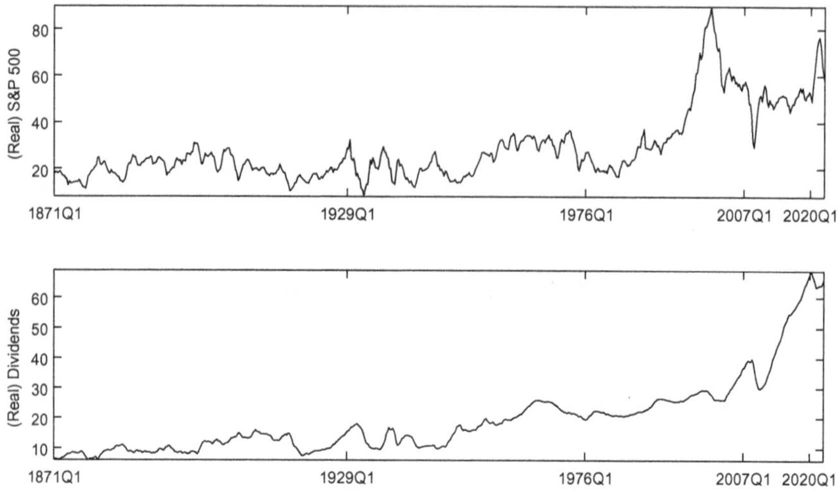

Figure 8.1. S&P 500 (real) prices and dividends.

research efforts on that front. In so doing, we first discuss the pricing of assets in a seminal dynamic stochastic general equilibrium model that takes the determination of income as a given. We then discuss some empirical issues this model presents us with when confronted with data. We conclude with a discussion of deviations from the main conclusion of the model, also known as bubbles.

8.2 The Lucas Model

8.2.1 Assumptions

Consider an endowment economy in which there is a representative agent who discounts exponentially utility from consumption

$$u(C_t), \tag{8.1}$$

where u is strictly increasing, concave and twice differentiable. The agent lives in a world in which there are N trees that each produce seedless fruit (or dividends) randomly in every period t. Let D_{it} denote this fruit from the ith tree and assume that this variable follows an exogenous stochastic process. Note that the fruit is perishable and since the fruit is seedless, there is no growth in this economy.

The representative agent has a endowment of 1 share (S_{it}) in each tree at time 0. In every period t, the D_{it} for every tree is distributed to shareholders in proportion to their shareholdings and then the shares are traded at price P_{it} in competitive markets. Note that since we assume a representative agent we need only focus on a single optimization problem whose constraint is given by

$$C_t + \sum_{i=1}^{N} P_{it} S_{it+1} = \sum_{i=1}^{N} S_{it}(P_{it} + D_{it}). \tag{8.2}$$

8.2.2 Optimization

The representative agent solves

$$\max_{\{C_t\}_{t=0}^{\infty}} \quad \Gamma = E_0 \sum_{t=0}^{\infty} \beta^t u(C_t), \tag{8.3}$$

$$\text{s.t.} \quad C_t + \sum_{i=1}^{N} P_{it} S_{it+1} = \sum_{i=1}^{N} S_{it}(P_{it} + D_{it}). \tag{8.4}$$

Substituting the constraint into the objective function yields an unconstrained optimization whose choice variable is how many shares to hold next period (S_{it+1}).

The main first-order condition for each asset i can be written as

$$P_{it} = E_t \left\{ \beta \frac{u'(C_{t+1})}{u'(C_t)} (P_{it+1} + D_{it+1}) \right\}, \tag{8.5}$$

whose interpretation is that the current price of a share is equal to the discounted, expected future payoff from holding that share (stemming from price appreciation and dividends) adjusted by the marginal rate of consumption substitution across time from holding that share instead of selling it and consuming the proceeds.

8.2.3 Equilibrium and analysis

Clearly, given the endowment nature of this economy, the equilibrium condition that has been imposed on the budget constraint is

$$C_t = \sum_{i=1}^{N} D_{it}. \tag{8.6}$$

Finally, given specifications for exogenous stochastic processes for the D_{it} and the Euler condition (8.5), we have a system of nonlinear expectational difference equations that characterize the equilibrium prices for all assets. We now examine the intuition of the model further.

Return to the Euler condition (8.5) and re-write it as

$$P_{it} = E_t\left\{\beta\frac{u'(C_{t+1})}{u'(C_t)}(P_{it+1} + D_{it+1})\right\} \tag{8.7}$$

$$= \frac{\beta}{u'(C_t)}E_t\left\{u'(C_{t+1})\left(P_{it+1} + D_{it+1}\right)\right\} \tag{8.8}$$

$$\rightarrow u'(C_t) = \beta E_t\left\{u'(C_{t+1})\frac{(P_{it+1} + D_{it+1})}{P_{it}}\right\} \tag{8.9}$$

$$u'(C_t) = \beta E_t\left\{u'(C_{t+1})R_{it+1}\right\}, \quad R_{it+1} = \frac{(P_{it+1} + D_{it+1})}{P_{it}}, \tag{8.10}$$

where R_{it+1} is the gross return on the ith asset consisting of any price appreciation and the dividend (or yield).

Consider the case of a single risky asset (the following analysis carries through generally), then

$$u'(C_t) = \beta E_t\left\{u'(C_{t+1})R_{t+1}\right\}, \tag{8.11}$$

$$\rightarrow u'(C_t) = \beta E_t\left\{u'(C_{t+1})\frac{(P_{t+1} + D_{t+1})}{P_t}\right\}, \tag{8.12}$$

$$\leftrightarrow u'(C_t)P_t = \beta E_t\left\{u'(C_{t+1})\left(P_{t+1} + D_{t+1}\right)\right\}, \tag{8.13}$$

$$u'(C_t)P_t = \beta E_t\left\{u'(C_{t+1})P_{t+1} + u'(C_{t+1})D_{t+1}\right\}. \tag{8.14}$$

Clearly, we can now substitute in for $u'(C_{t+1})P_{t+1}$ to get

$$u'(C_t)P_t = \beta E_t\left\{u'(C_{t+1})D_{t+1} + \beta E_{t+1}[u'(C_{t+2})(P_{t+2} + D_{t+2})]\right\} \tag{8.15}$$

and employing the LIE and the method of repeated substitution, we obtain

$$u'(C_t)P_t = E_t\left\{\sum_{j=1}^{J}\beta^j u'(C_{t+j})D_{t+j}\right\} + E_t\left\{\beta^J u'(C_{t+J})P_{t+J}\right\}. \tag{8.16}$$

Now, let J tends to $+\infty$ and rearrange the above to get

$$P_t = E_t\left\{\sum_{j=1}^{\infty}\beta^j \frac{u'(C_{t+j})}{u'(C_t)}D_{t+j}\right\} + \lim_{J\to\infty} E_t\left\{\beta^J u'(C_{t+J})P_{t+J}\right\}. \tag{8.17}$$

The 'no bubble' condition for an asset price is that

$$\lim_{J\to\infty} E_t\left\{\beta^J u'(C_{t+J})P_{t+J}\right\} = 0 \tag{8.18}$$

in which case the asset price only reflects fundamentals, that is,

$$P_t = E_t\left\{\sum_{j=1}^{\infty}\beta^j \frac{u'(C_{t+j})}{u'(C_t)}D_{t+j}\right\} \tag{8.19}$$

and thus an asset price (P_t) reflects the present discounted value of dividends adjusted for risk as reflected in the stochastic discount factor $\beta^j \frac{u'(C_{t+j})}{u'(C_t)}$. What makes the Lucas (1978) model interesting is that equation (8.19) holds regardless of whether an economy is an endowment economy or production economy.

Now, assuming risk neutrality (so that the marginal utility of consumption is constant versus declining in stochastic consumption) yields

$$P_t = E_t\left\{\sum_{j=1}^{\infty}\beta^j D_{t+j}\right\} \tag{8.20}$$

or in the case of multiple assets

$$P_{it} = E_t\left\{\sum_{j=1}^{\infty}\beta^j D_{it+j}\right\}. \tag{8.21}$$

Consider the case again of risk neutrality with a single asset, and assume further that the only other investment option available to the agent, other than the risky asset, is a riskless asset. Then, it is relatively straightforward to argue that given risk neutrality

$$\beta = \frac{1}{1+r}, \quad r > 0, \tag{8.22}$$

where r is the rate of return on the riskless asset. For instance, the riskless asset could be physical capital so that r represents the net marginal product of that physical capital, or it could be a riskless bond. Substituting in these assumptions into equation (8.19) yields

$$P_t = E_t\left\{\sum_{j=1}^{\infty}\beta^j\frac{u'(C_{t+j})}{u'(C_t)}D_{t+j}\right\} \tag{8.23}$$

$$\rightarrow P_t = E_t\left\{\sum_{j=1}^{\infty}\left(\frac{1}{1+r}\right)^j D_{t+j}\right\} \tag{8.24}$$

so that the price of an asset is simply the expected, discounted value associated with its dividend stream.

8.3 Empirical Asset Pricing Puzzles

Return to equation (8.5)

$$P_{it} = E_t\left\{\beta\frac{u'(C_{t+1})}{u'(C_t)}(P_{it+1}+D_{it+1})\right\}, \quad R_{it+1} = \frac{(P_{it+1}+D_{it+1})}{P_{it}} \tag{8.25}$$

and rewrite it as

$$E_t(R_{it+1}\mathcal{M}_{t,t+1}) = 1, \quad \mathcal{M}_{t,t+1} = \beta\frac{u'(C_{t+1})}{u'(C_t)}, \tag{8.26}$$

where $\mathcal{M}_{t,t+1}$ is known as the *stochastic discount factor*. Equivalently, we can write the above as

$$E_t(R_{it}\mathcal{M}_{t-1,t}) = 1. \tag{8.27}$$

Realize that for any two random variables X and Y we have that COV $(X,Y) = E(XY) - E(X)E(Y)$ and so

$$\text{COV }(R_{it}, M_t) + E_t(R_{it})E_t(\mathcal{M}_{t-1,t}) = 1 \tag{8.28}$$

and thus shares in assets with high expected returns are those for which the covariance of the asset's return with the stochastic discount factor is low. So, the agent pays a high price for an asset which is likely to have high dividends when aggregate consumption is low (e.g. in a recession). We now describe two important puzzles encountered when confronting theory with facts.

8.3.1 The equity premium puzzle

Mehra and Prescott (1985) used such characterizations of the model to argue that an implausible value of risk aversion would be required to reconcile the data on risk-free assets and risky assets. Let utility be of the CRRA variety with coefficient θ. Let there be one risky asset and one risk free asset. Let $G = \frac{C_{t+1}}{C_t}$ be the gross growth rate of consumption (possibly stochastic due to shocks). Then, the Euler equation for the risky asset can be written as

$$\frac{1}{\beta} = E_t\left[G^{-\theta}R\right]. \tag{8.29}$$

A second-order Taylor series expansion of the above equation evaluated at $\{1, 1\}$ yields

$$E(G^{-\theta}R) \approx E(1 + (R-1) - \theta(G-1) \tag{8.30}$$
$$+\frac{1}{2}[\theta(1+\theta)(G-1)^2 \tag{8.31}$$
$$-2\theta(G-1)(R-1)]). \tag{8.32}$$

Let $r = R - 1$ and $g = G - 1$ and realize that $E(gr) = E(g)E(r) + \text{cov}\ (g, r)$ and $E(g^2) = [E(g)]^2 + \text{var}\ (g)$ to get

$$E(G^{-\theta}R) \approx 1 + E(r) - \theta E(g) \tag{8.33}$$
$$+\frac{\theta(1+\theta)}{2}\left[[E(g)]^2 + \text{var}\ (g)\right] \tag{8.34}$$
$$-\theta E(g)E(r) - \theta\ \text{cov}\ (g, r). \tag{8.35}$$

Similarly, for the risk-free asset (whose gross rate of return would be fixed at $\overline{R}$), we would get

$$E(G^{-\theta})\overline{R} \approx 1 + \overline{r} - \theta E(g) \tag{8.36}$$
$$+\frac{\theta(1+\theta)}{2}\left[[E(g)]^2 + \text{var}\ (g)\right] \tag{8.37}$$
$$-\theta E(g)\overline{r}. \tag{8.38}$$

Ignore all terms involving $E(g)E(r)$ and $[E(g)]^2$ as they are likely to be small.

Subtract the two approximations from one another to obtain in general that

$$E(r_i) - \overline{r} \approx \theta \text{ cov } (g, r_i) \tag{8.39}$$

$$= \theta \times \text{ corr } (g, r_i) \times \text{ std. dev } (g) \times \text{ std. dev } (r_i), \tag{8.40}$$

where r_i refers to the rate of return on a risky asset (e.g. S&P 500 share).

Mehra and Prescott (1985) used annual data from 1890 to 1979 to compute $E(r_i) - \overline{r} = 0.06$, corr $(g, r_i) = 0.04$, std. dev $(g) = 0.167$, and std. dev $(r_i) = 0.036$. Plugging in these numbers into the above allows us to compute an estimate of θ as

$$\widehat{\theta} \approx 25. \tag{8.41}$$

If an agent had this level of risk aversion, it is unlikely that they would ever leave their house.

8.3.2 The excess volatility puzzle

Shiller (1981) raised the possibility that observed asset prices are too volatile relative to the data, known as the excess volatility puzzle, as follows. Assuming risk neutrality for a single asset, we have that

$$P_t = E_t\left\{\sum_{j=1}^{\infty} \beta^j D_{t+j}\right\}, \quad \beta = \frac{1}{1+\overline{r}}, \quad \overline{r} > 0 \tag{8.42}$$

$$\rightarrow P_t = E_t\left\{\sum_{j=1}^{\infty} \frac{D_{t+j}}{(1+\overline{r})^j}\right\}, \tag{8.43}$$

where $\overline{r}$ is the risk-free rate.

Suppose that future dividends were known with certainty, then the corresponding asset price would simply be

$$\widetilde{P}_t = \sum_{j=1}^{\infty} \frac{D_{t+j}}{(1+\overline{r})^j}. \tag{8.44}$$

Rational expectations would therefore suggest that

$$\widetilde{P}_t = P_t + \varepsilon_t, \quad E(\varepsilon_t | P_t) = 0 \tag{8.45}$$

implying that

$$\text{Var}\ (\widetilde{P}_t) \ = \ \text{Var}\ (P_t) \ + \ \text{Var}\ (\varepsilon_t). \tag{8.46}$$

Re-arranging yields

$$\frac{\text{Var}\ (P_t)}{\text{Var}\ (\widetilde{P}_t)} \leq 1. \tag{8.47}$$

That is, since P_t is a forecast of $\widetilde{P}_t$, P_t should be less volatile as measured by the variances. Shiller (1981) showed that in many datasets we have that

$$\frac{\text{Var}\ (P_t)}{\text{Var}\ (\widetilde{P}_t)} \approx 5, \tag{8.48}$$

which is clearly not less than or equal to one.

8.4 Bubbles

We first realize that if the risk neutral investor is choosing between a single risky versus a riskless asset in a competitive market, then she should be expected to arbitrage between the two assets. That is, the expected rate of return on the risky asset should equal the rate of return on the riskless asset. The rate of return on the riskless asset is obviously r. The rate of return on the risky asset equals the expected capital gain from selling the asset plus the real dividend from holding it, in any given time period t. Thus, the no arbitrage condition in a competitive market would be

$$\frac{E_t P_{t+1} - P_t}{P_t} + \frac{D_t}{P_t} = r. \tag{8.49}$$

Note how equation (8.24) follows directly from equation (8.49)! Thus, in explaining bubbles, we can work directly with equation (8.49). There can be two types of bubbles: deterministic bubbles and stochastically bursting bubbles. We first describe the former case.

Rewrite (8.49) as

$$P_t = RE_tP_{t+1} + RD_t, \quad R = \frac{1}{1+r} < 1. \tag{8.50}$$

Then, the rational expectations 'fundamental' solution to (8.50) by repeated substitution is

$$P_t = RE_t\left\{\sum_{j=0}^{\infty} R^j D_{t+j}\right\} = E_t\left\{\sum_{j=1}^{\infty}\left(\frac{1}{1+r}\right)^j D_{t+j}\right\} \tag{8.51}$$

and we denote it by P_t^*. Now, we relax the no bubble condition, that is, there may be other solutions to (8.50) as functions of P_t^*, that is,

$$P_t = P_t^* + B_t \tag{8.52}$$

can also be a solution to (8.50). We show that P_t which contains the bubble term B_t is also a solution of (8.50), as follows.

Using (8.52) compute E_tP_{t+1} as

$$E_tP_{t+1} = E_tP_{t+1}^* + E_tB_{t+1}. \tag{8.53}$$

Now, insert (8.52) and (8.53) into (8.50) to get

$$P_t^* + B_t = RE_tP_{t+1}^* + RE_tB_{t+1} + RD_t. \tag{8.54}$$

Inserting (8.51) into (8.54) yields

$$B_t = RE_tB_{t+1} \tag{8.55}$$

$$\rightarrow E_tB_{t+1} = R^{-1}B_t. \tag{8.56}$$

Thus, any process for B_t that satisfies (8.56) such that $P_t = P_t^* + B_t$ will also be a solution to (8.51).

In the deterministic case, consider for instance

$$B_{t+1} = \zeta B_t \tag{8.57}$$

with some initial condition B_0. Then,

$$E_tB_{t+1} = \zeta B_t \tag{8.58}$$

which implies, using (8.56), that any $\zeta = R^{-1}$ is also a solution!

Now, consider a simple stochastic process for the dynamics of the bubble term B_t, according to which the bubble keeps alive with some (known) probability $\pi \in (0,1)$ and bursts with probability $(1-\pi)$, conditional on the bubble being present at time t. Formally, if $B_t > 0$, then $B_{t+1} = \alpha B_t$ for some $\alpha > 0$ with probability π, and $B_{t+1} = 0$ with probability $(1-\pi)$.

We are interested in the restrictions on the constant α, if any, under which $P_t = P_t^* + B_t$ is also a solution the no arbitrage condition in a competitive market, i.e. a solution to

$$P_t = RE_tP_{t+1} + RD_t, R = \frac{1}{1+r}.$$

Since

$$E_tP_{t+1} = E_tP_{t+1}^* + E_tB_{t+1} = E_tP_{t+1}^* + \pi\alpha B_t,$$

one has

$$P_t^* + B_t = R\left(E_tP_{t+1}^* + \pi\alpha B_t\right) + RD_t$$

which, P_t^* being the fundamental solution, in turn yields

$$B_t = R\pi\alpha B_t$$

and thus $\alpha = (R\pi)^{-1}$ is necessary and sufficient for any random process B_t with arbitrary initial condition $B_0 > 0$ and conditional probability distribution as described above to satisfy the no arbitrage condition. Note that, relative to the case of deterministic bubbles, as long as the bubble keeps growing, its growth rate exceeds the interest rate and gets larger the larger the probability of bubble burst.

8.5 The Price-Dividend Ratio

Returning to the no-bubbles case, we now consider another empirical specification under rational expectations that has a precise prediction, namely that the price-dividend ratio is a constant. In the single risky-asset case the Euler is

$$P_tD_t^{-\gamma} = \beta E_t\left\{D_{t+1}^{-\gamma}\left(P_{t+1} + D_{t+1}\right)\right\}, \tag{8.59}$$

when $u(C_t) = \frac{C_t^{1-\gamma}}{1-\gamma}$, $\gamma > 0$. In steady state,

$$PD^{-\gamma} = \beta D^{-\gamma}(P + D),$$

$$P - \beta P = \beta D \rightarrow \bar{P} = \frac{\beta \bar{D}}{1 - \beta}.$$

To log-linearize the Euler equation

$$P_t D_t^{-\gamma} = \beta E_t \left\{ D_{t+1}^{-\gamma} \left(P_{t+1} + D_{t+1} \right) \right\}, \tag{8.60}$$

define

$$\tilde{d}_{t+1} = \ln D_{t+1}, \; \tilde{d}_t = \ln D_t, \tag{8.61}$$

$$\tilde{p}_{t+1} = \ln P_{t+1}, \; \tilde{p}_t = \ln P_t, \tag{8.62}$$

and rewrite the Euler equation as

$$\exp(\tilde{p}_t) \exp(-\gamma \tilde{d}_t) = \beta E_t \left\{ \exp(-\gamma \tilde{d}_{t+1}) \left(\exp(\tilde{p}_{t+1}) + \exp(\tilde{d}_{t+1}) \right) \right\}. \tag{8.63}$$

The first-order Taylor approximation requires derivatives evaluated at steady state as follows:

$$\frac{\partial \cdot}{\partial \tilde{p}_t} = \exp(\tilde{p}_t) \exp(-\gamma \tilde{d}_t) = \bar{P} \bar{D}^{-\gamma}, \tag{8.64}$$

$$\frac{\partial \cdot}{\partial \tilde{d}_t} = -\gamma \exp(\tilde{p}_t) \exp(-\gamma \tilde{d}_t) = -\gamma \bar{P} \bar{D}^{-\gamma}, \tag{8.65}$$

$$\begin{aligned} \frac{\partial \cdot}{\partial \tilde{d}_{t+1}} &= \gamma \beta \exp(-\gamma \tilde{d}_{t+1}) \left(\exp(\tilde{p}_{t+1}) + \exp(\tilde{d}_{t+1}) \right) \\ &\quad - \beta \exp(-\gamma \tilde{d}_{t+1}) \exp(\tilde{d}_{t+1}) \qquad (8.66) \\ &= \gamma \beta \bar{D}^{-\gamma} \left(\bar{P} + \bar{D} \right) - \beta \bar{D}^{1-\gamma}, \qquad (8.67) \end{aligned}$$

$$\frac{\partial \cdot}{\partial \tilde{p}_{t+1}} = -\beta \exp(-\gamma \tilde{d}_{t+1}) \exp(\tilde{p}_{t+1}) = -\beta \bar{P} \bar{D}^{-\gamma}, \tag{8.68}$$

and thus the linearized system is

$$\begin{aligned} \bar{P}\bar{D}^{-\gamma} \hat{p}_t - \gamma \bar{P} \bar{D}^{-\gamma} \hat{d}_t = \beta E_t \Big\{ &\left(\beta \bar{D}^{1-\gamma} - \gamma \beta \bar{D}^{-\gamma} \left(\bar{P} + \bar{D} \right) \right) \hat{d}_{t+1} \\ &+ (\beta \bar{P} \bar{D}^{-\gamma}) \hat{p}_{t+1} \Big\}, \qquad (8.69) \end{aligned}$$

$$\hat{p}_t - \gamma \hat{d}_t = E_t \left\{ (1 - \beta - \gamma) \hat{d}_{t+1} + \beta \hat{p}_{t+1} \right\}, \tag{8.70}$$

where log-deviations from steady state are denoted as $\hat{p}_t = \ln(P_t) - \ln(\bar{P})$ and $\hat{d}_t = \ln(D_t) - \ln(\bar{D})$.

The first step to solve the equation under rational expectations is to rewrite it more compactly as

$$\hat{p}_t - \gamma\hat{d}_t = E_t\{(1-\beta-\gamma)\hat{d}_{t+1} + \beta\hat{p}_{t+1}\} \tag{8.71}$$

$$= \beta E_t(\hat{p}_{t+1}) + (1-\beta-\gamma)E_t(\hat{d}_{t+1}) \tag{8.72}$$

and note that under the AR(1) assumption for $\hat{d}_t$ we have that

$$\hat{d}_{t+1} = \rho_{\hat{d}}\hat{d}_t + \varepsilon_{t+1} \rightarrow E_t(\hat{d}_{t+1}) = \rho_{\hat{d}}\hat{d}_t, \tag{8.73}$$

thus

$$\hat{p}_t - \gamma\hat{d}_t = \beta E_t(\hat{p}_{t+1}) + (1-\beta-\gamma)\rho_{\hat{d}}\hat{d}_t \tag{8.74}$$

$$\rightarrow \hat{p}_t = \beta E_t(\hat{p}_{t+1}) + ((1-\beta-\gamma)\rho_{\hat{d}} + \gamma)\hat{d}_t. \tag{8.75}$$

Now, we guess

$$\hat{p}_t = \phi\hat{d}_t \rightarrow E_t(\hat{p}_{t+1}) = \phi E_t(\hat{d}_{t+1}) = \phi\rho_{\hat{d}}\hat{d}_t \tag{8.76}$$

and insert the guess into $\hat{p}_t = \beta E_t(\hat{p}_{t+1}) + ((1-\beta-\gamma)\rho_{\hat{d}} + \gamma)\hat{d}_t$ to obtain

$$\hat{p}_t = \beta\phi\rho_{\hat{d}}\hat{d}_t + ((1-\beta-\gamma)\rho_{\hat{d}} + \gamma)\hat{d}_t \tag{8.77}$$

$$\rightarrow \hat{p}_t = (\beta\phi\rho_{\hat{d}} + ((1-\beta-\gamma)\rho_{\hat{d}} + \gamma))\hat{d}_t \tag{8.78}$$

and equating coefficients we have

$$\phi = \beta\phi\rho_{\hat{d}} + ((1-\beta-\gamma)\rho_{\hat{d}} + \gamma), \tag{8.79}$$

$$\phi - \phi\beta\rho_{\hat{d}} = ((1-\beta-\gamma)\rho_{\hat{d}} + \gamma), \tag{8.80}$$

$$(1-\beta\rho_{\hat{d}})\phi = ((1-\beta-\gamma)\rho_{\hat{d}} + \gamma), \tag{8.81}$$

$$\phi = \frac{(1-\beta-\gamma)\rho_{\hat{d}} + \gamma}{1-\beta\rho_{\hat{d}}} = \phi^{REE}. \tag{8.82}$$

Thus, prices equal a constant times dividends under rational expectations; Figure 8.2 suggests this may not be the case in reality.

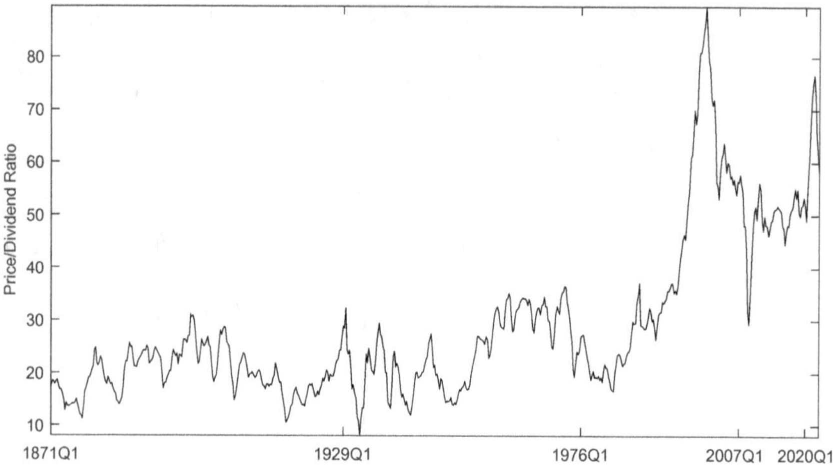

Figure 8.2. The price-dividend ratio.

8.6 Conclusion

We have seen that with the standard model of asset pricing, empirical puzzles exist when confronting theory with data. Thus, macroeconomists have offered up some solutions, e.g. exotic preferences (habits, temptation, loss aversion, etc.), incomplete markets (uninsured idiosyncratic risk, borrowing constraints, etc.), Knightian uncertainty, among others. One view is that there are no puzzles, just that historical returns on stocks were unexpected and the real riskiness of stocks is higher than what is observed in sample data. This remains a very active area of research as it offers the possibility of predicting risky asset prices.

Chapter 9

Overlapping Generations Models

9.1 Introduction

In this chapter, we consider a macroeconomic model whose features are a drastic departure from the standard representative agent (RA) framework. As we have seen in models by Solow, Ramsey, Cass, and Koopmans, economic outcomes can be described as the result of the interaction of identical agents that live for an infinite time period. The assumption of identical agents ensure that one can use symmetry arguments to get to the equilibrium solution, while the assumption that they live forever is useful in that one does not set an arbitrary terminal date for the whole economy. While these are simplifying assumptions, they allow us to analyze otherwise complex economies both in the short run (business cycles) and in the long run (growth). These models however have some shortcomings and do not allow for the inclusion of some salient features of actual economies. For example, one cannot analyze the impact of social security or the optimal provision of pensions in a model that doesn't distinguish between younger and older generations. In addition, standard RA models do not allow for the analysis of monetary policy, as money will typically end up being a 'strictly dominated asset', meaning that it is always better for individuals to invest in say, capital, than it is to keep them in money which may only depreciate as a result of inflation.

Overlapping generation (OLG) models allow for a natural setting in which to consider the roles of both money and government redistributive policy, in particular as it relates to the optimal provision of pensions and social security. Pioneered by Samuelson (1958), OLG models consider an economy populated by successive generations of finitely lived agents; they also assume that these generations overlap; the young will work and interact with other generations (the very young or the old) who may not be engaged in productive activities. This setting allows one to consider Fisher's life-cycle hypothesis in a general equilibrium setting: how do life-cycle issues affect interest rates at the aggregate level? By considering the competitive equilibrium outcome, one can see whether there is room for government intervention or whether in fact society will reach an optimal outcome without the need for redistributive policies. As we shall see, OLG models demonstrate in very simple settings that competitive equilibrium outcomes are not necessarily desirable and that government-induced redistribution can lead to Pareto-improving outcomes.

9.2 The Basic OLG Model

9.2.1 The general environment

We consider an economy where each agent lives for a finite number of periods. The simplest such setting is to assume that a typical agent lives for two periods or stages of life, denoted young and old. We also assume that each time period is populated by both types of agents. Time begins in period $t = 0$ and the economy is populated by $L_{-1} > 0$ of the initial old; in any period t, $L_t = L_0(1 + n)^t$ young people are born.

9.2.2 A pure endowment economy

Initially, we analyze an endowment economy, meaning that there is no production and agents receive an endowment of the consumption good in each period. A typical agent will receive $e_1 \geq 0$ when young and $e_2 \geq 0$ when old. The initial old are endowed with $e_2 \geq 0$ of the consumption good. Throughout this chapter (unless stated otherwise), we assume that the good perishes completely from one period to the next. Later, we will consider production in this economy, but for now, we uncover some of the issues that crop up in typical OLG settings.

As a first step, we solve for the golden rule level of consumption. Consider a social planner who controls all resources and whose objective is to maximize the utility of a typical agent. Suppose that a typical agent has preferences described by a utility function of the form $v(c_1, c_2)$ with the usual properties. Now, in any period t, the social planner has access to the following resources: $L_t e_1 + L_{t-1} e_2$. So, the objective of the social planner is to solve the following problem:

$$\max_{c_1, c_2} \quad v(c_1, c_2) \tag{9.1}$$

subject to

$$L_t c_1 + L_{t-1} c_2 \leq L_t e_1 + L_{t-1} e_2. \tag{9.2}$$

Note that this problem is stationary. Indeed, the last equation can be rewritten as

$$c_1 + \frac{c_2}{1+n} \leq e_1 + \frac{e_2}{1+n}. \tag{9.3}$$

This problem will yield an interior solution when under standard assumptions on utility. For example, suppose for now that $n = 0$, and also suppose that the utility function is symmetric in c_1 and c_2 then the optimal level of consumption is $\frac{e_1+e_2}{2}$ in each period. As we shall see, this result cannot be obtained as a competitive equilibrium outcome, at least not without making some additional assumptions.

To see this, let's simplify the problem a bit further. Suppose that the endowment profile is of the form

$$(e_1, e_2) = (y, 0). \tag{9.4}$$

So, young people produce $y > 0$ units of the consumption good and retire when old (and therefore do not produce during this stage of their lives). Because agents in this economy have standard preferences, they prefer average to extreme consumption bundles; in particular, they would prefer any bundle (c_1, c_2) such that $c_1 > 0$ and $c_2 > 0$ and $c_1 + c_2 = y$ over the consumption bundle $(y, 0)$, and yet a 'decentralized outcome' would yield precisely this result. To see this, note that the young, who would like to smooth their consumption by having only the current old to trade with. But they have no incentive to trade with them because the old will not be around next period to pay them back. As a result, the competitive equilibrium leads to an autarky outcome where each person in the economy consumes exactly her endowment. This is true for any endowment profile, for example, if

$$(e_1, e_2) = (0, y), \tag{9.5}$$

then what a typical agent wants to do is borrow against future income to smooth out her consumption. Once again, she cannot do that since her only trading partners are the current old, and they wish to consume whatever endowment is available to them.

Clearly, the competitive outcome does not lead to the golden rule outcome. There are a number of ways to interpret this result. On the one hand, one can state that there is room for government intervention. Consider for example the case where the typical endowment profile is $(e_1, e_2) = (y, 0)$. What the government can do is impose a tax on the current young and use tax proceeds to finance consumption for the current old. So, while the competitive outcome is $(y, 0)$, such a taxation system would lead to an outcome of the type $(y - \varepsilon, \varepsilon)$ (keep in mind that we are assuming that there is no population growth). Clearly, the consumption profile $(y - \varepsilon, \varepsilon)$ Pareto dominates the consumption profile $(y, 0)$ for small ε.

Similarly, suppose that the typical endowment profile is $(e_1, e_2) = (0, y)$. Here, a tax-transfer system implemented by the government would yield a typical generation $(\varepsilon, y - \varepsilon)$. Suppose that the government begins to do this in period t, then the current old will consume $y - \varepsilon$ instead of y, but generations born in period t and onward will consume $(\varepsilon, y - \varepsilon)$, which is better for them than to consume the autarky outcome $(0, y)$. As you can see, the outcome is better for all generations born in period t and onward but makes the current old worse off. Technically, one cannot say that this outcome Pareto dominates the competitive outcome (in fact, they cannot be Pareto ranked), but reasonable people might agree that making one generation worse off for the benefit of an infinite number of generations (including the current young) might be a worthwhile trade-off.

This 'reasonableness' criterion is why we are focusing on the golden rule outcome as being the desirable outcome. Let's formalize the above analysis in a slightly more specific setting.

9.2.3 Dynamic efficiency

We now assume that preferences over consumption take the following form:

$$v\left(c_{1t}, c_{2t+1}\right) = u\left(c_{1t}\right) + \frac{u\left(c_{2t+1}\right)}{1+\rho}, \tag{9.6}$$

where $\rho > 0$ is the rate of time preference or discount rate ($\beta = \frac{1}{1+\rho}$ is the discount factor). Here, (c_{1t}, c_{2t+1}) is the consumption profile of a typical agent born in period t. We assume the existence of a saving technology – this is not an additional assumption, rather it simplify formalizes the notion that individuals can 'save' their endowment by trading with others. The objective of this agent is to choose how much to consume and save. If s_t denotes savings, her objective is to

$$\max_{s_t} \quad \Gamma = u(e_1 - s_t) + \frac{u(e_2 + (1 + r_{t+1})s_t)}{1+\rho}. \tag{9.7}$$

This yields the following FONC:

$$-u'(e_1 - s_t) + \frac{(1 + r_{t+1})u'(e_2 + (1 + r_{t+1})s_t)}{1+\rho} = 0 \tag{9.8}$$

$$\rightarrow 1 + \widetilde{r} = \frac{u'(e_1)\left(1+\rho\right)}{u'(e_2)}, \tag{9.9}$$

where we note that $\widetilde{r}$ is introduced in order to define the notion of an autarkic interest rate, that is, the interest rate at which agents don't want to save. As we have argued in the previous section, this is an equilibrium outcome. Indeed, note that the budget constraint of a typical agent is satisfied when $(c_{1t}, c_{2t+1}, r_{t+1}) = (e_1, e_2, \widetilde{r})$:

$$c_{1t} + \frac{c_{2t+1}}{1 + r_{t+1}} = e_1 + \frac{e_2}{1 + r_{t+1}}. \tag{9.10}$$

Finally, we need to check that markets for the unique good clear each period when $(c_{1t}, c_{2t}) = (e_1, e_2)$ in the following equation:

$$L_t c_{1t} + L_{t-1} c_{2t} = L_t e_1 + L_{t-1} e_2. \tag{9.11}$$

To compare this with the golden rule outcome, let's solve for the FONC of the golden rule optimization problem. This is to

$$\max \quad u\left(c_1\right) + \frac{u\left(c_2\right)}{1+\rho} \tag{9.12}$$

subject to

$$L_t c_1 + L_{t-1} c_2 = L_t e_1 + L_{t-1} e_2, \tag{9.13}$$

or

$$c_1 + \frac{c_2}{1+n} = e_1 + \frac{e_2}{1+n}, \tag{9.14}$$

for all periods t. The FONC for this problem is

$$-u'(c_1) + \frac{(1+n)u(c_2)}{1+\rho} = 0. \tag{9.15}$$

Although the golden rule is thought of as being implemented by a government (and therefore doesn't involve markets), we can compute an imputed interest rate r_g to allow us to compare it to the competitive equilibrium outcome. This imputed interest rate must solve

$$1 + r_g = 1 + n = \frac{u'(c_{1g})\,(1+\rho)}{u'(c_{2g})}. \tag{9.16}$$

In all cases, the golden rule outcome is an improvement over the competitive equilibrium outcome beginning with the current generation. In the previous section however, we discussed a case where the current old would be worse off if the golden rule were implemented at the onset of their old age. This was the case where the endowment profile was $(e_1, e_2) = (0, y)$. In this case, note that

$$\frac{u'(0)\,(1+\rho)}{u'(y)} > \frac{u'(c_{1g})\,(1+\rho)}{u'(c_{2g})}. \tag{9.17}$$

This signals that the interest rate $\widetilde{r}$ in the competitive equilibrium outcome is bigger than the imputed interest rate of the golden rule outcome, which is equal to the population growth rate n. We define a Samuelson economy as one in which $\widetilde{r} < r_g = n$ and a classical economy as one in which $\widetilde{r} > r_g = n$. The economy with $(e_1, e_2) = (0, y)$ is a classical economy because the government cannot offer a Pareto-improving allocation. All classical economies share this feature.

Symmetrically, there exist Pareto improvements for all Samuelson economies. Because of this property, we say that classical economies are dynamically efficient while Samuelson economies are dynamically inefficient. One way to implement a Pareto improvement for a dynamically inefficient economy is to consider a tax of ε on the current young that is transferred to the current old. Since there are $(1+n)$ more young than there are old, each old person receives $(1+n)\,\varepsilon$. Consider $v(e_1-\varepsilon, e_2+\varepsilon) = u(e_1-\varepsilon) + \frac{u(e_2+(1+n)\varepsilon)}{1+\rho}$; this is the typical lifetime utility of an agent under this tax and transfer system. What is the effect on her utility of a small change from $\varepsilon = 0$?

$$\frac{dv}{d\varepsilon} = -u'(e_1) + \frac{(1+n)u'(e_2)}{1+\rho} > 0. \tag{9.18}$$

It is easy to show that this number is positive if and only if $\widetilde{r} < n$. Thus, a policy of tax transfers is welfare enhancing for Samuelson economies.

9.3 An Economy with Production

We now consider an economy with production. We assume that young people work, while the old do not. Young people are born with no wealth, generate income through their work, and when they become old, they consume any savings. We assume that the old do not leave bequests. This may be for example because the old derive utility only from their own current (and past) consumption.

To simplify matters, we assume that each young person supplies one unit of labor inelastically; leisure is therefore not an argument in the utility function. This is similar to the Ramsey model. Output is used either for consumption or for investment. We assume that physical capital is owned by households and rented to firms. Finally, the production technology is assumed to be CRTS, and all markets are perfectly competitive. Output is the usual numeraire good in that its price is set to unity.

We first consider the relevant interest rate in our economy. The rate of return on capital must satisfy

$$\frac{r_{\kappa t}K_t - \delta K_t}{K_t} = r_{\kappa t} - \delta, \tag{9.19}$$

where $r_{\kappa t}$ is the rental rate of capital and δ is the rate of depreciation of capital. If r is any interest rate (say on savings), no arbitrage implies that

$$r_t = r_{\kappa t} - \delta \tag{9.20}$$

in any time period. This means that the interest rate r_t on any financial instrument will adjust so that it pays off exactly $r_{\kappa t} - \delta$. We can now focus on r_t exclusively and put capital accumulation in the background. Since we will look at the decentralized equilibrium outcome, the next step is to define the problems faced by the agents.

9.3.1 Household behavior

Each young person plans for a two-period lifetime, thus they solve the following optimization problem:

$$\max_{c_{1t}, c_{2t+1}} \quad \Gamma = u(c_{1t}) + \frac{u(c_{2t+1})}{1+\rho} \tag{9.21}$$

$$s.t. \quad c_{1t} + s_t = w_t, \quad u' > 0, \quad u'' < 0, \tag{9.22}$$

$$c_{2t+1} = (1 + r_{t+1})s_t, \tag{9.23}$$

taking w_t and r_{t+1} as given; w_t is the real wage rate, and s_t is the amount saved from period t to period $t+1$.

9.3.2 Firm behavior

The representative firm solves a static problem,

$$\max_{K_t, L_t} \quad \Pi = F(K_t, L_t) - r_{\kappa t}K_t - w_t L_t, \tag{9.24}$$

which under perfect competition and CRTS yields

$$F_K = r_{\kappa t} = r_t + \delta \leftrightarrow f'(k_t) = r_t + \delta, \tag{9.25}$$

$$F_L = w_t \leftrightarrow f(k_t) - k_t f'(k_t) = w_t, \tag{9.26}$$

where $f' > 0$ and $f'' < 0$ as usual.

9.3.3 Market clearing

Note that $K_t^d = k_t^d L_t^d$ and since all markets clear at time t,

$$K_t^d = K_t^s = K_t, \tag{9.27}$$

$$L_t^d = L_t^s = L_t, \tag{9.28}$$

$$L_t^s = L_0(1+n)^t. \tag{9.29}$$

Thus,

$$k_t^d = \frac{K_t^d}{L_t^d} = \frac{K_t}{L_t}, \tag{9.30}$$

and so,

$$r_t = f'(k_t) - \delta \equiv r(k_t), \tag{9.31}$$

$$w_t = f(k_t) - k_t f'(k_t) = w(k_t), \tag{9.32}$$

which implies that

$$r'(k_t) = f'' < 0, \tag{9.33}$$

$$w'(k_t) = -k_t f'' > 0. \tag{9.34}$$

9.3.4 The model solution and the savings function

The household problem yields the FONC

$$\frac{d\Gamma}{ds_t} = -u'(w_t - s_t) + \frac{u'((1+r_{t+1})s_t)(1+r_{t+1})}{1+\rho} = 0, \tag{9.35}$$

$$\to u'(c_{1t}) = \frac{u'(c_{2t+1})(1+r_{t+1})}{1+\rho}. \tag{9.36}$$

The attendant second-order sufficiency condition (SOSC) is

$$\frac{d^2\Gamma}{ds_t^2} = u'' + \frac{u''(1+r_{t+1})^2}{1+\rho} < 0. \tag{9.37}$$

The SOSC is negative, so the optimality condition is both necessary and sufficient to describe the optimal outcome. A useful way to organize the problem is to derive the savings function of the households. The FONC determines s_t as a function of w_t and r_{t+1}, thus $s_t = s(w_t, r_{t+1})$.

Totally differentiate the FONC to get

$$-u''(c_{1t})(dw_t - ds_t) + \frac{u''(c_{2t+1})[(1+r_{t+1})ds_t + s_t dr_{t+1}](1+r_{t+1}) + u'(c_{2t+1})dr_{t+1}}{1+\rho} = 0. \tag{9.38}$$

The differential implies that

$$s_w = \frac{u''(c_{1t})}{u''(c_{1t}) + (1+\rho)^{-1}u''(c_{2t+1})(1+r_{t+1})^2} \in (0,1), \tag{9.39}$$

$$s_r = \frac{-(1+\rho)^{-1}[u'(c_{2t+1}) + c_{2t+1}u''(c_{2t+1})]}{u''(c_{1t}) + (1+\rho)^{-1}u''(c_{2t+1})(1+r_{t+1})^2} \lesseqgtr 0. \tag{9.40}$$

The first expression tells us that an increase in wages would cause a typical agent to increase her savings. Next, an interest rate rise causes both income and substitution effects. Here, the substitution effect would cause the agent to save more because consumption 'tomorrow' is now cheaper. This would result in lower consumption today. The income effect however would cause higher consumption today, as the agent does not need to save as much to get the same consumption tomorrow. If the coefficient of relative risk aversion of the period utility u is greater than unity, then savings will fall with interest rates.

9.3.5 The fundamental difference equation

The current young use existing capital K_t to produce the consumption good in period t. They consume part of it and save the rest. The current old own the existing capital stock K_t, which they consume before the end of the period so that capital in period $t+1$ is exactly equal to the savings of the young. This is expressed in the following equation:

$$K_{t+1} = L_t s(w_t, r_{t+1}). \tag{9.41}$$

Since $K_{t+1} = k_{t+1}L_{t+1}$ and $L_{t+1} = (1+n)L_t$, we have that

$$k_{t+1} = \frac{s(w(k_t), r(k_{t+1}))}{1+n}. \tag{9.42}$$

The current and future capital to labor ratio can be determined by employing the firms' first-order conditions; what results is the fundamental difference equation. Since s is nonlinear, constructing the phase diagram in (k_t, k_{t+1}) is not straightforward. To obtain the slope of the implicit function $k_{t+1}(k_t)$, totally differentiate (9.42) with respect to k_t and k_{t+1} to get

$$(1+n)dk_{t+1} = s_w w'(k_t)dk_t + s_r r'(k_{t+1})dk_{t+1} \tag{9.43}$$

$$\rightarrow \frac{dk_{t+1}}{dk_t} = \frac{-s_w(w(k_t), r(k_{t+1}))k_t f''(k_t)}{1+n-s_r(w(k_t), r(k_{t+1}))f''(k_{t+1})}. \tag{9.44}$$

This will be useful later once we consider the issue of the stability of the solution. For now, let's consider an example to simplify matters and solve directly for the dynamic equation. First, suppose that $u = \log c_t$. This utility function has a CRRA coefficient equal to 1, implying $s_r = 0$. This means that the income and substitution effects of an increase in the interest rate cancel each other out, which is a useful simplification: in particular, it means that the savings function is not a function of r_{t+1}:

$$s_t = \frac{w_t}{2+\rho}.$$

In addition, suppose that $F = A_t K_t^{\alpha} L_t^{1-\alpha}$, then $w_t = Ak^{\alpha} - \alpha A k^{\alpha-1}$. This allows us to rewrite the above equation as

$$k_{t+1} = \frac{(1-\alpha)A_t k_t^{\alpha}}{(1+n)(2+\rho)}, \tag{9.45}$$

which is plotted in Figure 9.1.

Here, we have k_t on the horizontal and k_{t+1} on the vertical. Clearly, steady states must lie on the 45 degree line.

Let us now consider the issue of stability of the solution. First, note that since the savings of the young cannot exceed their income, there is a bound to the curve, given by the dashed line which equals $\frac{f(k_t)}{1+n}$ as shown in Figure 9.2.

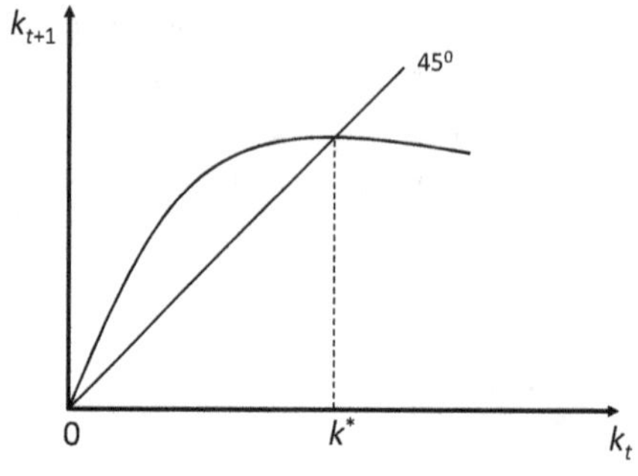

Figure 9.1. The fundamental difference equation.

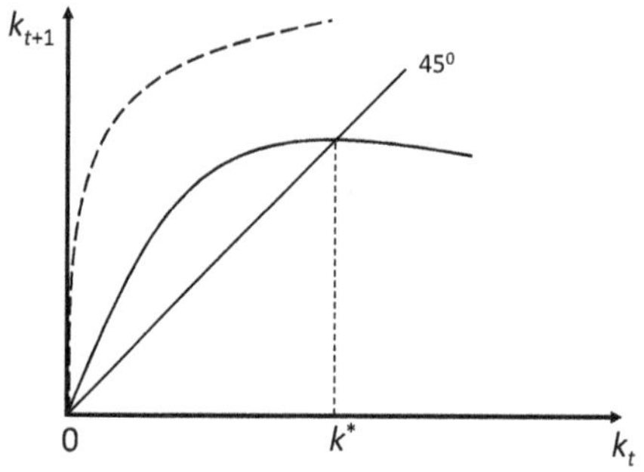

Figure 9.2. Production limits.

Next, note from

$$\frac{dk_{t+1}}{dk_t} = \frac{-s_w(w(k_t), r(k_{t+1}))k_t f''(k_t)}{1 + n - s_r(w(k_t), r(k_{t+1}))f''(k_{t+1})} \tag{9.46}$$

and that as long as $s_r(w(k_t), r(k_{t+1}))f''(k_{t+1}) \neq 1 + n$, we have that

$$\frac{dk_{t+1}}{dk_t} > 0 \longleftrightarrow s_r(w(k_t), r(k_{t+1})) > \frac{1+n}{f''(k_{t+1})}, \tag{9.47}$$

$$\frac{dk_{t+1}}{dk_t} < 0 \longleftrightarrow s_r(w(k_t), r(k_{t+1})) < \frac{1+n}{f''(k_{t+1})}. \tag{9.48}$$

This holds because s_w is always negatively signed (and of course $f'' < 0$. See the previous section). In the case of log utility, note that $s_r = 0$, so the condition always holds (indeed f'' is always negative). Further, we want to ensure that k_{t+1} as a function of k_t crosses the

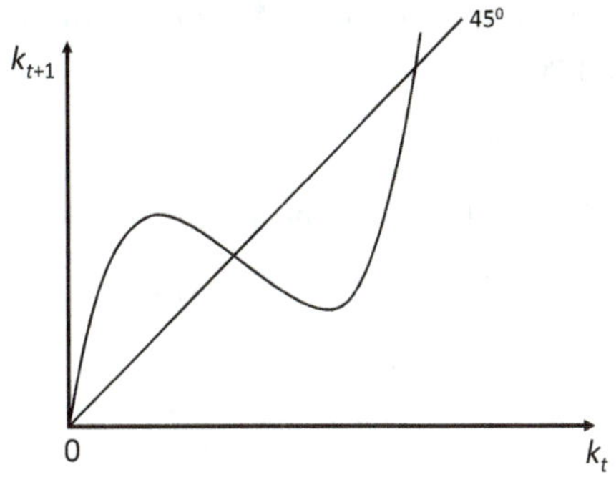

Figure 9.3. Stable vs. unstable steady states.

45 degree line. If this function is concave, a sufficient condition for this is that the slope of the curve is greater than unity near $k_t = 0$:

$$\lim_{k_t \to 0} \frac{dk_{t+1}}{dk_t} > 1. \tag{9.49}$$

This ensures that at the very least there is one steady state; it does not rule out the type of behavior shown in Figure 9.3.

One way to rule this out is to make sure k_{t+1} is a strictly concave function of k_t. This is straightforward to show, as the numerator of the expression $\frac{dk_{t+1}}{dk_t}$ tends to zero since $f'' \to 0$ and the denominator tends to $1+n$. A weaker sufficient condition is to prove that k_{t+1} as a function of k_t is a concave function.

9.4 Dynamic Efficiency and the Golden Rule

We now ask whether the savings behavior in the steady state is 'optimal' at least to the extent that it reaches the golden rule. Here, this means that consumption per worker is maximized in the steady state. Let us solve for the golden rule rate of savings. First, recall that aggregate consumption in period t is

$$C_t = L_t c_{1t} + L_{t-1} c_{2t}. \tag{9.50}$$

In terms of the current young, this gives

$$c_t = c_{1t} + \frac{1}{1+n} c_{2t}. \tag{9.51}$$

This consumption per current young and investment from the current young must equal production:

$$c_t + i_t = f(k_t). \tag{9.52}$$

Finally, overall capital evolves according to

$$K_{t+1} = I_t + (1-\delta) K_t. \tag{9.53}$$

In terms of the current young, this equals

$$(1+n) k_{t+1} = i_t + (1-\delta) k_t. \tag{9.54}$$

Replacing this gives us the aggregate resource constraint for period t:

$$c_t = f(k_t) + (1-\delta)k_t - (1+n)k_{t+1}, \tag{9.55}$$

which in steady state is

$$c = f(k) - (n+\delta)k \tag{9.56}$$

and when this above condition is maximized with respect to k yields

$$f' - (n+\delta) = 0, \tag{9.57}$$

and thus k_g is implicitly defined by

$$f'(k_g) - \delta = n \longleftrightarrow r_g^* = n, \tag{9.58}$$

where r_g^* is the golden rule (steady-state) interest rate. This gives us a simple criterion to see whether a particular economy is close or far away from the golden rule in the steady state. If the prevailing interest rate is r^* in the steady state with a corresponding steady-state value of the capital to labor ratio k^*, we have

$$k^* < k_g \longleftrightarrow r^* > n. \tag{9.59}$$

In this case, we say that the economy is dynamically efficient: the economy is underaccumulating capital. In the example with logarithmic utility and Cobb–Douglas production function, the steady-state k satisfies

$$(k^*)^{1-\alpha} = \frac{(1-\alpha) A}{(1+n)(2+\rho)}. \tag{9.60}$$

As ρ becomes large, k^* falls; this is because the young become more impatient and would rather consume while young than save for old age. In this case, the economy is dynamically efficient: any transfer of capital from the old to the current young would make the current old worse off.

Conversely, when ρ is close to zero, k^* becomes large and may become larger than k_g. In this economy, the young are overaccumulating capital. This is very much the same situation as in the Solow growth model. There, we showed that if the savings rate s^* was greater than s_g^* (the golden rule savings rate), then a fall in the savings rate would cause capital per worker to fall and consumption per worker to rise in the steady state. Unlike the Solow growth model, the savings rate is endogenous and yet, the economy is not maximizing consumption per worker. So clearly, some feature of this economy prevents us from applying the first welfare theorem. The reason for this inefficiency is as follows: when ρ is very small, agents in period t tend to save a lot and accumulate lots of capital per worker; this causes interest rates r_{t+1} to fall, which in turn forces the young in period $t+1$ to save more than they would have to ensure that their savings are sufficiently large in period $t+2$. The reason that the first welfare theorem doesn't apply is that the current old do not internalize the effects of the externality they impose on future generations through the (low) interest rate. The government can step in and impose a tax on the current young in favor of the current old, and overall steady-state welfare (as measured by $u(c_1, c_2)$, where c_1 and c_2 are consumption by the current young and old, respectively) is enhanced. Another way to make this point is that the government is forcing the interest rate to fall, hence causing the current young to save less.

Finally, note here that Ricardian equivalence does not hold: government policy, even when anticipated, has an effect on economic outcomes. As we shall see in the following section, anticipating government policy is but one necessary condition for Ricardian equivalence.

9.5 Bequests and Dynamic Efficiency

People leave bequests for many reasons. For example, if someone is unsure about the date of her death, she will usually engage in precautionary savings. If her death happens prematurely, then bequests will be positive. In addition, people leave bequests because they care about the welfare of the current young. The introduction of bequests allows us to consider issues related to Ricardian equivalence and may also mitigate the potential dynamic inefficiency encountered in the standard model. We adopt the same model as before but now consider a utility function of the form

$$\Gamma_t = u(c_{1t}) + \frac{u(c_{2t+1})}{1+\rho} + \frac{1+n}{1+R}\Gamma_{t+1}. \tag{9.61}$$

The term Γ_{t+1} is the utility of those born in period $t+1$. Since there are $(n+1)$ more of them, the above altruistic utility function adjusts for this. The term R is the rate of preference for discounting the utility of the next generation (Γ_{t+1}). As R tends to $+\infty$, we should retrieve the results from the previous sections. One can write a rate of time preference that is adjusted for population growth. Set $\widetilde{R}$ so that it satisfies the following expression:

$$\frac{1}{1+\widetilde{R}} = \frac{1+n}{1+R}. \tag{9.62}$$

The term $\frac{1}{1+\widetilde{R}}$ is less than 1 if and only if $R > n$ (if and only if $\widetilde{R} > 0$). The next step is to rewrite the utility function in terms of the direct utility,

$$v_t = u(c_{1t}) + \frac{u(c_{2t+1})}{1+\rho}, \tag{9.63}$$

and the indirect utility, $\frac{1}{1+\widetilde{R}}\Gamma_{t+1}$:

$$\Gamma_t = v_t + \frac{1}{1+\widetilde{R}}\Gamma_{t+1} \tag{9.64}$$

Use recursive substitution to obtain

$$\Gamma_t = \sum_{i=0}^{T} \frac{1}{\left(1+\widetilde{R}\right)^2} v_{t+i} + \frac{\Gamma_t}{\left(1+\widetilde{R}\right)^{T+1}}, \tag{9.65}$$

and take the limit as T tends to $+\infty$ to obtain

$$\Gamma_t = \sum_{i=0}^{\infty} \frac{v_{t+i}}{\left(1+\widetilde{R}\right)^i}. \tag{9.66}$$

So, although each generation cares about only the next, it turns out that each generation acts as if it cared about the utility of all future generations. Let b_t be the bequest received at the end of the first period of life by a member of generation t from the previous generation. We do not allow for negative bequests, so the budget constraints faced by an individual born at time t are

$$c_{1t} + s_t = w_t + b_t, \tag{9.67}$$

$$c_{2t+1} + (1+n)b_{t+1} = (1 + r_{t+1})s_t, \tag{9.68}$$

$$b_{t+1} \geq 0. \tag{9.69}$$

Thus, the optimization problem is

$$\max_{s_t, b_{t+1}} \quad \Gamma_t = \sum_{i=0}^{\infty} \frac{v_{t+i}}{\left(1+\widetilde{R}\right)^i} \tag{9.70}$$

$$s.t. \quad c_{1t} + s_t = w_t + b_t, \tag{9.71}$$

$$c_{2t+1} + (1+n)b_{t+1} = (1 + r_{t+1})s_t, \tag{9.72}$$

$$b_{t+1} \geq 0. \tag{9.73}$$

Note that since each generation cares about the next, it must be that $b_{t+1} > 0$, so we ignore the boundary condition $b_{t+1} \geq 0$. The FONC are

$$u'(c_{1t}) = \frac{1 + r_{t+1}}{1+\rho} u'(c_{2t+1}), \tag{9.74}$$

$$\frac{1}{1+\rho} u'(c_{2t+1}) = \frac{1}{1+\widetilde{R}} \frac{u'(c_{1t+1})}{1+n}. \tag{9.75}$$

The first FONC says that the current young will increase their savings until the marginal utility of current consumption equals the marginal utility of consumption tomorrow adjusted for additional capital accumulation. The second FONC says that the utility cost of increasing the bequest by one unit must be equal to the discounted utility benefit derived from the next generation having $\frac{1}{1+n}$ more units per member for consumption in the same period. Now, combine the two FONC to obtain

$$u'(c_{1t}) = \frac{1 + r_{t+1}}{1+\widetilde{R}} \frac{u'(c_{1t+1})}{1+n}, \tag{9.76}$$

which says that the utility cost of decreasing consumption of the young in period t equals the discounted utility increase next period for the next generation, which will be able to consume $\frac{1+r_{t+1}}{1+n}$ more units, that is, intertemporal *and* intergenerational optimality. Equations that are added for equilibrium are as usual:

$$r_{t+1} = f'(k_{t+1}) - \delta, \tag{9.77}$$

$$c_{1t} = f(k_t) + (1-\delta)k_t - (1+n)k_{t+1} - \frac{c_{2t}}{1+n}. \tag{9.78}$$

Now, use (9.76) and the steady-state conditions $k_t = k^*, c_{1t} = c_1^*, c_{2t} = c_2^*$ to obtain

$$1 + r^* = 1 + f'(k^*) - \delta = (1+\widetilde{R})(1+n) = 1 + R, \tag{9.79}$$

so the interest rate from the firm side r^* equals that from the household side R and the allocation is therefore dynamically efficient with the modified golden rule:

$$1 + f'(k^*) - \delta = (1+\widetilde{R})(1+n) \tag{9.80}$$

$$= 1 + n + \widetilde{R} + \widetilde{R}n \approx 1 + n + \widetilde{R} \tag{9.81}$$

$$\to f'(k^*) - \delta = n + \widetilde{R}. \tag{9.82}$$

Because current generations care about future generations, the externality that we discussed in the previous section is internalized by the current young when they make their savings decision. In addition, note that when $b_t > 0$, a lump-sum transfer will be matched by a one-for-one decrease in b_t, and thus Ricardian equivalence holds.

In our model without bequests, Ricardian equivalence does not hold. Indeed, we argued that a government tax and transfer scheme can be used to achieve an outcome that is closer to the golden rule. In that case, we argued that the government would transfer wealth from the current young to the current old, distorting the prevailing interest rate in the process. Note that in both models (with and without bequests), agents are forward looking. So, the (interest rate) effects of any change in government policy is fully anticipated by all agents in the economy. However, it is only in the model with bequests that individuals care about future generations and are therefore willing to change their behavior when faced with changes in government policy. In particular, if the current old care about the current young, they will nullify any changes in government policy; if they do not, they are better off keeping any transfer from the government.

9.6 Social Security and Optimal Capital

In the initial OLG model we covered (the pure endowment economy), we concluded that the equilibrium outcome was always autarky. Depending however on the endowment profile, the autarky outcome may not be dynamically efficient. For example, in the case where $(e_1, e_2) = (1, 0)$, it is possible for the social planner to take a bit of the endowment from the current young and give it to the current old. If it does this for all periods beginning in period t, then all generations benefit from this tax transfer system, including the initial old generation in period t. This system of course is simply a pay-as-you-go (PAYG) scheme of social security. Let's see what happens in the production economy we covered, without bequest motives. In each period, the government takes $\tau > 0$ from the young and gives it to the current old. With a population growing at a rate of $(1+n)$, this means that the old in period t each receive $\tau(1+n)$. Each generation takes this tax and transfer as a given, and its objective is to

$$\max_{c_{1t}, c_{2t+1}} \quad \Gamma = u(c_{1t}) + \frac{u(c_{2t+1})}{1+\rho} \tag{9.83}$$

$$s.t. \quad c_{1t} + s_t = w_t - \tau, \tag{9.84}$$

$$c_{2t+1} = (1 + r_{t+1}) s_t + \tau (1+n). \tag{9.85}$$

Here, the FONC for this problem is

$$u'(c_{1t}) = \frac{1 + r_{t+1}}{1+\rho} u'(c_{2t+1}). \tag{9.86}$$

Taking the case of log utility for simplicity, one can solve for the level of savings:

$$s_t = \frac{w_t - \tau}{2+\rho} - \frac{(1+\rho)(1+n)}{(2+\rho)(1+r_{t+1})} \tau. \tag{9.87}$$

As in the previous analysis, because $\log c$ has CRRA equal to unity, the interest rate r_{t+1} has no effect on the level of savings when τ is nil. When $\tau > 0$ however, an increase in interest rates causes the agent to save less unambiguously: the substitution effect always dominates.

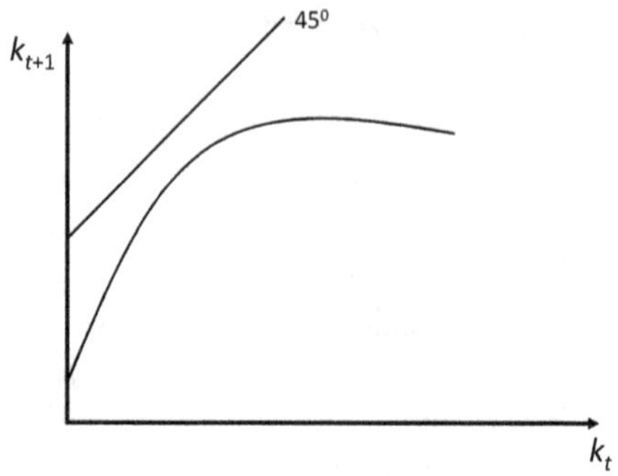

Figure 9.4. Tax example.

Next, we consider the effects on capital accumulation. Recall that

$$(1+n)\,k_{t+1} = s_t, \tag{9.88}$$

so

$$k_{t+1} = \frac{w_t - \tau}{(1+n)\,(2+\rho)} - \frac{(1+\rho)\,\tau}{(2+\rho)\,(1+r_{t+1})}. \tag{9.89}$$

Recall that $w_t = f(k_t) - k_t f'(k_t)$ and that $r_t = f'(k_t) - \delta$. Let's assume once more that $f(k_t) = Ak_t^{\alpha}$. Then, $w_t = (1-\alpha)\,Ak_t^{\alpha}$ and $r_{t+1} = A\alpha k_{t+1}^{\alpha-1} - \delta$. One obtains the following expression for capital accumulation:

$$k_{t+1} = \frac{(1-\alpha)\,Ak_t^{\alpha} - \tau}{(1+n)\,(2+\rho)} - \frac{(1+\rho)\,\tau}{(2+\rho)\left(1 + A\alpha k_{t+1}^{\alpha-1} - \delta\right)}. \tag{9.90}$$

Here, even the assumption that the utility function is of CRRA equal to unity does not allow us to have an expression where k_{t+1} can be expressed purely as a function of k_t.

In this setting, a steady state may not exist. Consider for example the following parametrization: $A = 1$, $\alpha = 0.3$, $\rho = 1/0.9 - 1$, $\delta = 0.3$, and $n = 0$. Let's see what happens if $\tau = 0.15$. Then, we obtain the following phase diagram (through simulation).

The x-axis is k_t and the y-axis is k_{t+1}. The lower curve is k_{t+1} as an implicit function of k_t, while the upper curve is the 45 degree line. Here, taxes are so high that a sustainable steady state is out of reach as in Figure 9.4. In the following example, we set $\tau = 0.13$.

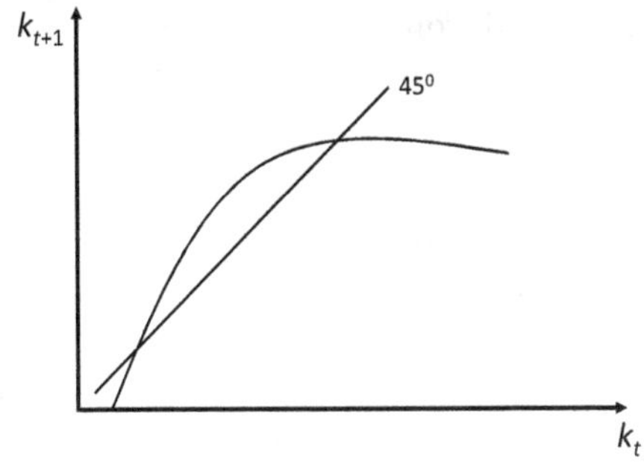

Figure 9.5. Two steady states.

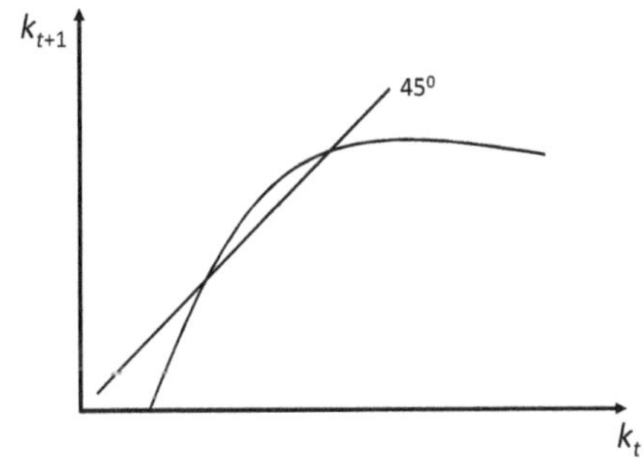

Figure 9.6. Steady states changing.

Here in Figure 9.5, note that there exist two steady states. The one to the left is unstable (the slope of the curve at the steady state is greater than unity), while the steady state to the right is stable. As the tax rate rises, the low steady state rises while the one with high capital to labor ratio falls. Indeed, consider the case where $\tau = 0.14$ as in Figure 9.6.

With a bit of algebra, one can show that a steady-state value of k^* (if it exists) falls with the tax rate if and only if it is stable.

9.7 Conclusion

In the Solow growth model, we saw that economies could exhibit dynamic inefficiencies. In that setting, if the savings rate was too high, it was possible for the social planner, or government, to intervene by taxing the savings of the representative agent. In the Ramsey model, the savings rate is endogenous and the outcome is Pareto optimal. More specifically, the steady state is at the golden rule savings rate. The endogeneity of savings is not enough to guarantee Pareto optimality. Indeed, one also requires that the conditions of the first welfare theorem hold.

As the OLG models in this chapter demonstrate, an endogenous savings rate does not guarantee Pareto optimality. When there is overaccumulation of capital, there is room for welfare-improving government intervention. The reason that outcomes are sometimes dynamically inefficient has to do with overaccumulation of capital and the corresponding 'low' interest rates. The latter force the current young to overaccumulate capital. The reason that the interest rate doesn't adjust is that the current young have no incentive to internalize the externality they impose on future generations. Allowing for a bequest motive ensures that the savings rate adjust to the (suitably modified) golden rule. By ensuring that current generations effectively care for future generations, decisions are made with a view to ensuring that future interest rates are sufficiently 'high'.

Chapter 10

Heterogeneous-Agent Models

10.1 Introduction

For a long time, economic science has almost invariably developed models of economic behavior on the presumption that economic actors – e.g. consumers, firms, financial intermediaries, and public authorities – share identical within-group characteristics (representative-agent hypothesis). On top of a fundamental lack of analytical tools and numerical methods to handle highly sophisticated frameworks embodying agent heterogeneity along with time and risk features, there was a widespread tendency to believe that incorporating household and/or firm heterogeneity into macroeconomic models was, at most, of second-order importance for uncovering the deep roots of aggregate business cycle dynamics and long-run patterns of growth. This view had long been supported by leading economists Per Krussel and Anthony A. Smith Jr., who, in a seminal article (Krussel and Smith, 1998), formally proved that an incomplete markets model with heterogeneous agents who are subject to both idiosyncratic and aggregate shocks mostly 'behaves' as its representative-agent counterpart: the aggregate law of motion is (almost) linear, and the incorporation of inequality is (almost) immaterial. A main message from Krussel and Smith's early work is that there is little need for heterogeneous-agent models to substitute their representative-agent analogues for business cycle analyses.

Heterogeneity and inequality are undoubtedly signs of our times. Over recent decades, casual observation suffices to reveal a persistent and dramatic rise in cross-sectional disparities in several facets of life and on disparate layers, e.g. saving rates, wealth, health and longevity, politics, and migration. Absent heterogeneities of any kind in models that should serve as a guidance for story-telling and policy prescriptive purposes, natural problems stemming from the interaction of diverse agents and from the coordination of their beliefs and choices are simply assumed away, allowing unrealistic aggregation properties – and thus an impassable bridge from microeconomic to macroeconomic analysis – to hold. Against this backdrop, the academic community has gradually embraced the idea that the representative-agent hypothesis in macroeconomic modeling (i) is not well suited to investigate the roots of empirically documented inequalities that still escape standard aggregation theorems and (ii) is likely to produce erroneous evaluations of the impact and welfare effects of macroeconomic policies that have distributional implications (Kirman, 1992). In parallel, empirical work on large databases containing detailed information on individual agents characteristics (microdata) has long revealed the existence of forms of profound dispersion and individual volatility for workers and firms which could not be traced back to random deviations from the average of a representative-agent abstraction (e.g. Attanasio, 2005).

In general, individual heterogeneities that are economically sensible can be cast in two broad, concurrent categories: (*ex ante*) heterogeneity in innate characteristics, which are largely determined by genetic makeup and family background (e.g. cognitive abilities); and (*ex post*) heterogeneity in unanticipated changes in fundamentals (or *shocks*) agents are exposed to over the life cycle, as determined by a variety of socioeconomic forces (e.g. income shocks in the absence of insurance markets). Both kinds of heterogeneity trigger endogenous differences in decision-making and strategy design (e.g. labor supply, portfolio choice, and job search) across economic units, in turn leading to inequality in economic outcomes of interest. Interpreting individual heterogeneity as the output of a complex interaction between inborn traits, unavoidable variation in exogenous fundamentals, and the ensuing endogenous reactions raises two important and intimately related questions, with significant implications for the design of policies and social institutions. First, what is the relative importance of *ex ante* heterogeneity vis-à-vis *ex post* shocks in shaping the cross-sectional dispersion in economic outcomes that we observe in the real world? And second, with the aim of devising realistic theoretical foundations for modeling individual heterogeneity, which factors can be considered to be exogenously determined and which, by contrast, should be traced to the endogenous behavior of individuals?

In this Chapter, we offer a brief, largely non-technical overview of first attempts and more recent advances in heterogeneous-agent macroeconomic modeling that explicitly incorporate distinct types of heterogeneity pertaining to (i) household income profiles and (ii) expectations formation in order to answer some of the questions highlighted above. A special focus will be devoted to the brand-new generation of structural, multivariate models in the new Keynesian tradition, known as heterogeneous-agent new Keynesian (HANK) models, which have been recently exploited to produce dispersion in economic agents' responses to shocks by matching empirical distributions of income and wealth and then to evaluate the implications of heterogeneity for macroeconomic stability and the transmission of monetary policy and other kinds of public intervention. Since a more formal treatment of these topics requires tools and methods that are well beyond the scope of the current book, we refer the interested reader to the many references provided in the following and in particular to Krussel and Smith (2006), Branch and McGough (2018), and Acharya and Dogra (2020) for details on the economic environments and the various technical tools adopted therein.[1]

10.2 Household Income Heterogeneity

The main building block of the macroeconomic analysis of household heterogeneity is the *incomplete market model* (IMM henceforth): a world where a large number of agents are *ex ante* homogeneous and yet are subject to non-insurable shocks to productivity (thus earnings), which in turn shape their individual choices for consumption,

[1]Further sources of household (*ex ante* or *ex post*) heterogeneity, such as agent-specific preferences and idiosyncratic rates of returns on financial wealth, have been fruitfully investigated in the literature to account for e.g. right-skewed and thick-tailed empirical wealth distributions; see, among others, Benhabib and Bisin (2018).

savings, portfolio composition, and labor supply. At the core of this model is the idea that, absent markets where individual risks can be traded and wealth/resources transferred across any two dates and/or states of the world, agents cannot fully insure against idiosyncratic shocks, opening room for cross-sectional dispersion in labor income, savings, and other variables; this in turn is reflected in the accumulation of output and capital in the economy and the endogenous determination of prices in a general equilibrium environment. The IMM merges insights from the standard theoretical treatment of intertemporal consumption/saving choices in the presence of non-insurable risk (the so-called income fluctuation problem popularized by Bewley, 1977, 1983; Aiyagari, 1994) while allowing for general equilibrium interactions; and from the neoclassical growth model with aggregate uncertainty, which at the time was the workhorse model for business cycle analysis (e.g. Kydland and Prescott, 1982) in the representative-agent paradigm.

10.2.1 Income fluctuation

As emphasized by Heathcote *et al.* (2009), the IMM approach to modeling market incompleteness is centered around the *income fluctuation problem*, i.e. a stochastic income version of the conventional intertemporal allocation problem studied in introductory textbooks for microeconomic analysis. Importantly, the only source of heterogeneity in the early quantitative heterogeneous-agent, incomplete-market models hinges on exogenous uninsurable endowment (or earnings) shocks, inducing fluctuations in (labor) income over the horizon of interest for economic agents. The *ex post* heterogeneity in shock histories across *ex ante* identical individuals then induces consumption and wealth differentials via heterogeneous intertemporal consumption (and thus saving) decisions.

On the empirical front, statistical evidence derived from longitudinal microeconomic data – e.g. the US Panel Study of Income Dynamics (PSID) – robustly suggest that individual earnings processes exhibit both a considerable degree of serial correlation, transitory components with unequal persistence properties, and time variation in the parameters capturing the dynamic relationship between current and past earnings, all factors that microfounded models of income and consumption (and also wealth) inequality are therefore required to embed, at the very least, among the exogenous components.[2]

From a modeling perspective, consider a discrete-time economy, where infinitely lived agents (households), who benefit from consumption streams, have to optimally decide on how to allocate their resources (wealth) to consumption and saving in the face of stochastic income endowments in each time period. Importantly, in the absence of state-contingent assets to insure against endowment risk (incomplete markets), agents can only save or borrow at a constant risk-free rate, possibly subject to credit constraints or other natural limits to borrowing. In the most basic setup, preferences are time- and state-separable, with period utility being captured by a smooth, increasing (non-satiation), and strictly concave (risk-aversion) function of consumption. In such a setting, agents who discount the future (at some constant, subjective rate) may desire to smooth consumption via asset accumulation for standard intertemporal reasons and also for a precautionary saving motive, which commands building a buffer against the non-insurable risk of future low-endowment realizations (*self-insurance*).

What are then the equilibrium features of an economy populated by a large number of non-interactive households, each facing uncorrelated shocks to their own endowments? Since different individuals will experience different histories for the endowments shocks and will accordingly make heterogeneous consumption and saving choices, the model delivers – under appropriate regularity conditions – (i) individual decision rules, linking state variables (wealth) to optimal consumption and saving plans; and (ii) an ensuing invariant (stationary) distribution for household wealth, which exhibit cross-sectional dispersion and mobility of individuals across wealth classes. Thanks

[2]It must be remarked that lifetime earnings dispersion can be shaped by further factors, such as family background and human capital formation, that are predetermined at the time individuals enter the labor market and are, at least partly, endogenous to educational and saving decisions of agents within lineages. Disentangling the importance of unequal initial conditions from that of *ex post* shocks in shaping cross-sectional inequality is crucial, insofar as they deliver different implications for the design of policy intervention aimed at mitigating disparities across individuals. The conventional IMM approach deliberately disregards this distinction and solely focus on the latter dimension.

to this stark prediction, the IMM has gained central stage in the theoretical analysis of the determinants of the evolution of the equilibrium distributions for consumption, savings, and wealth and for the analysis of the dynamics of inequality.

In its baseline version, the income fluctuation problem reads as follows:

$$\max_{c_t} \mathbb{E}_0 \sum_{t=0}^{\infty} \beta^t u(c_t) \tag{10.1}$$

$$s.t\, a_{t+1} + c_t \leq R\, a_t + y_t,\, c_t \geq 0,\, a_t \geq 0\, t = 0, 1, \ldots \tag{10.2}$$

where $\beta \in (0,1)$ is the subjective discount factor, a_t denotes assets before interests at time t, c_t is consumption, y_t is the (exogenously given) stochastic endowment (e.g. labor income), and R is the gross interest rate on savings. The goal of the locally non-satiated ($u' > 0$) and risk-averse ($u'' < 0$) household is to optimally select a state-contingent consumption plan $\{c_t\} \geq 0$ that maximizes the discounted sum of period utilities from consumption streams over an infinite horizon, under the no-borrowing constraint $a_t \geq 0$ (which might be replaced by relatively weaker restrictions on the amount of admissible borrowing). To sharpen the results, it is typically assumed that the utility function satisfies limiting conditions of the form $\lim_{c \to 0} u' = \infty$ to rule out corner solutions, e.g. Ma *et al.* (2020).

In the model, the unique source of risk is represented by the agent-specific (non-insurable) stochastic additive shock y_t, which can induce occasionally binding constraints and promotes the emergence of precautionary saving behavior. In general, once assumptions about the stochastic evolution of the endowment process y_t are stated, the objects of interest are (i) a feasible consumption path $\{c_t^*\}$, i.e. a measurable consumption sequence (i.e. a sequence of functions of random outcomes y_s up to time $s \leq t$ and current asset holdings a_t) solving problem (10.1); and (ii) the induced asset path $\{a_t\}$ evolving according to

$$a_{t+1} = R\, a_t - c_t^* + y_t$$

whose limiting properties – e.g. the existence and uniqueness of a stationary asset distribution – can be studied using tools from the theory of stochastic processes. The first-order (necessary) condition for optimality is

$$u'(c_t) = \beta R \mathbb{E}_t \left[u'(c_{t+1}) \right] + \lambda_t, \tag{10.3}$$

where the expectation is taken over the distribution of y_{t+1} and $\lambda_t \geq 0$ denotes the Lagrange multipliers on the no-borrowing constraint. Note the two forces shaping asset accumulation. The first is the effective rate of time preference, embodied by the term βR: the higher this rate, the more the agents prefer future consumption over current one, and the higher the incentive to accumulate assets. The second force is risk. Agents save and accumulate assets to shield their consumption from bad endowment realizations, so the higher this downside risk and the stronger the precautionary saving motive of agents. Figure 10.1 plots the consumption policy rule, i.e. the consumption sequence solving the expected utility maximization problem, as a function of asset holdings: uninsured shocks to endowments and the ensuing precautionary savings entail a concavification of the optimal consumption function.

It turns out that the convergence of the consumption sequence $\{c_t^*\}$ crucially depends on the effective rate of time preference: relative to its deterministic counterpart, under precautionary behavior, the model delivers unbounded asset accumulation on the part of households in cases when $\beta R \geq 1$, whereas additional conditions are required to guarantee the convergence of the accumulation process when $\beta R < 1$. For instance, Schechtman and Escudero (1977) show that decreasing absolute risk aversion in household's preferences is sufficient in this respect when y_t are i.i.d. shocks: in this case, saving incentives tend to taper off over wealth states, where

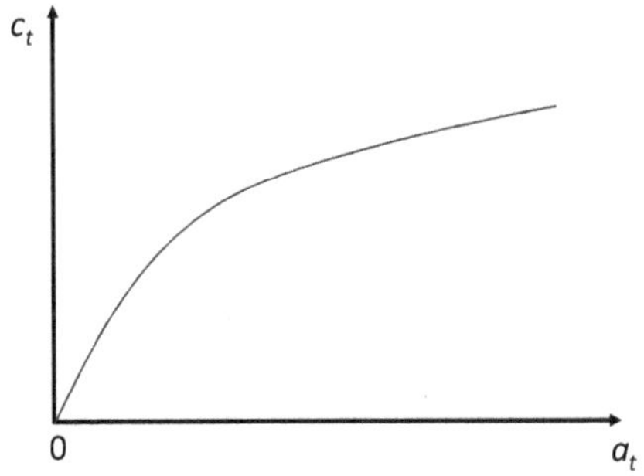

Figure 10.1. Consumption policy rule.

asset holdings become sufficiently large. Huggett (1993) generalizes this insight to environments in which households exhibit constant relative risk aversion (CRRA) utility and their labor income follows a two-state Markov chain.

When the interest rate R is endogenously determined in the asset market – i.e. it is the price at which net asset aggregate demand (the sum of all the positive and negative asset holdings in the stationary distribution) and net supply meet – an equilibrium exists such that the net interest rate $R-1$ lies below the discount rate $1/\beta - 1$. Intuitively, the tendency of households toward saving more than under complete markets for precautionary reasons pushes the equilibrium interest rate below the complete markets level, and such a lower interest rate prevents the aggregate demand for assets from growing without bound.

With the aim of enhancing coherence between theory and measurement, the baseline IMM sketched above has been generalized to encompass further salient features of market economies, such as – among many others – production sectors (e.g. Aiyagari, 1994), demographic stratification and the ensuing life-cycle dynamics in labor supply (e.g. Imrohoroglu *et al.* 1995; Huggett 1996), the interplay between idiosyncratic risk and aggregate shocks, and in particular the mechanisms by which individual-level risk impacts on the aggregate economy (Krussel and Smith, 1998).

10.2.2 The endogenous grid method: Remarks

To illustrate some computational aspects of the solution of heterogeneous-agent models, consider the IMM problem (10.1) where (i) the period utility function is isoelastic, i.e. $u(c_t) = \frac{c_t^{1-\gamma}}{1-\gamma}$, $\gamma > 0$ ($\gamma \neq 1$), and (ii) the endowment process y_t is assumed to follow a well-defined two-state Markov chain with transition probabilities $\pi_{t+1,t} = \pi(y_{t+1}|y_t)$.

The states of the consumer's problem are (a_t, y_t), and so a solution to this problem – a so-called *saving policy rule* – can be represented as a function, $\sigma = \sigma(a_t, e_t)$, that provides the choice for a_{t+1}. To this end, consider the Euler equation

$$c_t^{-\gamma} = \beta R \mathbb{E}_t[c_{t+1}^{-\gamma}] \tag{10.4}$$

so that, given the savings policy rule, the budget constraint can be used to derive the consumption function $c^*(a_t, y_t) = Ra_t + y_t - \sigma(a_t, y_t)$. The endogenous grid method is routinely employed as an iterative algorithm, whereby, upon guessing a policy rule, the algorithm provides the next candidate policy rule – if the two agree within some pre-specified degree of numerical tolerance, the algorithm stops. To illustrate the endogenous grid approach to solving the model, suppose that, for some generic period t, we know y_t but not a_t. Suppose that, with states (a_t, y_t), there is a given amount of savings $\bar{\sigma}$, so that $\sigma(a_t, y_t) = \bar{\sigma}$; from the Euler equation, one has

$$(c^*(a_t, y_t))^{-\gamma} = \beta R \mathbb{E}_{y_{t+1}}[(R\bar{\sigma} + y_{t+1} - \sigma(\bar{\sigma}, y_{t+1}))^{-\gamma}]. \tag{10.5}$$

Thus, given a guess for the policy rule σ, we can compute the right-hand side and solve this equation for the consumption policy $c^*(a_t, y_t)$ and finally exploit the budget constraint to solve for (the yet-unknown) state $a_t = R^{-1}(c^*(a_t, y_t) + \bar{\sigma} - y_t)$. This provides us with a policy rule mapping the states (a_t, y_t) into savings $\bar{\sigma}$, which can be in turn used as a new guess of the saving policy rule σ; these steps can be repeated until convergence is achieved – meaning the guess of σ maps into itself up to some arbitrarily small discrepancy.

How can we approximate the saving policy rule σ? We can start with an educated guess: assume the policy rule is strictly increasing in a_t when the no-borrowing constraint does not bind. Let σ denote a grid of $N_{\bar{\sigma}}$ points on the values of y_{t+1}, with the first grid point at the borrowing constraint (zero). Now, let Σ be a $N_{\bar{\sigma}} \times 2$ matrix in which each column is a strictly increasing $N_{\bar{\sigma}}$-dimensional vector that represents the policy rule as a function of the state a_t for one of the values of y_t. This means that, corresponding to states $(\Sigma_{i,j}, y_j)$, the policy rule calls for saving $\bar{\sigma}_i$. Simple interpolation techniques can be used to approximate the σ function for asset values between grid points $\Sigma_{i,j}$ and $\Sigma_{i+1,j}$.

10.2.3 Endogenous labor income heterogeneity

While idiosyncratic endowments (or labor income) were modeled as purely exogenous forces in the early literature on heterogeneous-agent macroeconomics, individual earnings dynamics are apparently endogenous to educational investment, occupational choice, and thus labor supply behavior. In a general equilibrium setting, earnings heterogeneity and the ensuing dispersion in consumption and wealth is in fact the outcome of the interplay between exogenous shocks and endogenous reactions of optimizing agents, reflecting their different saving behavior over the income (and wealth) distribution.

Initial differences in human capital endowments and cognitive abilities naturally translate into inequality in lifetime earnings and consumption by impacting the process of skill formation during working life. By the same token, educational investment choices interact with labor income risk by inducing self-selection into different education groups that bear more or less risk and thus exhibit heterogeneous propensities to save at the margin.

Even in the presence of competitive labor markets, assuming (as is reasonable) that agents engage in an explicit decision of how many hours to supply to the market, uninsurable risk necessarily transmits from earnings to hourly wages and eventually to consumption dynamics, according to the trade-offs shaped by substitution and income effects, which in turn stem from agents' own preferences and market incompleteness. In general, shocks that tend to persist over time engender large income effects, which mitigate the volatility of earnings, whereas short-lived shocks produce almost negligible income effects, allowing further amplification of wage shocks in the transmission to earnings.

When labor markets are not fully competitive, labor market uncertainty stems from both productivity disparities at the individual level and from labor market transitions. In fact, individual wage dynamics do not respond proportionally to individual productivity, but rather reflect the complex interaction between productivity shocks and the transitions between employment status or across jobs, which are partly determined by agents' own choices. Interestingly, search frictions in labor markets can entail additional (precautionary) saving motives, whereby high-wage earners want to self-ensure against the risk of losing their wage status through a layoff.

What is more, other types of fundamental differences across economic agents can filter the pass-through of labor income risk, producing heterogeneous responses in terms of consumption smoothing and precautionary saving. For instance, substantial evidence provided by applied work in labor economics reveal significant gender differences in the estimated intertemporal elasticity of labor supply, with women exhibiting historically higher elasticity than males.

More generally, confining attention to exogenous earnings processes may undermine the robustness of the economic implications of theoretical results in terms of e.g. the relative strength of the forces that ultimately govern the dispersion of income and consumption over the population of interest as well as the mobility frictions experienced by agents at different layers of the wealth distribution; or underestimate the role of feedback effects from policies (such as income taxation) to relative wages of skilled and unskilled workers. In fact, in the baseline IMM, fiscal policies that target labor earnings and redistribute revenues in a top-down fashion would increase social welfare. Things become far more complicated when earnings dynamics is endogenous to occupational choice and labor supply decisions: taxes can in fact severely distort the efficient choices for educational investment, job search effort, and hours worked, breaking the tight connection between market luck (i.e. high realizations of income shocks) and location in the wealth distribution (lucky agents becoming rich). This, in turn, renders optimal policy design a challenging yet extremely relevant issue to address.

10.3 Heterogeneous Expectations

A further source of heterogeneity that is central in modern macroeconomic analysis pertains to the mechanism by which economic agents form expectations (or beliefs) in dynamic and uncertain environments. Even in simple partial equilibrium settings, such as the baseline IMM, decision-making is intertemporal in nature and must account for (idiosyncratic and/or aggregate) uncertainty about future states of the economy. The feedback loop between expectations and decisions in models of economic behavior calls for a careful evaluation of alternative approaches to modeling the expectations formation mechanism.

Since Muth (1961) and Lucas (1972), the benchmark approach in macroeconomics – particularly in dynamic stochastic general equilibrium (DSGE) theory – is to posit that all economic operators (e.g. consumers, investors, firms, and public authorities) hold homogeneous *rational expectations* (RE). Under the RE hypothesis, agents are assumed to fully understand the economic model they face, to exploit all the publicly available information (so that any forecast error must be unpredictable on the basis of such information), and to hold beliefs that accurately reflect the likelihood of any regime holding in future dates. The two key 'ingredients' of the RE construct are thus (i) homogeneity of the forecasting rule employed and (ii) the possibility of conditioning forecasts of the economic variables of interest (e.g. prices, interest rates, and government policies) on an homogeneous set of observables.

Against this backdrop, a large body of empirical and experimental work has offered robust evidence on the fact that individuals and firms rather form expectations according to heterogeneous information sets and/or heterogeneous forecasting rules. For instance, the Survey of Professional Forecasters (SPF) typically reveals the presence of substantial and time-varying heterogeneity among professional forecasters in terms of inflation probability forecasts. In several controlled laboratory experiments, Hommes (2013) finds strong evidence of heterogeneous beliefs among participants.

In the presence of expectational heterogeneity, the main theoretical questions of interest revolve around the derivation of individual behavior under given, pre-specified forecast rules (e.g. adaptive learning vis-à-vis heuristics) and around the aggregate implications for the dynamics of endogenous variables of the interaction of heterogeneous forecasting rules, when the distribution of agents across the latter is possibly endogenously determined as an equilibrium object. A full account of these issues is far beyond the scope of the current overview. Rather, we survey a number of alternative efforts exerted by macroeconomists towards incorporating expectational heterogeneity (of information sets and/or forecasting models) into dynamic, stochastic model environments, and the main implications of these departures from the overly restrictive assumption of homogeneous, full-information RE. Put simply, expectational heterogeneity involves two conceptually distinct issues: how to make forecasts given the asymmetrically allocated information, on the assumption that all agents in the economy follow the same forecast rule; and how to form forward-looking beliefs under heterogeneous forecast models, which in turn begs the question of how to aggregate diverse expectations and the ensuing decision rules.

10.3.1 Limited information and heterogeneous expectations

The literature on solving RE models with limited information structures has a long tradition. The study of the implications of partial current information ('observability') about endogenous variables traces back to the well-known Lucas (1972) model of spatially separated markets. In the case of partial current information, the forecaster is aware of the values of some endogenous variables only with a lag but can observe other current endogenous variables at the time the forecast is made. Hence, specific tools (such as the Kalman filter) are needed to extract information from observables regarding current disturbances.

Along these lines, there are two main approaches to modeling informational heterogeneity within the standard RE construct, i.e. maintaining that all the economic agents form expectations rationally, though conditional on agent-specific information sets.

A first strand of literature in computational economics has recently focused attention on macroeconomic environments in which some state variables of interest (e.g. a subset of the aggregate shocks, such as to TFP) are unobserved in the current period or observed with some lag by some decision-makers and where some endogenous variables that adjust to observed states can serve as additional states forcing variation in other endogenous variables that rather are the output of optimal decision-making by fully informed agents. This approach acknowledges the fact that it is not the date at which expectations are formed that matters, but rather the date and the structure of the information set upon which expectations are framed. In this context, restricted (or limited) information means that, in the face of exogenous shocks that do not occur simultaneously, agents' expectation formation and the ensuing decision rules are to be conditioned on heterogeneous information sets.

Model-wise, timing restrictions are naturally formalized by means of fictitious *informational sub-periods* characterized by heterogeneous (across rational decision-makers) information sets and the associated process of expectations formation and the timing of decisions. Remarkably, being rooted in the theory of perturbation of nonlinear systems, this approach allows one to embed the assumed set of timing restrictions directly into the nonlinear equilibrium conditions that fully characterize a given DSGE model; approximated (up to second-order) optimal decision rules can then be derived on the basis of the imposed informational structure. When an RE equilibrium exists in the restricted information environment, it is certainty equivalent and is generically (in a measure-theoretic sense) unique provided the homogeneous, full-information RE model admits a locally unique (first-order approximate) solution – see Kormilitsina (2013) and Sorge (2020).

On a positive side, a burgeoning number of studies in modern macroeconomic writing has underscored the role of informational frictions in reconciling theoretical predictions of otherwise standard rational expectations frameworks with observed features of the data, e.g. the persistent and hump-shaped responses of inflation and output measures to unanticipated monetary shocks (Mankiw and Reis, 2002), the relationship between inflation illusion and asset prices (Piazzesi and Schneider, 2008), or the excess return predictability in financial markets (Bacchetta *et al.*, 2009).

Heterogeneity of information sets – and ensuing beliefs – can also be imagined to drive a permanent informational gap between economic operators, e.g. public authorities vis-à-vis private agents, who typically have access to highly differentiated sources of information and information processing technologies. Dispersed information among different economic actors and the ensuing effects on their strategic behavior have been shown to produce important implications for the amplification and propagation of economic shocks; see among others Nimark (2008), Angeletos and La'O (2013), and Acharya *et al.* (2021). Unfortunately, when information sets are non-nested, the equilibrium representation of the structural framework of analysis is not finite dimensional, thereby posing severe analytical challenges. Lubik *et al.* (2023) rather consider a general environment where two kinds of agents engage in optimal decision-making in forward-looking fashion: fully informed agents observe histories of all exogenous and endogenous variables; boundedly informed agents observe only a strict subset of the full information set and need to solve a dynamic signal extraction problem to gather information about the non-observables. In this peculiar setting, information sets are nested and yet persistently asymmetric, allowing the models to deliver a finite-state reduced-form representation of the equilibrium under RE, with two novel and noteworthy results. First, heterogeneous information sets can produce *local non-uniqueness* (also known as equilibrium indeterminacy) of the model's solution, thus opening room for so-called *sunspot shocks* to shape the dynamics of endogenous variables: the interaction of the two expectation formation processes allows agents' forecast errors to depend (arbitrarily) on structural aggregate shocks, capturing unanticipated variation in the underlying fundamentals, and on extrinsic noise embodying any non-structural, observed variable which coordinates agents' beliefs, making these latter self-fulfilling along the equilibrium path. Second, the interplay of expectations based on heterogeneous information sets can produce first-order approximate equilibrium outcomes which fail to be certainty equivalent, despite the linear Gaussian setting; as a result, the coefficients of the equilibrium law of motion will depend on the shock variances and thus on the second-moment properties of the RE solution.

10.3.2 Heterogeneous forecast rules

Departing from the homogeneous, full-information RE benchmark and thus explicitly modeling heterogeneous forecast rules in micro-founded macroeconomic frameworks requires taking a stand on four distinct, yet intimately related, issues: first, how are non-fully rational expectations formed (e.g. are they the outcome of some adaptive-like learning process that evolves over time, or are they persistently biased away from RE and rather respond to some heuristic reasoning)? Second, how to model individual (belief-specific) behavior conditional on any given forecast rule (assuming there is more than one), and how to aggregate heterogeneous beliefs? Third, how are the dynamics of endogenous variables shaped by the distribution of forecast rules across the population of agents? And last, can the distribution of agents across forecasting rules be taken to be endogenous and thus determined as an equilibrium object itself within a given model environment?

On the first two questions, a large strand of literature has adopted a simple *reduced-form approach*, according to which the conditional forecast in the model's defining equations derived under RE are simply replaced with a convex combination of heterogeneous expectations operators, capturing agent-specific forecast models, with weights given by the proportions of agents in the population who exploit each specific forecast rule. While analytically appealing, this approach prevents modelers from decoupling the expectation formation and decision-making stages and thus disregards the fact that boundedly rational beliefs held by agents may force them into forecast-based boundedly optimal behavior.

Acknowledging that aggregate implications of boundedly rational decision-making for equilibrium relationships should only occur after imposing bounded rationality at the outset and then deriving the resulting optimal decision rules, recent work has put forward an *agent-level approach* by virtue of which a variety of behavioral primitives (e.g. adaptive vs. rational, or structurally different learning rules) is over-imposed to allow different sets of agents to engage in economic forecasting upon recognizing the presence of expectational heterogeneity; see Brock and Hommes (1997), Honkapohja and Mitra (2006), and the excellent survey by Branch and McGough (2018).

Regarding behavioral primitives, the literature has traditionally followed two different routes. The first one – called the *anticipated utility approach* – has long served as a benchmark in theoretical studies of boundedly rational decision-making and stipulates the following: beliefs are determined via some learning process, and agents take the evolution of such (individual) beliefs as a constraint when formulating optimal decisions. Compared to (homogeneous) full-information RE, whereby agents know all the parameters of the model and hold time-invariant beliefs, under learning the true state equation determining the transition (time evolution) of the model is unknown and must be estimated by the agents at each time step conditional on available (current and past) data, with estimates updated via recursive least squares algorithms or the application of Bayes' theorem. As a result, time-varying decision rules will emerge, which depend on period-specific beliefs on the unknown state transition: incoming data fuel belief updating, which in turn enforces time variation in optimal decisions – see e.g. the *shadow price learning* approach to modeling boundedly optimal behavior (Evans and McGough, 2016) or the alternative *Euler-equation learning* popularized by Honkapohja *et al.* (2013).

One major drawback of the anticipated utility approach is that, while taking the dispersion of beliefs (i.e. the heterogeneity of forecast rules as functions of past data) as given, it explicitly treats the model's parameters as random objects (to be estimated by economic operators) within the learning stage and deterministic items in the decision-making stage. In plain words, agents can look backward and see the whole path along which their beliefs have evolved over time and thus are aware that learning has in fact occurred in the past; and yet, looking forward, they solve for optimal decisions – about e.g. consumption, financial investment, and labor supply – over their planning horizon *as if* beliefs will perpetually keep constant in the future, however distant. Agents thus fail to recognize (and then to internalize in their optimal decisions) the fact that learning is not a completed process: as their beliefs shift, they will relinquish on their plan and formulate a new one on the assumption that beliefs would not change in the future – they *pretend* no further learning will occur (e.g. Evans and Honkopohja, 2001).

In reaction to this, Cogley and Sargent (2008) have advocated for an *internal rationality* approach to modeling boundedly rational beliefs and ensuing decision-making in a Bayesian fashion. Acknowledging that Bayesian agents would condition their choices on the uncertainty surrounding the formation of beliefs and thus treat them as an evolving state variable, Cogley and Sargent (2008) contrast anticipated utility consumption decisions with a fully Bayesian plan according to which consumers holding a prior about future consumption paths maximize an expected utility objective where the expectation is taken with respect to the distribution of posterior probabilities. A rather surprising result, which lends strong support to the anticipated utility assumption, is that the former serves as a good approximation to fully Bayesian intertemporal optimization, i.e. the two assumptions generate fairly similar model-based implications for the dynamics of macroeconomic variables of interest.

The second question emphasized above also revolves around the issue of aggregating belief-specific individual decisions at the macro level. The most popular approach to aggregation hinges on the notion of *temporary equilibrium*: given the distribution of agents across forecast rules and the ensuing heterogeneity in decision rules, market-clearing conditions can be exploited to derive a temporary equilibrium law of motion that – under sufficiently mild regularity conditions – depends on the aggregate expectations operator (i.e. a weighted average of heterogeneous expectations) and is expressed entirely in terms of aggregate state variables. Such an aggregation property also offers a straightforward way to address the third question about the determination of endogenous variables in heterogeneous expectations environment: under the reduced-form approach, a convex combination of beliefs – embedded into diverse expectations operators – is imposed directly into the expectational equilibrium representation of the model; under a micro-founded approach, a temporary equilibrium is rather constructed by aggregating individual decision rules (as shaped by heterogeneous forecasts) and imposing market clearing.

The last (fourth) question – what forces contribute to determining the distribution of agents across forecast rules as an endogenous object – has proven rather challenging, and several mechanisms have been put forward in the recent macroeconomic literature as an attempt to provide a compelling answer. Two of them have revealed to be highly promising, and we briefly (and non-technically) review them here.

The first approach – labeled *rational expectational heterogeneity*, see Brock and Hommes (1997) – posits that agents form beliefs by selecting from a finite set of predictors exhibiting different 'processing costs', measuring individuals' preference or relative ease of exploiting heterogeneous predictors. As a result, the cross-sectional distribution of the processing costs will determine, via endogenous selection, the intensity of choice for any given predictor and thereby the distribution of agents across forecast rules.

The second approach – labeled *intrinsic heterogeneity*, see Branch and Evans (2006, 2010, 2011) – has agents engage in expectation formation by choosing from a set of heterogeneously misspecified (parametric) forecast rules (*perceived laws of motion*). The parameters of the forecast models and the distribution of agents across these latter are jointly determined in a so-called *restricted perceptions equilibrium*, with the property that only the best-performing statistical models are selected, and agents do not recognize the misspecification of their employed forecast rule.

10.4 Heterogeneous-Agent New Keynesian Models

10.4.1 A short review

A crucial building block of the first generation of new Keynesian macroeconomic models is the *representative-agent assumption*: all agents (on some side of the market, e.g. the consumers) are alike, meet in complete markets, and face uncertainty that comes in aggregate forms solely. The ability to borrow and save without bounds enables the representative agent to smooth out all temporary changes to income, so that only unanticipated shocks at the macroeconomic level can produce short-lived fluctuations in aggregate consumption, output, and inflation rate. While offering key insights into the behavior of macroeconomic systems, such a modeling approach is, by construction, unable to study macroeconomic questions in terms of cross-sectional facts (and the rich interaction between distributions of microeconomic variables and the macroeconomy) rather than merely aggregates.

Based on results from Campbell and Mankiw (1989) on the low sensitivity of consumption to changes in interest rates or variables other than current income, economists started considering, along with standard agents, groups of hand-to-mouth (HtM) households that are excluded from participation in financial markets (or, equivalently, find themselves continuously against a binding borrowing constraint) and are therefore highly exposed to unexpected shifts in their labor income profile over time. This generation of two-agent new Keynesian models (TANK) has naturally lend itself to the analysis of the effects of fiscal measures which shape the risk-return structure of labor income. As a leading example, Galì *et al.* (2007) prove that a large enough share of HtM consumers in an otherwise standard environment is able to qualitatively match the empirically observed positive reaction of aggregate consumption to fiscal expansion, breaking the postulate of Ricardian equivalence: key to the result is the agent heterogeneity in marginal propensities to consume (MPCs), with HtM consumers exhibiting highest (nearly unitary) MPCs because of their inability to access credit markets to meet their consumption needs.

On the widespread presumption that, in the long run, monetary policy is neutral regarding the structure of income and wealth distributions, research in the monetary policy realm had largely neglected, up until quite recent times, the redistributive implications of agent heterogeneity and the consequences for inequality in the short term. In fact, swings in monetary policy behavior tend to favor net savers and net borrowers in an asymmetric fashion, e.g. heterogeneity in household balance sheets (and, on top of that, cross-sectional differences in income sources and portfolio compositions) matters for the transmission of monetary policy via interest rate changes. Starting with Bernanke and Gertler (1995), varying degrees of intertemporal impatience across consumers have been introduced in macroeconomic models in order to explore the role of credit market imperfections in shaping monetary policy transmission, e.g. Iacoviello (2005).

But it was only recently that the new Keynesian view of macroeconomic behavior has started exploring the implications of uninsurable (idiosyncratic) income shocks and borrowing constraints – combined with the kind of nominal rigidities that are the hallmark of new Keynesian models – for optimal consumption and saving decision rules of forward-looking agents and the implications for business cycle fluctuations and the design of monetary policy. HANK models – after Kaplan *et al.* (2018) – have then been developed by positing market incompleteness, which forces cross-sectional disparities in agents' saving rates due to the wealth-contingent response to income shocks against which full insurance is not achievable. As a result, households are heterogeneous *ex post*, and there is imperfect risk sharing among them.

A distinctive feature of such HANK models is the emergence of *precautionary savings* across the time-varying wealth distribution: absent insurance contracts, agents' current decisions reflect the likelihood of being financially constrained in the future, creating a demand for extra saving vis-à-vis the certainty scenario (no income risk) for precautionary reasons; even mid-wealth (non-HtM) consumers who may be hit by negative income shocks might face an analogous time-varying incentive for saving provided they fear downside risk (i.e. if they exhibit prudence, see Kimball, 1990). In general, three groups of households (with endogenous mobility across them) emerge in HANK models: HtM agents, displaying low liquidity and high MPCs; a middle class, engaging in precautionary saving to stay away from borrowing limits; and high net-worth individuals, who hold highly liquid positions and are less exposed to income uncertainty. The ensuing heterogeneity in saving rates in the population in turn imparts asymmetric responses to contractionary and expansionary monetary policy shocks, with the largest share of the policy-induced variation in macroeconomic aggregates stemming from indirect general equilibrium effects (asset prices/returns, fiscal policies, and labor income) rather than through the direct intertemporal substitution channel affecting the incentives to save and consume, as suggested by the representative-agent framework. Remarkably, the transmission of monetary policy and its aggregate effects may change significantly conditional on the prevailing fiscal regime since the latter contributes to shaping the channel through which monetary policy influences the distribution of individual income and wealth among agents displaying different MPCs. In this environment, fiscal policy can achieve aggregate demand management goals and also prove better suited relative to monetary policy for redistribution (or public insurance) tasks for it can be more precisely targeted to those in need of support.

More generally, the HANK project embracing a full spectrum of individual *ex post* heterogeneities differs from its representative-agent counterparts along two crucial dimensions: first, it can easily predict differences in average consumption at any point in time between the groups of constrained and unconstrained households, making group composition (and the endogenous transitions in and out of each group) significant for the quantitative assessment of the models against real-world data; and second, and differently from unsophisticated TANK models, the fraction of agents who are subject (or operate as if subject) to binding borrowing constraint is endogenous and may change over time as a result of the interplay between aggregate shocks and the distribution and composition of wealth at any point in time. Some notable HANK models in the domain of monetary policy include, but are not limited to, McKay *et al.* (2016), Carroll *et al.* (2017), Guerrieri and Lorenzoni (2017), and Kaplan *et al.* (2018).

10.4.2 Two-agent new Keynesian model insights

Since early contributions to the HANK literature (e.g. Kaplan *et al.*, 2018), solving for the general equilibrium in HANK models routinely requires the adoption of non-trivial numerical techniques, given the need to keep track of the distribution of wealth and the ensuing compositional effects of aggregate shocks, as well as the computational issues arising from the presence of occasionally binding (borrowing) constraints at the individual level.

In order to clearly isolate some of the key mechanisms underlying the main differences between the predictions of HANK versus RANK models, we next present and fully work out a two-agent (TANK) model – based on Bilbiee (2008) – where the source of heterogeneity lies in individual types: the standard representative household that can freely borrow and save to smooth consumption, and the HtM household that is unable (or forced not) to participate in financial markets and thus consumes their disposable income at any point in time. In such a setting, there is no switching between types, and no precautionary saving behavior emerges. Still, the TANK model allows us to highlight the role of individual heterogeneity for the aggregate implications of the model, such as the role of asymmetric profits' distribution (across heterogeneous household types) for aggregate demand amplification, and the amplification of monetary policy effects via the elasticity of aggregate demand to real interest rates.

The model is a standard cashless new Keynesian model augmented with limited asset market participation, which is exogenously imposed. The failure to trade in asset markets could be due to, e.g. trading frictions, transaction costs, and/or market segmentation. As standard in the new Keynesian theoretical apparatus, the model comprises a continuum of households (with a positive measure share of HtM consumers), a single perfectly competitive final-good producer, and a continuum of monopolistically competitive intermediate-goods producers setting prices on a staggered basis. Price stickiness – due to inability of a given share of intermediate goods firms to re-optimize prices in each time period – will create room for monetary policy to affect the real economy. The nominal interest rate is assumed to be set by the central bank following a simple feedback instrument rule.

10.4.2.1 *Households*

Consider an infinite horizon economy populated by a unit mass continuum of households, all exhibiting the same preferences over consumption and leisure, captured by a separable utility function $U(\cdot, \cdot)$, specified as follows. A fraction $1 - \lambda \in (0, 1)$ of households are full *optimizers* that can save and borrow and have access to state-contingent securities: their problem is to choose, in a forward-looking fashion, consumption, working hours, and asset holdings by solving a standard intertemporal problem,

$$\max \mathbb{E}_t \sum_{i=0}^{\infty} \beta^i \ln C_{O,t+i} - \chi \frac{N_{O,t+i}^{1+\varphi}}{1+\varphi} \tag{10.6}$$

subject to the sequence of budget constraints

$$B_{O,t} + \Omega_{O,t+1} V_t \leq Z_{O,t} + \Omega_{O,t} (V_t + P_t D_t) + W_t N_{O,t} - P_t C_{O,t}, \tag{10.7}$$

where the subscript O denotes the representative optimizer, $\beta \in (0,1)$ is the subjective discount factor, $\chi > 0$ measures the importance of leisure relative to consumption, and $\varphi > 0$ is the inverse of the labor supply elasticity. The variables $C_{O,t}$ and $N_{O,t}$ are consumption and hours worked, respectively; $B_{O,t}$ is the end-of-period nominal value of a portfolio of contingent assets held (not including firm shares), $Z_{O,t}$ is beginning-of-period wealth, V_t is the average market value of shares in intermediate good firms, D_t are real dividend payoffs from firm shares, $\Omega_{O,t}$ are firm shares holdings, and P_t is the price of final good.[3]

In the absence of arbitrage opportunities, a stochastic discount factor, $\mathcal{M}_{t,t+1}$, will exist for the fundamental pricing of assets:

$$B_{O,t} = \mathbb{E}_t[\mathcal{M}_{t,t+1} Z_{O,t+1}]; \quad V_t = \mathbb{E}_t[\mathcal{M}_{t,t+1}(V_{t+1} + P_{t+1} D_{t+1})], \tag{10.8}$$

implying that the riskless (gross) nominal interest rate R_t solves $R_t^{-1} = \mathbb{E}_t[\mathcal{M}_{t,t+1}]$. Using the no-arbitrage conditions and the usual natural no-borrowing limit for each state, the usual intertemporal budget constraint obtains

$$\mathbb{E}_t \sum_{i=t}^{\infty} \mathcal{M}_{t,i} P_i C_{O,i} \leq Z_{O,t} + V_t + \mathbb{E}_t \sum_{i=t}^{\infty} \mathcal{M}_{t,i} W_i N_{O,i}, \tag{10.9}$$

[3]The additively (and state) separable utility specification with unitary elasticity in consumption generates constant steady-state equilibrium hours and is used for analytical tractability; yet, the main implications of the model remain unaltered under more general formulations (see Bilbiee, 2008).

under which maximizing utility yields the following first-order (necessary and sufficient) conditions:

$$\beta \frac{C_{O,t}}{C_{O,t+1}} = \mathcal{M}_{t,t+1} \frac{P_{t+1}}{P_t}, \tag{10.10}$$

$$\chi N_{O,t}^{\varphi} = \frac{1}{C_{O,t}} \frac{W_t}{P_t}, \tag{10.11}$$

along with the intertemporal budget constraint holding with equality.

A fraction λ rather collects HtM households – or non-asset holders – in the sense of Campbell and Mankiw (1989): they have no assets and consume all of their labor income (wage) each period. In each time period t, the representative HtM H solves

$$\max_{C_{H,t}, N_{H,t}} \ln C_{H,t} - \chi \frac{N_{H,t}^{1+\varphi}}{1+\varphi} \quad s.t. \quad W_t N_{H,t} \leq P_t C_{H,t}, \tag{10.12}$$

yielding the first-order (necessary and sufficient) condition

$$\chi N_{H,t}^{\varphi} = \frac{1}{C_{H,t}} \frac{W_t}{P_t}. \tag{10.13}$$

Note that, by virtue of the utility specification, labor supply of HtM consumers is fixed, with worked hours constant at their steady-state level given by $N_{H,t} = \chi^{-\frac{1}{1+\varphi}}$, which in turn delivers a simple consumption function for these agents that tracks the real wage to exhaust the budget constraint.

10.4.2.2 *Firms*

In each time period, the final good Y_t is produced by a representative firm using a CES production function (with elasticity of substitution ϵ) that aggregates a unitary continuum of j intermediate goods:

$$Y_t = \left(\int_0^1 Y_t(j) \frac{\epsilon - 1}{\epsilon} dj \right)^{\frac{\epsilon}{\epsilon - 1}}. \tag{10.14}$$

The producers of the final good operate under perfect competition and thus take the price index P_t as given when maximizing their period t profits

$$P_t Y_t - \int_0^1 P_t(j) Y_t(j) dj, \tag{10.15}$$

where $P_t(j)$ is the price of intermediate input (good) j, whose demand is

$$Y_t(j) = \left(\frac{P_t}{P_t(j)}\right)^{\epsilon} Y_t, \tag{10.16}$$

so that the price index is given by

$$P_t = \left(\int_{0,1} P_t(j)^{1-\epsilon} dj\right)^{\frac{1}{1-\epsilon}}. \tag{10.17}$$

Each intermediate good is produced by a monopolistic firm j according to the technology

$$Y_t(j) = \max\{A_t N_t(j) - F, 0\}, \tag{10.18}$$

where A_t is labor productivity and $F > 0$ is a fixed cost common to all firms. Cost minimization yields the common nominal marginal cost

$$MC_t = \frac{W_t}{A_t}, \tag{10.19}$$

and aggregate total profits (over all the intermediate good firms) in real terms are

$$D_t = \left[1 - \frac{MC_t}{P_t}\Delta_t\right] Y_t, \tag{10.20}$$

where $\Delta_t = \int_0^1 (P_t(j)/P_t)^{-\epsilon} dj$ denotes relative price dispersion. Total profits D_t accrue to firm shares holders (i.e. optimizing households solely) in terms of dividends.

Intermediate good firms are assumed to adjust their prices infrequently. Let $\theta \in (0, 1)$ denote the (time-invariant) fraction of firms that are unable to reset prices in each time period. Those who in equilibrium will hold all the shares in firms (market participants) maximize the value of the firm, i.e. the discounted sum of future nominal profits, by choosing the price $P_t(i)$ to maximize nominal profits

$$\mathbb{E}_t \sum_{k=0}^{\infty} \theta^k \mathcal{M}_{t,t+k} \left[P_t(j) Y_{t,t+k}(j) - MC_{t+k} Y_{t,t+k}(j)\right] \tag{10.21}$$

subject to the demand equation. The optimal price of the firm then obeys

$$P_t^* = \mathbb{E}_t \sum_{k=0}^{\infty} \frac{\theta^k \mathcal{M}_{t,t+k} P_{t+k}^{\epsilon-1} Y_{t+k}}{\mathbb{E}_t \sum_{n=0}^{\infty} \theta^n \mathcal{M}_{t,t+n} P_{t+n}^{\epsilon-1} Y_{t+n}} MC_{t+k}. \tag{10.22}$$

In equilibrium, each intermediate good firm that sets a new price will choose P_t^* and the same level of output, hence the price index is

$$P_t^{1-\epsilon} = (1-\theta)(P_t^*)^{1-\epsilon} + \theta P_{t-1}^{1-\epsilon}. \tag{10.23}$$

10.4.2.3 *Monetary policy*

Given the purposes of the analysis, we focus on simple instrument feedback rules for monetary policy that map relevant macroeconomic indicators into the policy instrument, i.e. the short-term nominal interest rate, within the family

$$R_t = \Phi\left(R_t^*, \frac{P_t}{P_{t-1}}, \mathbb{E}_t \frac{P_{t+1}}{P_t}, \frac{Y_t}{Y_t^*}\right), \tag{10.24}$$

where starred variables denote their flexible-price model analogues and $\Phi(\cdot)$ is an arbitrary function which is increasing in all their arguments.

10.4.2.4 *Equilibrium*

Under price taking (of all agents but the intermediate good producers who operate in a monopolistic fashion), a *rational expectations equilibrium* is collection of processes for all prices and quantities introduced above such that the optimality conditions hold for all the agents and all markets clear at any given time period t. Specifically:

(i) labor market clearing requires

$$N_t = \lambda N_{H,t} + (1-\lambda) N_{O,t}; \tag{10.25}$$

(ii) state-contingent assets are in zero net supply (markets are complete and agents participating in this market are identical);

(iii) Equity market clearing implies

$$\Omega_{O,t+1} = \Omega_{O,t} = \frac{1}{1-\lambda} := \Omega; \tag{10.26}$$

(iv) By Walras' law, the goods market also clears, i.e.

$$Y_t = C_t := \lambda C_{H,t} + (1-\lambda)C_{O,t}. \tag{10.27}$$

The dynamic properties of the TANK model can be locally studied by taking a (log-)linear approximation around the unique non-stochastic steady state. To obtain the latter, note that from the Euler equation of optimizing households, the steady-state riskless interest rate is $R = \beta^{-1}$, where $R := 1 + r$. Defining the steady-state net mark-up as $\mu := (\epsilon - 1)^{-1}$ and the share of the fixed cost in steady-state output as $F_Y := F/Y$, the share of labor income in total output is $WN/PY = (1 + F_Y)/(1 + \mu)$, whereas the profits' share in total output is $D_Y = D/Y = (\mu - F_Y)/(1+\mu)$. On the assumption that F_Y is equal to the net markup μ, one clearly has $D_Y = 0$. Given preference homogeneity across household groups, hours and consumption are also equalized in steady state, i.e.

$$N_O = N_H = \chi^{\frac{1}{1+\varphi}}; \quad C_O = C_H = \chi^{-\frac{1}{1+\varphi}} \frac{W}{P}, \tag{10.28}$$

in turn implying that steady-state consumption for each group will be equal to total steady-state consumption and output, i.e.

$$C_O = C_H = C = Y. \tag{10.29}$$

Taking a (log-)linear approximation of the equilibrium conditions around the above-derived steady state (denoting log-deviation by small-size letters for each variable involved other than profits, which are simply defined as a fraction of steady-state output) yields the following linearized equilibrium conditions that express the model's dynamics in terms of aggregate variables:

- Euler equation, O: $c_{O,t} = \mathbb{E}_t c_{O,t+1} + (r_t - \mathbb{E}_t \pi_{t+1})$
- Labor supply, O: $\varphi n_{O,t} = w_t - c_{O,t}$
- Budget constraint, O: $c_{O,t} = (w_t + n_{O,t}) + (1-\lambda)^{-1} d_t$

- Labor supply, H: $\varphi n_{H,t} = w_t - c_{H,t}$
- Budget constraint, H: $c_{H,t} = w_t + n_{H,t}$
- Production function $y_t = (1+\mu)(n_t + a_t)$
- Real marginal cost: $mc_t = w_t - a_t$
- Real profits: $d_t = -mc_t + \mu(1+\mu)^{-1}y_t$
- Phillips curve: $\pi_t = \beta\mathbb{E}_t\pi_{t+1} + \psi mc_t$, $\psi := (1-\theta)(1-\theta\beta)\theta^{-1}$
- Labor market clearing: $n_t = \lambda n_{H,t} + (1-\lambda)n_{O,t}$
- Aggregate consumption: $c_t = \lambda c_{H,t} + (1-\lambda)c_{O,t}$
- Good market clearing: $y_t = c_t$

Using these equilibrium conditions allows us to derive a straightforward three-equation representation of the aggregate behavior of the TANK model, similar to the one representative-agent new Keynesian benchmark. Specifically, upon deriving the consumption of the full optimizing households (those holding financial assets) in terms of aggregate output (recall that the consumption of HtM households by construction tracks the real wage), the dynamic IS equation is

$$y_t = \mathbb{E}_t y_{t+1} - \delta^{-1}[r_t - \mathbb{E}_t\pi_{t+1}] + (1+\mu)(1-\delta^{-1})[a_t - \mathbb{E}_t a_{t+1}], \tag{10.30}$$

where $\delta := 1 - \lambda(1-\lambda)^{-1}(1+\mu)^{-1}$ is the inverse of the elasticity of aggregate demand to real interest rate.

Focusing on aggregate supply and the dynamics of inflation, upon deriving the equilibrium relationship between real wage and total output, the new Keynesian Phillips curve becomes

$$\pi_t = \beta\mathbb{E}_t\pi_{t+1} + \kappa y_t - \psi(1+\varphi)a_t, \tag{10.31}$$

where $\kappa = \psi\gamma$ and $\gamma := 1 + \varphi(1+\mu)^{-1} \geq 1$.

Finally, recalling the definition of output gap $x_t := y_t - y_t^n$ (i.e. the difference between actual output y_t and natural output $y_t^n = (1+\varphi)\gamma^{-1}a_t$, which prevails in the flexible-price equilibrium where inflation is nil and real marginal cost and markup are constant), one can rewrite both the dynamic IS equation (10.30) and the new Keynesian Phillips curve (10.31) as

$$x_t = \mathbb{E}_t x_{t+1} - \delta^{-1}[r_t - \mathbb{E}_t\pi_{t+1} - r_t^n] \tag{10.32}$$

$$\pi_t = \beta\mathbb{E}_t\pi_{t+1} + \kappa x_t + u_t, \tag{10.33}$$

where $r_t^n = [1 + \mu(1-\delta/\gamma)][\mathbb{E}_t a_{t+1} - a_t]$ is the natural level of the real interest rate and u_t is a random (shock) component embodying variations in marginal cost not due to shifts in excess demand (also known as cost-push shocks). These two equations, along with an equation specifying the determination of the nominal interest rate – such as the instrument rule $r_t = \phi_\pi \mathbb{E}_t \pi_{t+1} + \phi_x x_t + \varepsilon_t$, where ε_t captures monetary policy surprises – fully determine the dynamics of endogenous variables as a function of exogenous shocks a_t and u_t.

10.4.2.5 *Aggregate implications of individual heterogeneity*

Introducing household heterogeneity via limited asset market participation into the new Keynesian model engenders two crucial effects on aggregate dynamics vis-à-vis the baseline (representative-agent) framework. First, the elasticity of aggregate demand to real interest rates is modified and varies nonlinearly with the share of HtM households: there exists a threshold $\lambda^* \in (0, 1]$ of such a share beyond which the parameter σ switches sign, so that for sufficiently low participation rates (sufficiently high fraction of HtM households), $\sigma < 0$, and surges in real interest rates become expansionary; in the limit case where as λ tends to 1 $-\sigma^{-1}$ tends to 0, monetary policy becomes totally ineffective in restraining aggregate demand.[4] Figure 10.2 depicts the region where the standard aggregate demand logic (SADL) applies, meaning that a rise in real interest rates depresses aggregate demand; and the region where the inverted aggregate demand logic (IADL) prevails, meaning that increasing interest rates fuel aggregate demand.

Why do rising interest rates push up aggregate demand in the presence of a large fraction of HtM households? Suppose the central bank pursues a fully unexpected, one-time discretionary increase in the short-term interest rate ($\epsilon_t > 0$), otherwise accommodating inflationary expectations ($r_t = \mathbb{E}_t \pi_{t+1} + \epsilon_t$). In the representative-agent economy, an increase in interest rates leads to a concurrent fall in aggregate demand, stimulating labor supply at a given real wage, while labor demand contracts because of sticky prices: the new equilibrium will features lower output, consumption, hours, and real

[4]We shall note that $\lambda^* = 1$ if and only if $\varphi = 0$, i.e. when labor supply from the fully optimizing households is infinitely elastic. In this case, consumption of households – whether participating in financial markets or not – is independent of wealth, making individual heterogeneity immaterial.

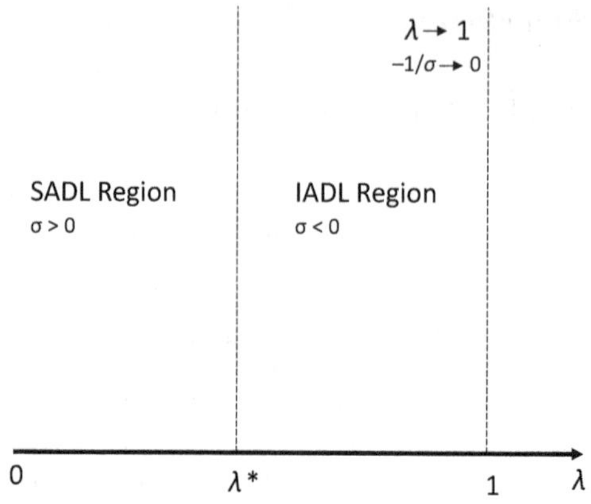

Figure 10.2. SADL region.

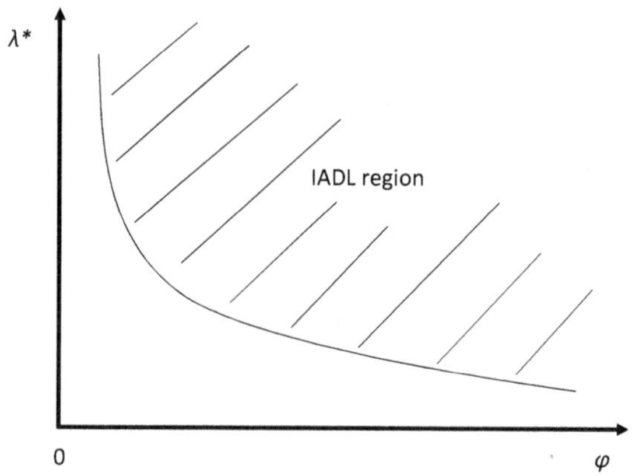

Figure 10.3. IADL region.

wage. Figure 10.3 depicts the threshold share of HtM households as a function of the inverse labor supply elasticity, for a given steady-state value of firms' markup: the larger the elasticity, the more likely the actual share of HtM households lies in the IADL region where aggregate demand increases with real interest rates.

Consider now the TANK structure, but let us assume for the moment that $\lambda < \lambda^*$; then, the fall in real wage induced by the intertemporal substitution of financial market participants further contracts aggregate demand since HtM households merely consume their labor income, producing a further shift in labor demand and thus tipping the economy into a new equilibrium with even lower output, consumption, hours, and real wage – this effect enhances the effectiveness of monetary policy in containing aggregate demand. In general equilibrium, however, the described demand effect that occurs because of the presence of HtM households also impacts profits because both marginal costs (wages) and sales (output and hours) fall. The relative size of these reductions (and the final effect on profits) depends on λ and on labor supply elasticity. Taking the latter as fixed, when $\lambda > \lambda^*$, an increase in profits would occur that would generate a positive income effect on fully optimizing households, which dominates both the initial intertemporal substitution effect on labor supply and the compressing effect of monetary policy on the demand of optimizing households. An equilibrium is then reached where consumption, output, hours, and the real wage all increase – a monetary contraction generates expansionary effects. However, as λ increases to its upper bound, this expansionary effect is muted: while in the standard region ($\lambda \in (0, \lambda^*)$), an increase in the share of HtM households improves the effectiveness of monetary policy, in the inverted region ($\lambda \in (\lambda^*, 1)$), monetary policy contractions are increasingly less expansionary as λ rises.

By contrast, the structure of the new Keynesian Phillips curve (and the ensuing inflation-output gap stabilization trade-off faced by the central bank) is invariant to the share of HtM households (i.e. the equation does not depend on λ), reflecting the assumption of equal steady-state consumption shares across groups. As a result, the response of inflation to aggregate demand variations due to limited asset markets participation is nil.

A further, important difference between the TANK models and its representative-agent counterpart pertains to the ability of the so-called Taylor principle in interest rate setting to induce a unique rational expectations equilibrium and thus safeguard the economy against extrinsic (sunspot) sources of uncertainty. In particular, when $\lambda > \lambda^*$, the Taylor principle is inverted: the central bank is required to adopt a passive stance according to which the nominal interest rate increases with inflation less than one-for-one, in order to tip the economy in a unique equilibrium where only structural shocks matter.

10.5 Conclusion

There are at least two broad categories of salient economic questions that call for an explicit account of heterogeneity in macroeconomic analysis. First, from an epistemological standpoint, understanding how far the predictions of heterogeneous-agent models are from those of a representative-agent benchmark vis-à-vis the reality helps economists to identify the types of individual risk and cross-sectional heterogeneity that are key to interpreting observed distributional phenomena and to discard those that play no role in this respect. For instance, the aggregate behavior of a model where the only source of heterogeneity resides in the absence of full insurance against idiosyncratic risk is almost indistinguishable from that of the underlying benchmark, which can thus robustly serve as a reliable guidance for investigating aggregate issues. Second, and most importantly, heterogeneous-agent general equilibrium models can be exploited to investigate, from both a positive and a normative perspective, fundamental forces and mechanisms shaping cross-sectional disparities, making them suitable for addressing issues of current policy debate associated with the re-distributional effects of government intervention and large-scale programs (e.g. tax policies and social security systems) in market economies. The methodological aspects of these questions are, apparently, non-trivial since they naturally hinge on solving highly nonlinear and sophisticated models encompassing stochastic dynamic optimization problems and equilibrium objects in large-dimensional function spaces.

References

Acemoglu, D. A., 2009. *Introduction to Modern Economic Growth*, Princeton University Press.

Acharya, A. and K. Dogra, 2020. "Understanding HANK: Insights From a PRANK," *Econometrica* 88(3): 1113–1158.

Acharya, S., Benhabib, J. and Z. Huo, 2021. "The Anatomy of Sentiment-Driven Fluctuations," *Journal of Economic Theory,* 195: 105280.

Aghion, P. and P. W. Howitt, 1997. *Endogenous Growth Theory*, MIT Press.

Aiyagari, S. R., 1994. "Uninsured Idiosyncratic Risk and Aggregate Saving," *Quarterly Journal of Economics* 109: 659–684.

Angeletos, G.-M. and J. La'O, 2013. "Sentiments," *Econometrica* 81(2): 739–779.

Attanasio, O., 2005. Consumption, Chapter 11 in J. Taylor and M. Woodford, eds., *Handbook of Macroeconomics*, North-Holland: 741–812.

Bacchetta, P., E. Mertens, and E. van Wincoop, 2009. "Predictability in Financial Markets: What do Survey Expectations Tell Us?," *Journal of International Money and Finance* 28(3): 406–426.

Benassy, J.-P., 2001. "The Phillips Curve and Optimal Policy in a Structural Signal Extraction Model," *Review of Economic Dynamics* 4: 58–74.

Benhabib, J. and A. Bisin, 2018. "Skewed Wealth Distributions: Theory and Empirics," *Journal of Economic Literature* 56: 1261–1291.

Bernanke, B. S. and M. Gertler, 1995. "Inside the Black Box: The Credit Channel of Monetary Policy Transmission," *Journal of Economic Perspectives* 9: 27–48.

Bewley, T., 1977. "The Permanent Income Hypothesis: A Theoretical Formulation," *Journal of Economic Theory* 16: 252–292.

Bewley, T., 1983. "A Difficulty with the Optimum Quantity of Money," *Econometrica* 51: 1485–1504.

Bilbiee, F. O., 2008. "Limited Asset Markets Participation, Monetary Policy and (Inverted) Aggregate Demand Logic," *Journal of Economic Theory* 140: 162–196.

Blanchard, O. J., 2000. "What do we know about Macroeconomics that Fisher and Wicksell did not?," *NBER Working Papers* No. 7550.

Blanchard, O. J. and C. M. Kahn, 1980. "The Solution of Linear Difference Models Under Rational Expectations," *Econometrica*, 48: 305–11.

Branch, W. A. and B. McGough, 2018. "Chapter 1 – Heterogeneous Expectations and Micro-Foundations in Macroeconomics," in *Handbook of Computational Economics*, Editor(s): Cars Hommes, Blake LeBaron, 3–62.

Branch, W. A. and G. W. Evans, 2006. "Intrinsic Heterogeneity in Expectation Formation," *Journal of Economic Theory* 127: 264–295.

Branch, W. A. and G. W. Evans, 2010. "Asset Return Dynamics and Learning," *Review of Financial Studies* 23: 1651–1680.

Branch, W. A. and G. W. Evans, 2011. "Monetary Policy and Heterogeneous Expectations," *Economic Theory* 47: 365–393.

Brock, W. A. and C. H. Hommes, 1997. "A Rational Route to Randomness," *Econometrica* 65: 1059–1095.

Campbell, J. Y. and N. G. Mankiw, 1989. *Consumption, Income, and Interest Rates: Reinterpreting the Time Series Evidence,* in: O. Blanchard, S. Fisher (Eds.), NBER Macroeconomics Annual, MIT Press, Cambridge, MA: 185–216.

Carroll, C., Slacalek, J., Tokuoka, K., and M. N. White, 2017. "The Distribution of Wealth and the Marginal Propensity to Consume," *Quantitative Economics* 8: 977–1020.

Chiang, A., 1999. *Elements of Dynamic Optimization*, Waveland Press.

Cogley, T. and T. J. Sargent, 2008. "Anticipated Utility and Rational Expectations as Approximations of Bayesian Decision Making," *International Economic Review* 49: 185–221.

Cogley, T. and T. J. Sargent, 2001. "Evolving Post-World War II Inflation Dynamics," *NBER Macroeconomic Annual* 16: 331–373.

Cogley, T. and T. J. Sargent, 2005. "Drifts and Volatilities: Monetary Policies and Outcomes in the Post-World War II U.S.," *Review of Economic Dynamics,* 8: 262–302.

Cooley, T. F. and E. C. Prescott, 1995. "Economic Growth and Business Cycles," in *Frontiers of Business Cycle Research*, T. F. Cooley, Ed. 1–38. Princeton University Press.

de la Fuente, A., 2000. *Mathematical Methods and Models for Economists*, Cambridge University Press.

DeJong D. N. and C. Dave, 2011. *Structural Macroeconometrics (2nd Ed.)*, Princeton University Press.

Dixit, A., 1990. *Optimization in Economic Theory*, Oxford University Press.

Domar, E. D., 1946. "Capital Expansion, Rate of Growth, and Employment," *Econometrica* 14: 137–147.

Dressler S. J. and V. E. Li, 2009: "Inside money, credit, and investment," *Journal of Economic Dynamics and Control* 33: 970–984.

Evans, G. W. and B., McGough, 2016. *Agent-level Adaptive Learning*, mimeo.

Evans, G. W. and S. Honkapohja, 2001. *Learning and Expectations in Macroeconomics*, Princeton University Press.

G. D. Hansen, 1985. "Indivisible Labor and the Business Cycle," *Journal of Monetary Economics*, 16: 309–327.

Gali, J., Lopez-Salido, J. D., and J. Valles, 2007. "Understanding the Effects of Government Spending on Consumption," *Journal of the European Economic Association* 5: 227–270.

Guerrieri, V. and G. Lorenzoni, 2017. "Credit Crises, Precautionary Savings, and the Liquidity Trap," *Quarterly Journal of Economics* 132: 1427–1467.

Heathcote, J., K. Storesletten and G. L. Violante, 2009. "Quantitative Macroeconomics with Heterogeneous Households," Annual Review of Economics, 1: 319–354.

Hamilton, J. D., 1994. *Time Series Analysis*, Princeton University Press.

Hommes, C. H., 2013. *Behavioral Rationality and Heterogeneous Expectations in Complex Economic Systems*. Cambridge University Press.

Honkapohja, S. and K. Mitra, 2006. "Learning Stability in Economies with Heterogeneous Agents," *Review of Economic Dynamics* 9: 284–309.

Honkapohja, S., Mitra, K. and G. W. Evans, 2013. "Notes on Agents' Behavioral Rules Under Adaptive Learning and Recent Studies of Monetary Policy," in *Macroeconomics at the Service of Public Policy*, ed. by T. Sargent, and J. Vilmunen. Oxford University Press.

Huggett, M. 1993. "The Risk-Free Rate in Heterogeneous-Agent Incomplete-Insurance Economies," *Journal of Economic Dynamics and Control* 17: 953–969.

Huggett, M. 1996. "Wealth Distribution in Life-cycle Economies," *Journal of Monetary Economics* 38: 469–494.

Iacoviello, M. 2005. "House Prices, Borrowing Constraints, and Monetary Policy in the Business Cycle," *American Economic Review* 95: 739–764.

Imrohoroglu, A., Imrohoroglu, S., and D. Joines, 1995. "A Life Cycle Analysis of Social Security," *Economic Theory* 6: 83–114.

Ireland, P. N., 2003. "Endogenous Money or Sticky Prices," *Journal of Monetary Economics*, 50: 1623–1648.

Ireland, P. N., 2004. "A Method for Taking Models to the Data," *Journal of Economic Dynamics and Control*, 28: 1205–1226.

Judd, K. L., 1998. *Numerical Methods in Economics*, Cambridge, MA: MIT Press.

Kaplan, G., Moll, B. and G. L. Violante, 2018. "Monetary Policy According to HANK," *American Economic Review* 108: 697–743.

Kimball, M. S., 1990. "Precautionary Saving in the Small and in the Large," *Econometrica* 58: 53–73.

Kirman, A. P., 1992. "Whom or What Does the Representative Individual Represent?," *Journal of Economic Perspectives*, 6: 117–136.

Klein, P., 2000. "Using the generalized Schur form to solve a multivariate linear rational expectations model," *Journal of Economic Dynamics and Control* 24: 1405–1423.

Kormilitsina, A., 2013. "Solving Rational Expectations Models with Informational Subperiods: A Perturbation Approach," *Computational Economics* 41: 525–555.

Kreps, D. M., 1990. *A Course in Microeconomic Theory*, Princeton University Press.

Krusell, P. and A. Smith, Jr., 1998. "Income and Wealth Heterogeneity in the Macroeconomy," *Journal of Political Economy* 106: 867–896.

Kydland, F. E. and E. C. Prescott, 1982. "Time to Build and Aggregate Fluctuations," *Econometrica*, 50: 345–70.

Kydland, F. E. and E. C. Prescott, 1996. "The Computational Experiment: An Econometric Tool," *Journal of Economic Perspectives*, 10: 69–85.

Ljungqvist, L. and T. J. Sargent, 2018. *Recursive Macroeconomic Theory (4th Ed.)*, MIT Press.

Lubik, T. A., Matthes, C., and E. Mertens, 2023. "Indeterminacy and Imperfect Information," *Review of Economic Dynamics* 49: 37–57.

Lucas, R. E., 1972. "Expectations and the Neutrality of Money," *Journal of Economic Theory* 4: 103–124.

Lucas, R. E., 1973. "Some International Evidence on Output-Inflation Tradeoffs," *American Economic Review*, 63: 326–334.

Lucas, R. E., 1978. "Asset Prices in an Exchange Economy," *Econometrica*, 46: 429–45.

Lucas, R. E. and N. Stokey, 1987. "Money and Interest in a Cash-in-Advance Economy" *Econometrica* 55: 491–513.

Ma, Q., Stachurski, J., and A. A. Toda, 2020. "The Income Fluctuation Problem and the Evolution of Wealth," *Journal of Economic Theory* 187: 105003.

Mankiw, N. G. and R. Reis, 2002. "Sticky Information Versus Sticky Prices: A Proposal to Replace the New Keynesian Phillips Curve," *Quarterly Journal of Economics* 117: 1295–1328.

Mas-Collel, A., Whinston, M. D. and J. R. Green, 1995. *Microeconomic Theory*, Oxford University Press.

McKay, A., Nakamura, E., and J. Steinsson, 2016. "The Power of Forward Guidance Revisited", *American Economic Review* 106: 3133–3158.

Mehra, R. and E. C. Prescott, 1985. "The Equity Premium: A Puzzle," *Journal of Monetary Economics*, 15: 145–61.

Muth, J. F., 1961. "Rational Expectations and the Theory of Price Movements," *Econometrica* 29: 315–335.

Mankiw N. G., 2018. *Macroeconomics (10th Ed.)*, Worth Publishers.

Nimark, K. 2008. "Dynamic Pricing and Imperfect Common Knowledge," *Journal of Monetary Economics* 55: 365–382.

Simon, P. and Blume, L., 1994. *Mathematics for Economists*, W. W. Norton & Company.

Piazzesi, M. and M. Schneider, 2008. *Inflation Illusion, Credit, and Asset Pricing*, In Asset Pricing and Monetary Policy, edited by John Y. Campbell, Chicago University Press: 147–181.

Rebelo, 1991. "Long-Run Policy Analysis and Long-Run Growth," *Journal of Political Economy* 99: 500–521.

Rogerson, R., 1988. "Indivisible Labor, Lotteries and Equilibrium," *Journal of Monetary Economics*, 21: 3–16.

Romer, D., 2018. *Advanced Macroeconomics*, McGraw-Hill.

Sameulson, P., 1958. "An Exact Consumption-Loan Model of Interest with or without the Social Contrivance of Money," *The Journal of Political Economy*, 66: 467–482.

Sargent, T. J., 1987. *Macroeconomic Theory*, 2nd Ed., London: Academic Press.

Schechtman, J. and V. L. S. Escudero, 1977. "Some Results on an Income Fluctuation Problem," *Journal of Economic Theory* 16: 151–166.

Shiller, R. J., 1981. "Do Stock Prices Move Too Much to be Justified by Subsequent Changes in Dividends?," *American Economic Review*, 71: 421–436.

Sims, C., 2001. "Solving Linear Rational Expectations Models," *Computational Economics*, 20: 1–20.

Solow, R., 1956. "A Contribution to the Theory of Economic Growth," *The Quarterly Journal of Economics*, 70: 65–94.

Sorge, M. M., 2020. "Computing Sunspot Solutions to Rational Expectations Models with Timing Restrictions," *The B.E. Journal of Macroeconomics* 2020: 20180256.

Swan, T. W., 1956. "Economic Growth and Capital Accumulation," *Economic Record,* 32: 334–361.

Uhlig, H., 1999. "A Toolkit for Analyzing Non-linear Dynamic Stochastic Models Easily," in Ramon Marimon and Andrew Scott Eds., *Computational Methods for the Study of Dynamic Economies*, Oxford University Press, New York, 30–61.

Varian, H. R., 2024. *Intermediate Microeconomics A Modern Approach* (10th Ed.), W. W. Norton

Varian, H. R., 1992. *Microeconomic Analysis (3rd Ed.)*, W. W. Norton and Company.

Woodford, M., 2000. "*Revolution and Evolution in Twentieth-Century Macroeconomics*," June 1999. [Presented at a conference, Frontiers of the Mind in the Twenty-First Century, U.S. Library of Congress, Washington, D.C., June 1999.]

Whiteman, C. H., 1983. *Linear Rational Expectations Models: A User's Guide,* Minneapolis: University of Minnesota Press.

www.ingramcontent.com/pod-product-compliance
Lightning Source LLC
LaVergne TN
LVHW011807200926
848484LV00005B/1092
9789811296208